IMAGES
of America

ROGERS, HASSAN TOWNSHIP, AND FLETCHER REMEMBERED

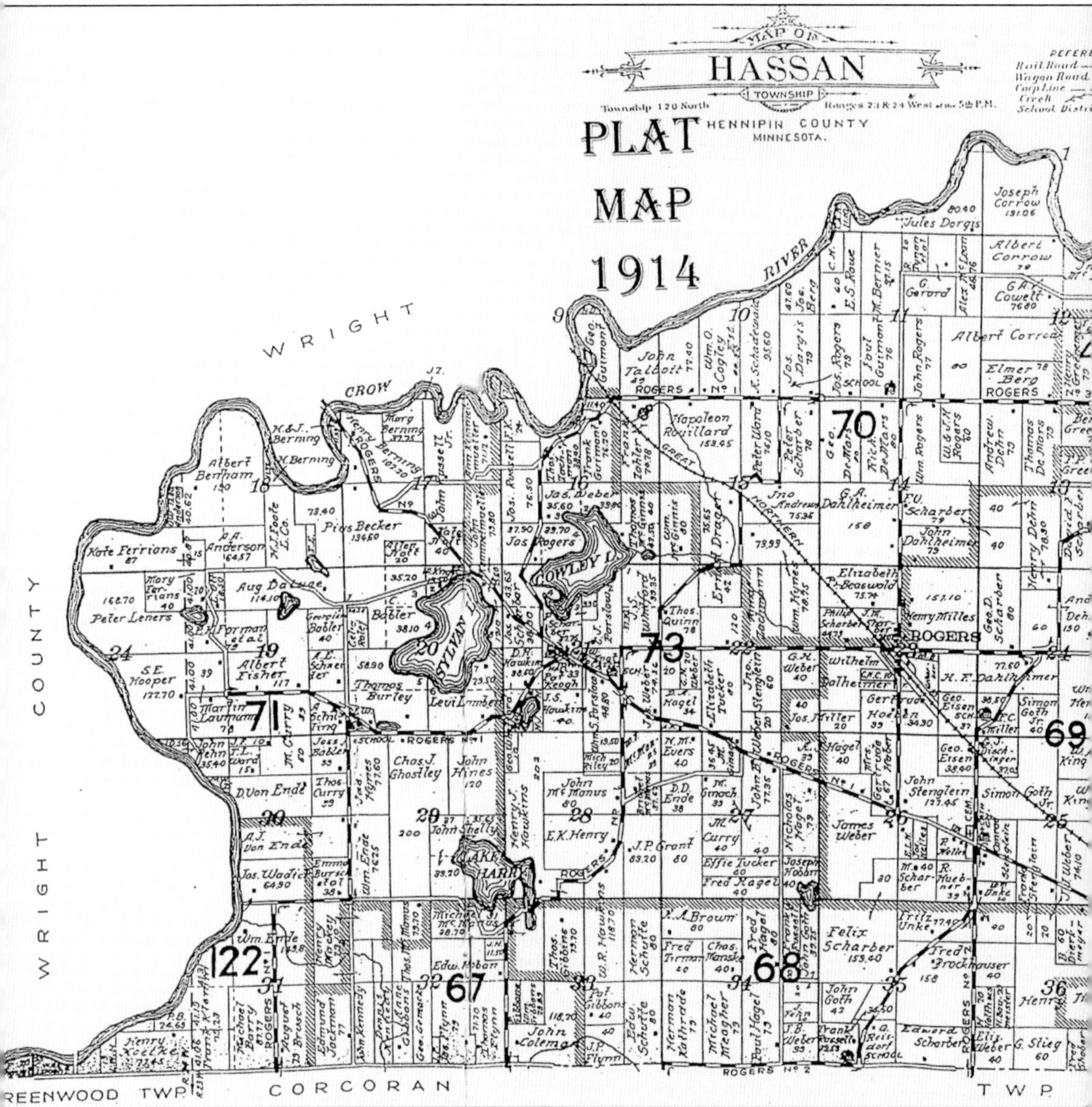

This plat map, dated 1914, illustrates the vast area of Hassan Township, denotes the location of the newly formed village of Rogers, and includes symbols identifying the Fletcher hamlet. The first documented settlers arrived in 1854 and 1855. These pioneers had the arduous task of clearing the land and preparing it to sustain their families. Hassan Township was organized in April 1860, the village of Rogers became incorporated in February 1914, and the Fletcher hamlet is currently eligible to become a historic district by the Minnesota Historical Society. (Courtesy of Jack Hines.)

On the cover: Fond memories of this building dance in everyone's mind as they reminisce about their childhood. The ice-cream parlor, owned by Katie Farrion, was a local hangout where people enjoyed sharing the events of their day while sipping an icy fountain drink or licking a double-scoop ice-cream cone. This image was captured by Marion Scharber in about 1940. (Courtesy of Leo Scharber.)

IMAGES
of America

Rogers, Hassan Township, and Fletcher Remembered

Paulie Skaja-Bell

ARCADIA
PUBLISHING

ISBN 978-0-7385-4111-2

Published by Arcadia Publishing
Charleston, South Carolina

Printed in the United States of America

Library of Congress Catalog Card Number: 2006930315

For all general information contact Arcadia Publishing at:
Telephone 843-853-2070
Fax 843-853-0044
E-mail sales@arcadiapublishing.com
For customer service and orders:
Toll-Free 1-888-313-2665

Visit us on the Internet at www.arcadiapublishing.com

To the pioneering families who settled the area
and all who have helped shape its future

Contents

Acknowledgments

This book was truly a community effort. Many contributed to its creation, and I would like to express a heartfelt thank-you to them for sharing their time, stories, pictures, and support. I ask forgiveness in advance from anyone I may forget to mention; however, everyone's participation was greatly appreciated. Contributors include Eugene Ahlstrom; Priscilla Arenz; JoAnn Bourgeois; Chuck, Dave, Jeff, and Clyde Christian; Jack, Peggy, Ray, Mary Lou, and Howard Dahlheimer; Danny and Janet Durant; Fire Chief Brad Feist; Jerome and Ferdella Gmach; John Hagel; Carmen Hawkins; Florian Heinen; Jane Heinrich; Evelyn Henry; Jack and Carol Hines; Grady Kinghorn; Leon LaVasseur; Florence and Bernard Lenz; Capt. Mike Miller; Bob Milless; Dennis Miltz; Danny Nadeau; Jim Rogers; Jim, Melvin, and Gordon Rouillard; Doug and Leo Scharber; Lenny, Lila, and Mary Beth Schlegel; Denny Stieg; Andrew Stueve; Harold Trombley; Judy and Norm Volkers; George Yankoupe; Norb Zahler; Crow River News; Luna Blu Coffee Company; Rogers Library; Hennepin History Museum; Minnesota Historical Society; Embers in Rogers; Antique Mall of Rogers; and Mary Queen of Peace, Joy Free, and Word of Peace Churches. There were also storytellers that contributed but requested to remain anonymous.

In addition to the endless contributions from the community, I received continuous support from my family and friends. If it had not been for the loving support of my husband, Rob Bell, and the ongoing patience of my children, Heather Osen and Taylor Bell, I would not have found the time or stamina to complete this project. I also need to thank my sister, Crystal Kokal, and my friend Sue Welch for helping me stay calm near the deadline.

Many thanks also go to Arcadia Publishing for believing in my vision, accepting the book proposal, and working patiently toward achieving the unreasonable timeline I requested. Thank you!

Introduction

In September 2005, I stopped by Eugene Ahlstrom's home to purchase some apples and got the opportunity to listen to many stories about his younger years. His stories were so enjoyable that I shared them with my children. That is when my son suggested I write a book so Mr. Ahlstrom's stories could be read by everyone. I pondered the idea but did not feel I needed another project to work on at the time.

In December of the same year, there was threatening activity at the Rogers High School. Although the officials handled the situation well, it was scary for parents with children going to the school. I began having conversations with Capt. Mike Miller about a K-9 unit for our community, primarily about the cost for this form of protection. Suddenly it became clear. A book capturing the stories of how our community was developed would be a fantastic fund-raiser to help defray the costs for a new K-9 unit!

Within this book, you will find historical facts, images and photographs, and stories shared by people who have lived in Rogers, Hassan Township, or Fletcher for a very long time. The last several months have been a trip back in time and a walk down memory lane for many; it has been a journey I am thankful to have taken and grateful so many shared.

Rogers, Hassan Township, and Fletcher Remembered will take you back to the pioneering days in 1854 when brave men carved a path through the "Big Woods" and created the first passageway between Minneapolis and Monticello. The road was known as Territorial Road and is still used today. You will also learn about the leaders of the community in the founding years and recognize many of the same names still in the community today.

Historical information about the area churches and schools will be revealed. You will learn about the families that started the churches and why and understand some of the hardships they had to face. Stories about the one-room schoolhouse share excellent arguments for going back to the basics.

Have you ever wondered what people did for fun "in the olden days"? You will find out in the pages of this book. Community members shared the games they played, what they did with their friends, what they enjoyed doing in the community, and what they think children are missing out on today. Life was simpler and people seemed happier than today; maybe readers will learn why. The community is honored to have several veterans living within it. Their wartime stories will enlighten readers of all ages and may encourage an increased level of patriotism in the lives this book touches.

It was my pleasure to meet with so many long-standing families of the community and to learn about its rich heritage. The village of Rogers, Hassan Township, and the Fletcher hamlet are all very unique communities that lay within a platted area of land. Our situation is uncommon; however, it seems that is one of the characteristics that draws people to the area: the diversity of charm. My desire is to provide an opportunity for each reader to relive "the good ole days" just a little bit through this book and to touch the lives of those who choose Rogers, Hassan Township, and Fletcher as their new hometown.

Dragonfly Journey will donate the proceeds from the sale of this book to help defray expenses associated with forming a K-9 unit for our community. Thank you for your support. I sincerely hope you enjoy the book!

—Paulie Skaja-Bell

One

Clearing the Way

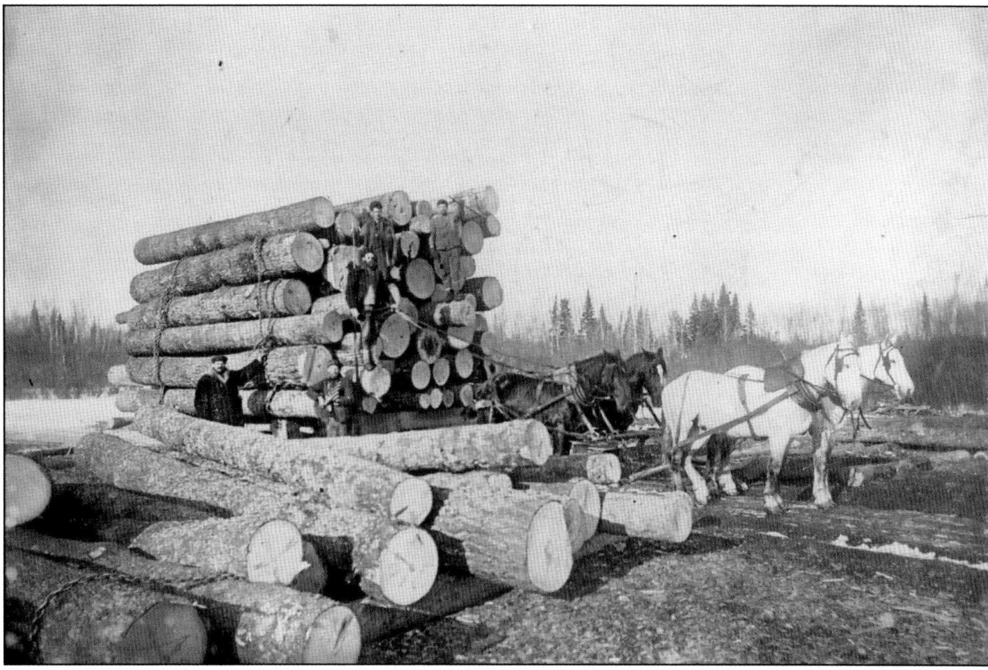

Settling this new territory, later named Hassan Township, was a daunting task. The land resided in the northwesternmost corner of Hennepin County in Minnesota and was laden with trees. The only access to the heavily wooded area was by water via steamboat on the Mississippi River or by small boat along the Crow River. In 1854, Alexander Borthwick and Harvey Hicks are said to have brought the first horses and wagon into the area, cutting a road through the timber. Dennis Ford, Alpheus Maservy, and Joseph Green followed that fall. In April 1855, Henry Parslow and Jasper Hawkins penetrated the "Big Woods" for their oxen-drawn wagon to pass. Other early pioneers were Tomas Rogers; Mortimer and Patrick Hynes; Horatio "Happy" Hawkins; Septimus, John, and Charles Parslow; Henry Ghostley; John Mitchell; Samuel Gowell; John Keegan; Patrick Burke; Owen McCabe; Ariel Begelow; A. Woodman; Harvey Norton; Charles Tucker; and William Demery. The government price for land was $1.25 per acre. (Courtesy of Jack and Peggy Dahlheimer.)

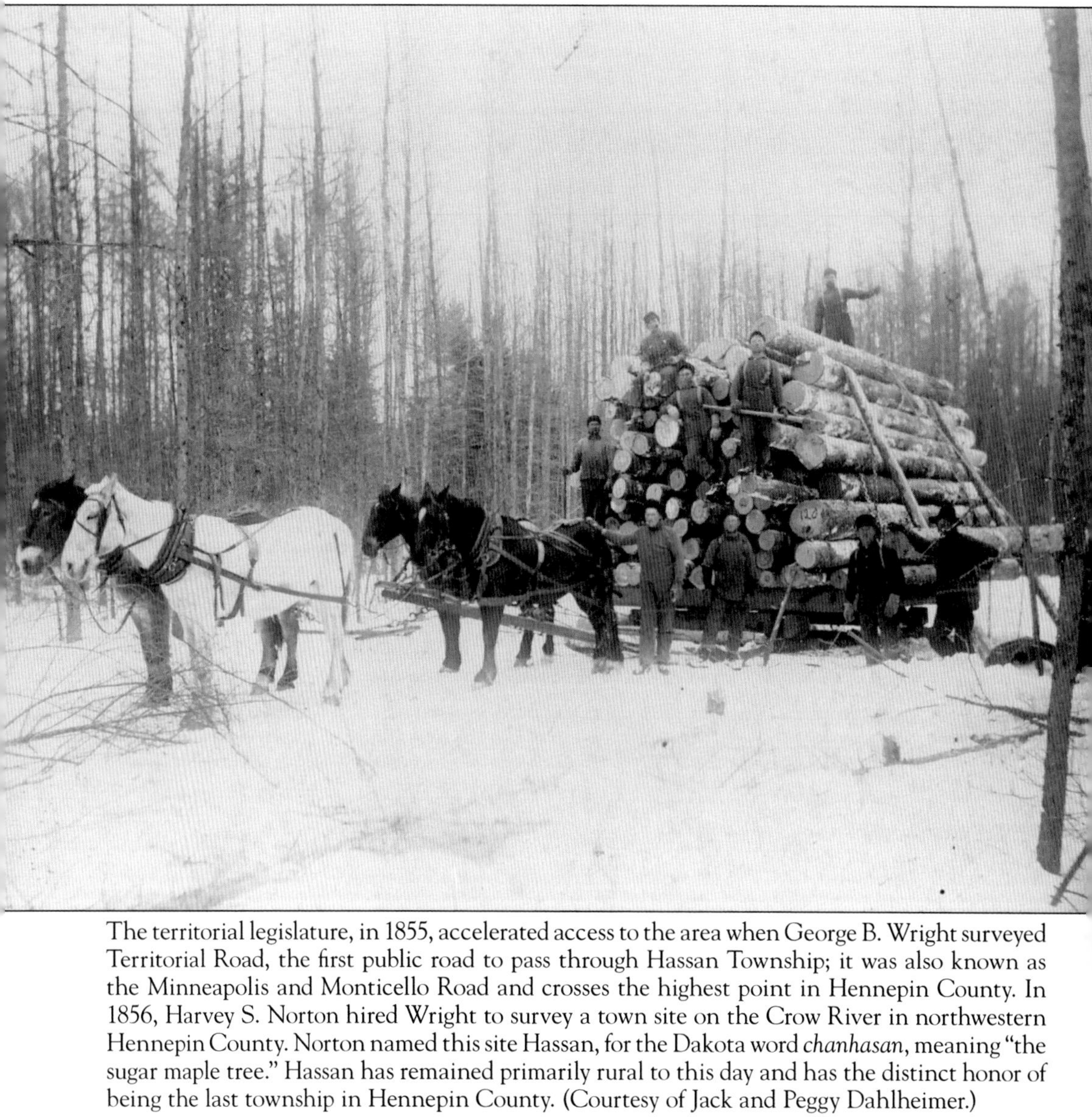

The territorial legislature, in 1855, accelerated access to the area when George B. Wright surveyed Territorial Road, the first public road to pass through Hassan Township; it was also known as the Minneapolis and Monticello Road and crosses the highest point in Hennepin County. In 1856, Harvey S. Norton hired Wright to survey a town site on the Crow River in northwestern Hennepin County. Norton named this site Hassan, for the Dakota word *chanhasan*, meaning "the sugar maple tree." Hassan has remained primarily rural to this day and has the distinct honor of being the last township in Hennepin County. (Courtesy of Jack and Peggy Dahlheimer.)

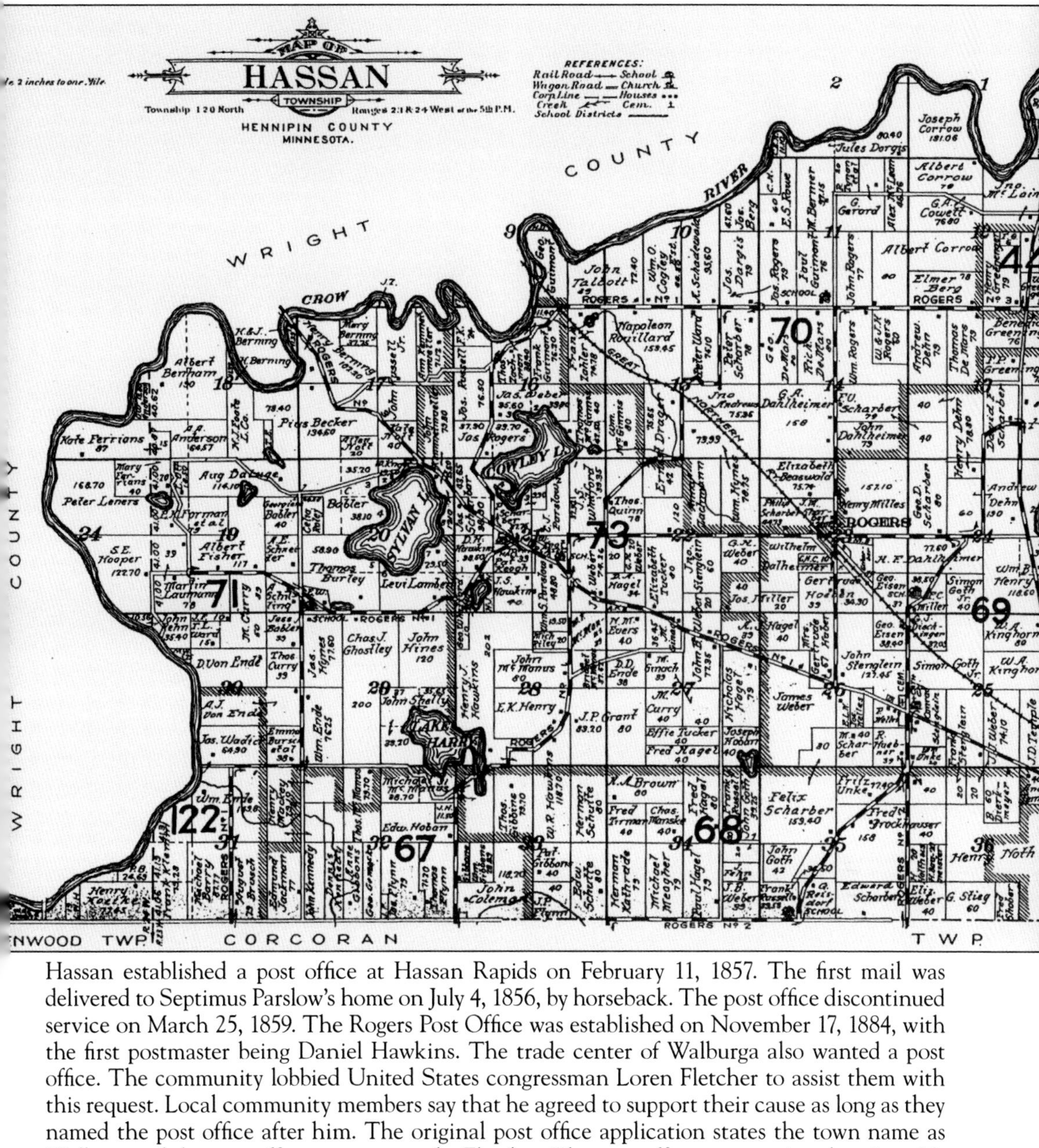

Hassan established a post office at Hassan Rapids on February 11, 1857. The first mail was delivered to Septimus Parslow's home on July 4, 1856, by horseback. The post office discontinued service on March 25, 1859. The Rogers Post Office was established on November 17, 1884, with the first postmaster being Daniel Hawkins. The trade center of Walburga also wanted a post office. The community lobbied United States congressman Loren Fletcher to assist them with this request. Local community members say that he agreed to support their cause as long as they named the post office after him. The original post office application states the town name as Walburg and the post office name was to be Fletcher. The post office was appointed on June 28, 1900. The first postmaster was Andrew N. Nelles, and John Stenglein was the final postmaster when the post office closed August 31, 1906; mail was forwarded to Rogers. (Courtesy of Jack and Carol Hines.)

34 ATLAS AND FARMERS' DIRECTORY OF HENNEPIN COUNTY, MINNESOTA.

Farmers' Directory of Hassan Township

Abbreviations: Sec., section; ac., acres; wf., wife; ch., children; ( ) years in county

Rogers Post Office.

Andrews, J. N., R1, sec 15, ac 75.60, wf Addie, ch Allen, Margaret, Robert, (5).

Babler, C., R3, sec 20, 19, ac 165.35, wf Georgiena, ch Jesse, Rudolph, Albert, Christ, Emma, Albertia, Frances, Helen, (35).

Beaswad, John, R3, sec 23, ac 75.74, wf Elizabeth, ch Henry, Joseph, Deloras, Rudolph, (45).

Becker, K., R3, sec 17, ac 4, wf Lena, ch Rose, Ambrose, Verner, Annie, Agnes, Albert, (12).

Becker, Pius, R3, B53, sec 17, 18, ac 266, wf Frances, ch Tresa, William, Joseph, Tillie, Alois, Margaret, Henry, Thomas, Clara, Minnie, (28). "Crow River Stock Farm."

Berndt, Charles, R1, sec 10, ac 88.30, wf Dorothy, ch Lillian.

Bernies, Medes, R3, sec 11, 2, ac 100, wf Blanche, ch Lawrence, Louise, Raymond, Albert, (3).

Berry, Mike, sec 23, 31, ac 91½, wf Minnie, ch Mathew, Thomas, Mary, (47).

Borck, M., sec 23, 16, ac 79.40, wf Lizzie, ch Emma, Elsie, (30).

Brockhaus, Fred, R2, sec 35, 36, ac 198, wf Emma, (44).

Brown, Thomas, R3, sec 21, ac 59, wf Luella, ch Howard, (23).

Burley, Thomas, R1, sec 20, ac 117.90, wf Nellie, ch Thomas, Charles, Ralph, (40).

Bursch, Robert A., R1, sec 30, ac 40, wf Emma, ch Evelyn, Vivian, Luella, Gladys, (30).

Bush, A., R1, sec 32, ac 40, wf Amelia, ch Hazel, Frank, Elmer, Julius, Walter, Frances, Alice, Victor, (47).

Carbin, Edward, R2, sec 13, ac ½, wf Lucy, ch Stella, Nettie, Roy, Edward, (40).

Carbin, Mose, R3, sec 13, ac 80, wf Annie, ch Lloyd, (24).

Carrow, Albert, R3, sec 11, 12, ac 160, wf Sadie, ch Neil, Celia, (25).

Carrow, Joseph, R3, sec 1, 12, ac 210, wf Caroline, ch Richard, Georgina, (35).

Cowette, G. A., R3, sec 12, ac 80, wf Manda, ch Raymond, Aleides, Richard, Leo, (41).

Curry, M., R1, sec 30, ac 90, wf Magdeline, (50).

Curry, Thomas, R1, sec 30, ac 40, wf Margaret, ch Margaret, Nellie, Walter, (51).

Dahlheimeir, George, R3, sec 14, ac 160, wf Dina, ch Leo, Bennie, Werner, Walter, (51).

Dahlheimer, Henry, R2, sec 24, 23, ac 120, wf Emma, ch Delrose, Bernice, (30).

Dahlheimer, William, R3, sec 14, ac 80, (31).

Daluge, August, R3, sec 19, ac 120, wf Lizzie, ch William, Minnie, Herman, Emma, Mabel, Sarah, (21).

Dargis, Joseph, R3, sec 2, ac 80.40, wf Clara, ch Edward, Louis, (20).

Dehn, Andrew, R2, sec 24, 13, ac 314, wf Josephine, ch Anthony, George, Andrew, Bennie, (49).

Dehn, H., R2, sec 24, 13, ac 100, wf Elizabeth, ch Rosella, (28).

DeMars, Fred, R1, sec 14, ac 80, wf Isabell, ch Angeline, Priscilla, (22).

De Mars, Richard, R3, sec 14, ac 80, wf Leah, (26).

De Mars, Thomas Jr., sec 23, ac 15, wf Stella, ch Gerald, (24).

Dichinger, George, R2, sec 25, ac 40, wf Maggie, ch Herman, Charles, (5).

Dirksmire, Joseph, R2, sec 25, 36, ac 60, (50).

Eisien, G., R2, sec 26, 23, ac 77, (57).

Ende, August, R1, sec 36, 22, ac 160, wf Bertha, ch Walter, (30).

Evers, N., R1, sec 27, 22, ac 40, wf Mary, ch Marie, William, Charlotte, Herbert, Arthur, Martha, (30).

Farrier, J., R1, sec 30, ac 15, wf Sarah, (35).

Fisher, A., R1, sec 19, ac 120, wf Harriet, ch Harry, (52).

Fitzgerald, N., R1, sec 22, 27, ac 7, wf Mary, ch William, George, (45).

Fitzgerald, Thomas, R2, sec 25, 144 rods, wf Katie, (43).

Flynn, J. P., R1, sec 32, ac 160, ows sec 33, ac 40, wf Elizabeth, ch Raymond, Mary, Mildred, John, (49).

Ghostley, C. H., R1, sec 21, ac 36, (29).

Ghostley, C. J., R1, sec 29, ac 200, wf Emma, ch Clifford, Mabel, James, Maude, Frank, Kenneth, Phyllis, (58).

Gibbons, Mrs. Thomas, R1, sec 33, ac 80, ch Martin, (45).

Gibbons, P., R1, sec 33, ac 40, wf Rose, (36).

Gmach, Mathew, R1, sec 27, ac 8, wf Lena, ch Marcellus, (1).

Goth, Andrew, R2, sec 24, ac 40, wf Mary, ch Henry, Raymond, (40).

Goth, John, R2, sec 35, 34, ac 103, wf Lena, ch Rose, Regina, Albert, Mary, Anthony, Agnes, (46).

Goth, J. J., sec 23, ac 14.85, wf Lizzie, ch Cornelia, (18).

Goth, S., R2, sec 25, 24, ac 116.25, wf Tresa, ch Frank, Lizzie, Margaret, Cecelia, George, Eurban, (45).

Grant, J. P., R1, sec 28, 27, ac 164, wf Emily, (4).

Greenenger, Ben, R3, sec 13, ac 80, wf Rose, ch Mary, Katie, Florence, Emelia, Dorothy, Emma, Walter, (38).

Greenenger, F., R3, sec 13, ac 160, wf Theresa, ch William, Casper, (40).

Greeninger, Henry, R3, sec 13, ac 80, wf Veronica, ch Victor, Theresa, Margaret, (40).

Greeninger, W., R3, sec 12, ac 40, (40).

Guemont, G., R3, sec 12, ac 50, wf Mary, ch Naploeon, Joseph, Josephine, Louis, (50).

Guimont, Paul, R3, sec 11, ac 80, wf Julia, ch Charles, Hattie, Virginia, Luella, (56).

Hagel, Fred, R2, sec 34, 27, ac 120, wf Gertie, ch Nellie, Arnold, Henrietta, (48).

Hagel, N., R1, B5, sec 27, ac 80, wf Christina, ch George, Joseph, Catherine, Margaret, (52).

Hagel, Paul, R2, sec 34, ac 80, wf Mary, ch Veronica, (51).

Hagel, P. J., R1, sec 27, 26, ac 80, wf Sarah, ch Laura, Robert, Wallace, (31).

Harves, Mary, R2, sec 26, 23, ac 77, ch Joseph, George, Fred, Anna, Katie, (30).

Hawkins, J. S., sec 21, ac 40, wf Alice, (60).

Hawkins, D. H., R1, sec 21, ac 40, wf Emma, ch Myrtle, Ethel, (56).

Hawkins, H. J., R1, sec 28, 21, ac 220, wf Emma, ch Gertrude, Marion, (57).

Hawkins, W. H., R1, sec 28, 21, ac 220, wf Marion, (28).

Hawkins, W. R., R1, sec 28, 33, ac 120, wf Effie, ch Horatio, Winnefred, Martha, Edward, William R. Jr., Herbert, Walter, Mina, (47).

Henry, E. K., R1, sec 28, ac 97, wf Winifred, ch Lois, Byron, Alfred, Charles, Robert, (45).

Henry, F. B., R2, sec 24, ac 160, wf Grace, ch Rhoda, (41).

Hines, John, R1, sec 29, ac 120, wf Ellen, ch John, (13).

Hoeben, Edward, R1, sec 32, ac 60, wf Katherine, ch Frances, Viola, (35).

Hoeben, Mrs. J. F., sec 23, 26, 27, 32, ac 195½, ch Andrew, Henry, (40).

Hoeben, T. L., sec 23, ac 1, wf Tresa, ch Lambert, (30).

Hubner, R., R2, sec 26, 36, ac 80, wf Sophie, ch August, Clara, Lena, (38).

Kaska, August, R2, sec 36, ac 170, wf Augusta, ch Herman, Albert, Richard, Eda, Bertha, Martha, (14).

Kemmetmueller, John, R3, sec 20, 17, ac 118, wf Susie, ch Edwin, Alvina, Clara, (30). "Sylvan Lake Stock Farm."

Kinghorn, W. A., R2, sec 25, ac 80, wf Linnie, ch Lester, Laren, Mildred, Victor, (52).

Lambert, Alex, R1, sec 20, ac 121, wf Jennet, ch Mary, (34).

Lambert, William, R1, sec 20, (brother of Alex).

Laymann, M., R1, sec 19, ac 120, wf Gertrude, ch John, Katie, Martin, Agnes, Lena, Peter, Herbertine, Annie, Felix, Mathias, (15).

McGinnis, Thomas, R1, sec 16, ac 82½, wf Katie, ch John, Jim, Joseph, (48).

McGinnis, William, R1, sec 15, ac 80, wf Johanna, ch William, Thomas, Tresia, (46).

McLean, Alex, R3, sec 11, ac 90, wf Sarah, ch Raymond, (34).

McLean, N., R3, sec 1, ac 90, wf Lydie, ch Marion, (31).

McLean, William, R3, sec 1, ac 100, ch Lizzie, Robert, Mary, Nellie, Wallace, (44).

McManus, John, R1, sec 28, ac 80, wf Mary, ch Anna, Margaret, Leonard, (37).

McManus, Thomas, R1, sec 32, ac 79.70, wf Tillie, ch Belle, Ellen, Anthony, Rosanna, Earl, (35).

McManus, William, R1, sec 28, ac 60.

McNeal, John, sec 23, ac 5, wf Sarah, ch Cornelia, Henrietta, Priscilla, Adolph, (42).

Mangzke, Carl, R2, sec 34, ac 40, wf Augusta, ch Augusta, Alma, Clara, Elsie, Albert, Tillie, (20).

Mathena, Newton, R1, sec 27, ac 40, wf Maggie, ch Dollie, Melvin, Leafy, (1).

Miller, Joseph, R1, sec 22, 23, ac 60, wf Susie, ch Susie, Margaret, Agnes, Carl, (54).

Milless, H., R3, sec 23, ac 157, wf Katie, ch Rudolph, Elmer, Mirandas, Katie, Hillerd, Henry, (49).

Natt, A., R3, sec 17, ac 20, (58).

Natti, William, R3, sec 20, 17, 21, ac 79, wf Sarah, ch Mabel, Harold, (36).

Nelles, E., R1, sec 26, ac 15, wf Florence, ch Virgil, (32).

Nelles, M. J., R1, sec 27, 22, ac 120, wf Elizabeth, ch John, Carrie, William, Annie, Catherine, Rose, Frank, Andrew, Clara, Lewis, (49).

Nelles, P. C., R2, sec 26, ac 30, wf Rose, ch Alice, (34).

Parslow, W. S., R2, sec 21, 28, ac 70, wf Nina, (53).

Quinn, Thomas, R1, sec 22, ac 78, wf Margaret, ch Mike, Thomas, Annie, Nellie, Rose, Elizabeth, (36).

Rehm, John, R1, sec 30, 25, ac 45, (22). Wright Co. Frankford twp., sec 30, ac 5.

Reisdorf, G., R2, sec 35, ac 38, wf Mary, ch John, (40).

Riley, M., R1, sec 28, ac 20, wf Celia, ch Hugh, Annie, Edwina, (33).

Rogers, James, R1, sec 16, ac 73, wf Allen, ch Lenora, Mamie, Margaret, James, Elizabeth, (53).

Rogers, Thomas, R1, sec 10, 11, ac 130, wf Laura, ch Raymond, (21).

Rogers, William, R3, sec 14, ac 160, wf Annie, ch Walter, Myrtle, Irene, Pearl, Earl, Nellie, Robert, Gilbert, Wilbur, (48).

Rouillard, Napoleon, R1, sec 15, ac 153.45, wf Adelia, ch Dean, Hazel, Henry, Elmer, Joseph, Lester, Edward, Wilfred, (54).

Russell, John, R3, sec 17, 16, ac 188.16, wf Katie, ch Mathew, (53).

Russell, Joseph, R3, sec 17, 16, ac 188.16, wf Katie, (27).

Russell, Mathew, R3, sec 17, (brother of Joseph).

Schadwald, Adolph, R1, sec 10, ac 95½, wf Cecelia, ch Walter, (34).

Scharber, D. F., R2, sec 13, ac 80, Dayton twp. sec 18, ac 67, wf Annie, ch Albert Alex, Emma, Margaret, Clarence, (46).

Scharber, Frank V., R3, sec 14, 13, ac 120, wf Frona, ch Rudolph, Agnes, Archie, Raymond, Ervin, (39).

Scharber, Mathew, R2, sec 26, ac 75, wf Rose, ch Lenora, Herbert, Clemons, (41).

Scharber, Phil, R2, sec 35, ac 159½, wf Lena, ch Andrew, Tresa, (46).

Scherber, Edward, R2, sec 35, ac 80, wf Mary, ch Cecelia, Leo, Adeline, (36).

Scherber, George D., R2, sec 24, ac 80, wf Lena, ch Mathilda, Emil, Adeline, Grace, Walter, (46).

Scherber, Joseph D., R3, sec 21, ac 80.60, wf Katherine, ch Joseph, Anthoney, Gilbert, Charles, Marion, Cyril, Erwin, Francis, (38).

Scherber, P. M., R3, sec 21, ac 49, wf Margaret, ch Petronella, Harold, Roland, (37).

Scherber, Peter, R1, sec 15, ac 80, wf Josephine, ch Gertrude, Clara, Clarence, Robert, (47).

Scherber, Phil, R3 sec 23, ac 44, wf Annie, ch Ralph, Irene, Priscilla, Wilfred, (42).

Schillig, S., R1, sec 19, ac 40, wf Emma, (22).

Schneider, Aaron, R1, sec 19, ac 40, wf Ada, ch George, Helen, (19).

Schutte, Edward, R2, sec 33, ac 80, wf Augusta, ch Edward, Walter, John, (56).

Stenglein, Conrad, R2, sec 25, ac 75, wf Katie, ch Max, Margaret, Andrew, (57).

Stenglein, F. C., R2, sec 25, 36, ac 96, wf Anna, (28).

Stenglein, Joseph, R1, sec 26, 22, ac 167.45, wf Emma, ch Marvel, parents, (25).

Talbot, John, R1, sec 10, 9, ac 112, wf Marian, ch Cyril, Alma, Vincent, Donald, Floyd, Dorothy, (4).

Tempel, A., R2, sec 36, ac 40, ch Lizzie, Joseph, (55).

Tempel, John P., R2, sec 25, ac 74, wf Josephine, ch Clara, (31).

Tempel, Joseph, R2, sec 36, 25, ac 120, (27).

Unk, W., R2, sec 25, ac 20, (44).

Unke, Frit, R2, sec 35, ac 80, wf Sophie, (47).

Von Ende, Albert, R1, sec 30, ac 107, wf Katie, ch Albert, William, Lawrence, Adie, Mary, Dougherty, (38).

Von Ende, Mrs. William, R1, sec 29, ac 80, ch Carrie, Fred, (26).

Ward, F., R1, sec 30, ac 15, wf Sarah, (35).

Ward, P. F., R1, sec 15, ac 80, wf Bridget, (38).

Weber, F., R2, sec 25, ac 20, wf Mary, ch Laura, Helen, Lucille, (39).

Weber, George, R1, sec 27, 22, ac 97.35, wf Mary, ch Walter, (28).

Weber, James, R1, sec 26, ac 130, wf Lizzie, ch William, Lizzie, Edward, Jacob, Mathilda, (57).

Weber, Joseph, R1, sec 21, ac 77¾, wf Catherine, ch Robert, Lawrence, Louis, (43).

Weier, A. E., R1, sec 21, ac 2¼, wf Minnie, ch Anita, (26).

Whitefard, James, R1, sec 21, ac 100, wf Helen, ch James, Joseph, John, Alice, Helen, (41).

Wiggen, Edwin, R1, sec 22, ac 120, wf Rose, ch Kenneth, Howard, (29).

Whitefard, George, R1, sec 33, ac 1, wf Margaret, ch Kenneth, Edward, mother Mrs. Wadick, (28).

Zohler, Frank, R1, sec 16, ac 154.78, wf Christina, ch Bert, Sylvester, Isadore, Victor, Harold, Florence, Alvina, Luella, Whihlmina, (19).

Zoldahn, E., R1, sec 16, 22, ac 152, wf Emma, ch Esther, Reinhart, (30).

Zoldahn, Paul, R1, sec 15, 22, ac 120, wf Katie, (30).

St. Michaels Post Office.

Ferrians, Louis, sec 13, ac 107, wf Katherine, ch Lizzie, John, Peter, Gertrude, Felix, (29).

Ferrians, Theodore, sec 19, 24, ac 60, wf Mary, ch Conrad, Fred, Louise, Annie, (29).

Kemmetmueller, Frank, sec 17, 16, 9, 8, ac 107.29, wf Anna, (30). "Riverside Farm."

Ott, L., sec 19, ac 20, wf Annie, ch Mamie, Grace, Caroline, (25).

Hanover Post Office.

Jackman, Edward, R1, sec 31, ac 80, wf Lillie, ch William, Earl, Alfred, Ethel, Thomas, James, Edmund, Luella, (43).

On April 3, 1860, the community of Hassan Township elected the first city council officers. The results were as follows: chairman, Gideon Reeves; supervisors, Harvey Hickes and Richard Quinn; town clerk, C. J. Parslow; treasurer, L. Parslow; assessor, A. Borthwick; justice of the peace, Henry Ghostley; constables, Patrick Hynes and John Parslow. This 1915 copy of the Farmers Directory of Hassan Township reflects the families owning land within Hassan Township. It includes the location of their land, how many acres they owned, to whom they were married, the names of their children, and how long they had lived in the county. While interviewing Carol (Berg) Hines, she shared that although she was a Berg, her dad's mother was a Dahlheimer and mother's dad was a Scharber; therefore, if the Hines family had not come from Ireland she could not imagine who she could have married. (Courtesy of Jack and Carol Hines.)

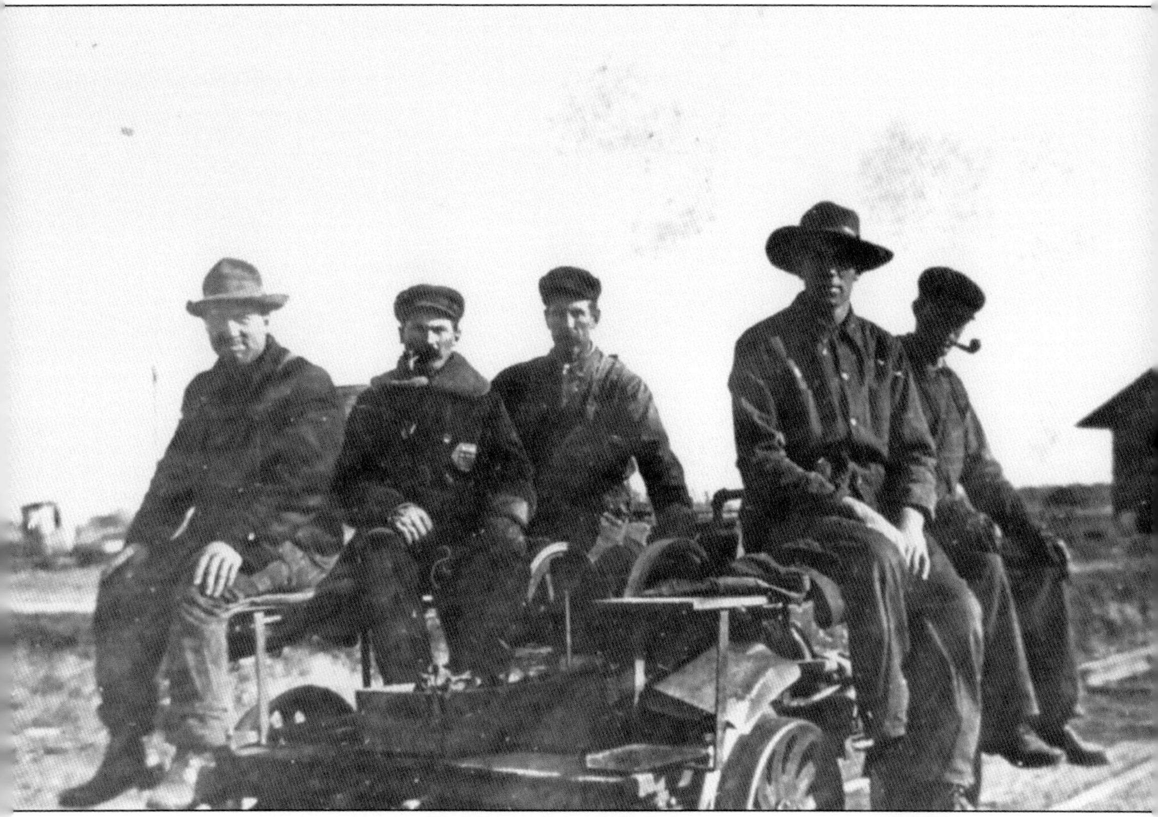

The legal description from a copy of the original purchase agreement between Thomas Rogers Jr. and Gustaves A. Austin on July 24, 1880, reflects that Thomas Rogers Jr. and his wife, Maggie, acquired the original land that became known as Rogers Siding. The sum of this transaction was $2,000. A copy of another agreement between Thomas and Maggie to sell about one acre of land for $200 to the St. Paul, Minneapolis and Manitoba Railway Company transpired on April 29, 1887. These original documents were provided by descendant Jim Rogers, which could explain how the area became known as Rogers Siding. However, some locals speculate the area was named after famous American surveyor Maj. A. B. Rogers who worked for James J. Hill. Major Rogers was known for finding a rail route through the Selkirk and Rocky Mountains in British Columbia, Canada. (Courtesy of Leo Scharber.)

TION III **THE NORTH HENNEPIN POST** Thursday, Apri

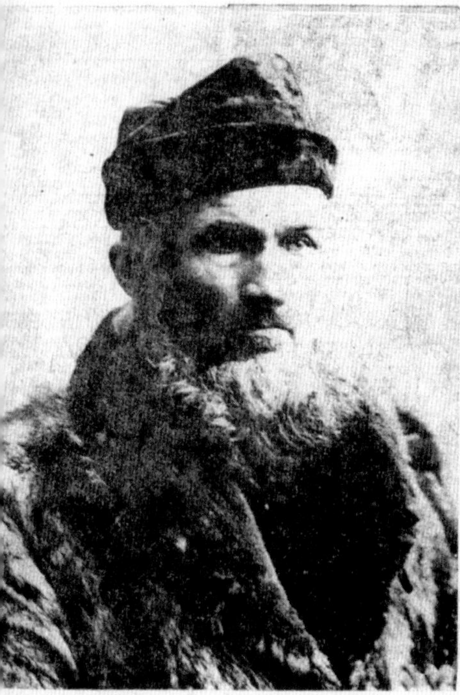

GEORGE SCHARBER was one of the early settlers in the Rogers a. He is pictured above prior to 1892 when he jointly operated general merchandise store in Rogers with his son, John.

Mr. Norton Platted First Hassan Town

Early in the summer of 1855, the excellent water power on the Crow river attracted the notice of Harvey S. Norton, an early settler in Hassan.

Norton suggested the founding of a village on the site (today, located south of St. Michael on the extreme western portion of Hassan township), and hired a surveyor, laid out a town plat and decided to name it Hassan, if it was ever born.

It never was.

The name remained unused until 1886, until a postoffice was started. In years to come, the original Hassan town was moved a few miles east to the present site.

The first mail was received July 4, 1856. The carrier made the trips on horseback. Soon afterward, the Territorial road from Minneapolis to Monticello was opened, and wheeled vehicles replaced the horses. In a matter of time, tri-weekly mail service was secured.

The first marriage in the town took place in 1856 when Charles Tucker took Elizabeth Hawkins as his bride.

The first school was taught by Miss Sarah Ward in a small log building in the west part of town.

In 1858, the county commissioners named the area Hassan. It was official then.

Pierre Bottineau Made Fir Claim at Osseo Site in 185

These Are Pioneers of Hassan Area

These are the pioneers of Hassan township—the Gadbois family, the James family, Reason and Mercy Lyons, Pat Ward, the Morris family, the Demaray family, John Rogers, Sr., Mike Hax, Horatio Hawkins, Jasper Hawkins, John Tucker, Charles Tucker.

The Whiteford family, three Parslow families, two Ghostley families, Johanthan Wiggings, the Burleigh family, Charles Hoag, the Tynan family, the Hord family, the Lundriggans, Mulreans, Pat Hynes, Mort Hynes, Con Dineen, the Klersys, the Russels, the Kemmetmuellers.

Tom Zachman, the Guimonts, the DeMars', the Caouttes, the Scherbers, the Dahlheimers, the Milless', the Rouses, the Hobansm, the Gothsm, the Millers, the Temples,

The Drapers, the Fishers, the Jackins, A. Lamson, the Gowells, the Notts, John Curry, Sr., John Shelly, Ed Lehr, the Quinns, the McManus', Mike Riley, the McHugos, the McGintys, the Gib-

Pierre Bottineau, the f the territory now know seo, made his first clai land that now includes th in the year 1852. With came Joseph Potvin, Pet and Peter Gervais, who claims near Bottineau.

The village of Osseo ted in 1856 by Warren and Isaac Labosiniere. S another village was laid B. Chaffee, adjoining Os southeast and called "C traction." This is now in the limits of Osseo.

Osseo was settled in Warren Sampson, Isaac iere, Clark Ellsworth Brown, James McRay Thayer.

Sampson built and store, and was postmas office, then called Palis ing 1855 and 1856, the ing country was occupie lers, among whom we Chaffee, D. C. Smith and

After the village was in 1856, the settlement A wood market was by Sampson in 1855. would buy green wood, it to families in M after allowing it to dr

The first blacksmith established in 1855 by C worth. Eli Haviland be partner two years later.

Osseo remained under

Almost one hundred years after the first pioneers began claiming land in Hassan Township, the North Hennepin Post chose to remember these adventurers. The Hassan country school was the first school in the area, with Sarah Ward teaching students in 1857, followed the next year by Helen Tilton. Pictured in this article is George Sebastian; there is speculation whether his last name was spelled Scherber or Scharber, and some believe it may have been Schirber in his home country of Germany. Regardless, it has been determined the family name has changed many times. This entrepreneur created a general merchandise store in 1892 that became a cornerstone for the community and a legacy for his family. The Modern Woodman of America built a hall just across the road from the Episcopal church in 1902. The building was used for lodge meetings and as a community center for social activities; it was torn down in the late 1930s. (Courtesy of Crow River News.)

Two

CHURCHES ARE THE CORNERSTONE

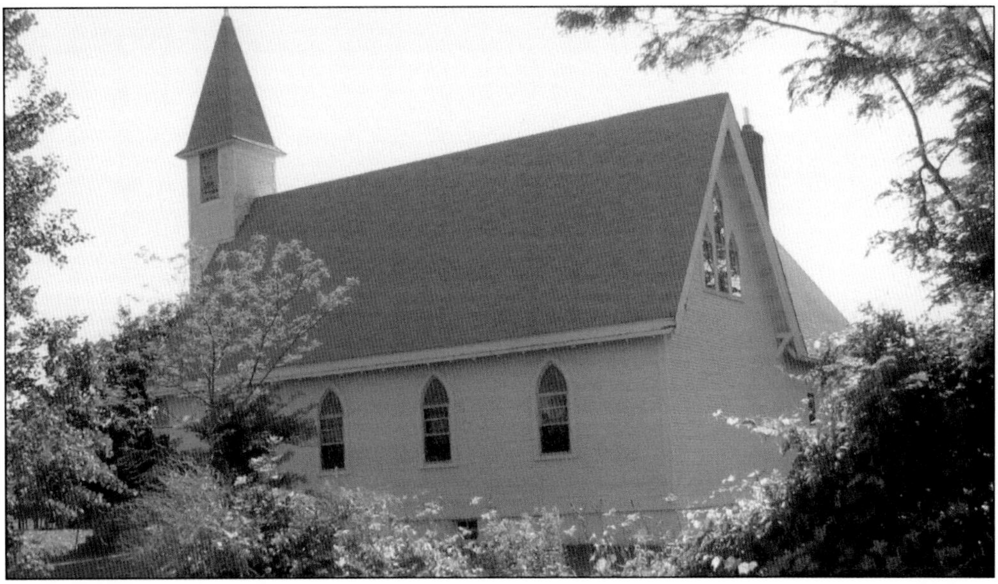

Henry Parslow and Jasper Hawkins cleared the land they claimed in anticipation of others joining them from Slymbridge, England. Their families arrived within five weeks, and after getting settled, these English people began holding monthly Anglican services of worship in the home of Septimus Parslow. On Easter Monday in 1857, the official church committee was formed under the name St. John's Parish, Crow River Woods, Minnesota, after St. John the Evangelist, and was the pioneer Episcopal church in Hennepin County outside of Minneapolis. Bishop Jackson Kemper visited the parish in 1859 and laid the foundation stone. Septimus and Catherine Parslow gave five acres of land to establish a church and cemetery. Through donations and hard work, the church was ready for its first service on July 9, 1860. The officiating reverend, J. S. Chamberlain, walked about 15 miles with bread, wine, and 12 copies of *The Book of Common Prayer*. (Courtesy of Rob Bell.)

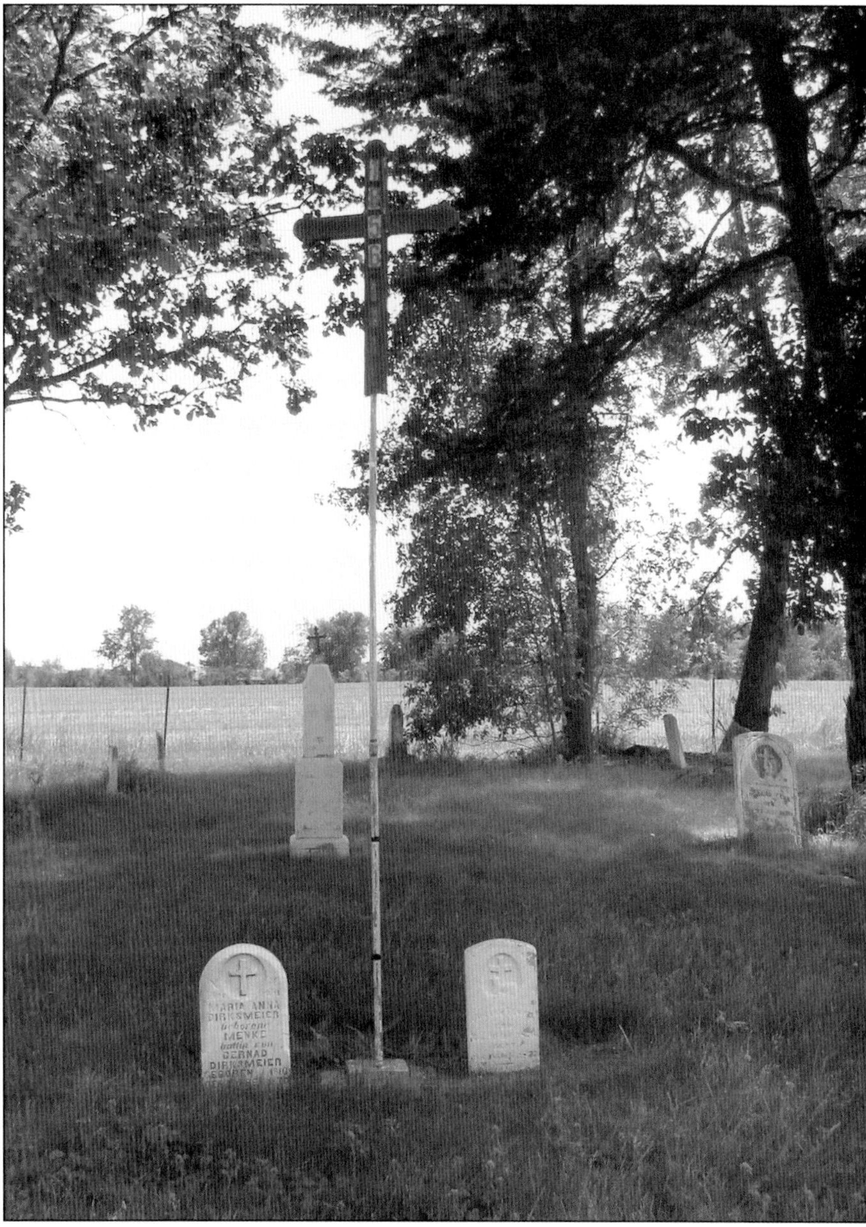

Fr. Demetrius de Marogna, O.S.B., founded the mission of St. Walburga two miles west of the present hamlet of Fletcher. The Benedictine father rode 60 miles on horseback from Collegeville to Fletcher for monthly services, which were initially held in the home of John Fehn in 1856. Early in 1857, the mission parish organized about 15 families, with the church committee being John Fehn, William Bennett, Peter Hagel, John Temple, Conrad Fehn, Andrew Stenglein, and Jacob Weber. This parish was one of the earliest in this part of Minnesota; the Diocese of St. Paul had only begun six years earlier. Within one year, in 1858, the committee established St. Walburga parish and built a log chapel on land donated by John Fehn. The parish was named in honor of John Fehn's wife, Walburga, whose saintly namesake came from Eichstatt, Germany. In 1882, the Catholic church was moved two miles east of the original mission. All that remains of the original dream are a few headstones in this preserved cemetery. (Courtesy of Rob Bell.)

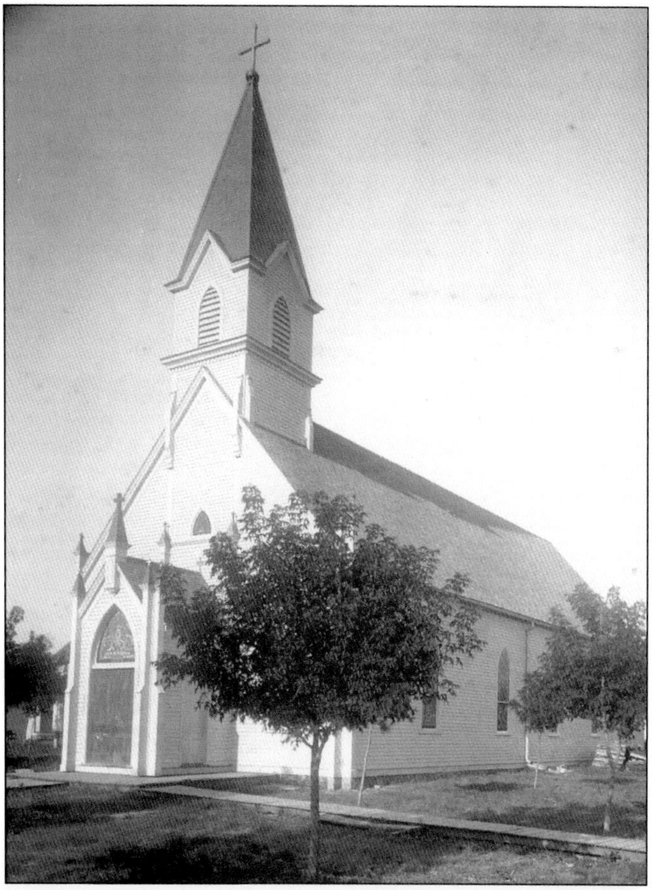

In 1882, Fr. Ignatius Schaller decided the church should be more centrally located between Dayton and Corcoran. He accepted a gift of two and a half acres from Conrad Stenglein at the intersection of Territorial Road and Corcoran-Dayton Road. In 1883, a $3,000 church was constructed directly across the street from Conrad's farm. Felix Scherber, John Stenglein, and John Fehn led the construction efforts. In the early 1900s, the church was enlarged 30 feet and a large sacristy was added. The craftsmanship of St. Walburga Church has withstood over 120 years of violent Minnesota winters, while its beauty and charm are timeless. Pictured are outside and inside views of St. Walburga in 1885. (Courtesy of Andrew Stueve.)

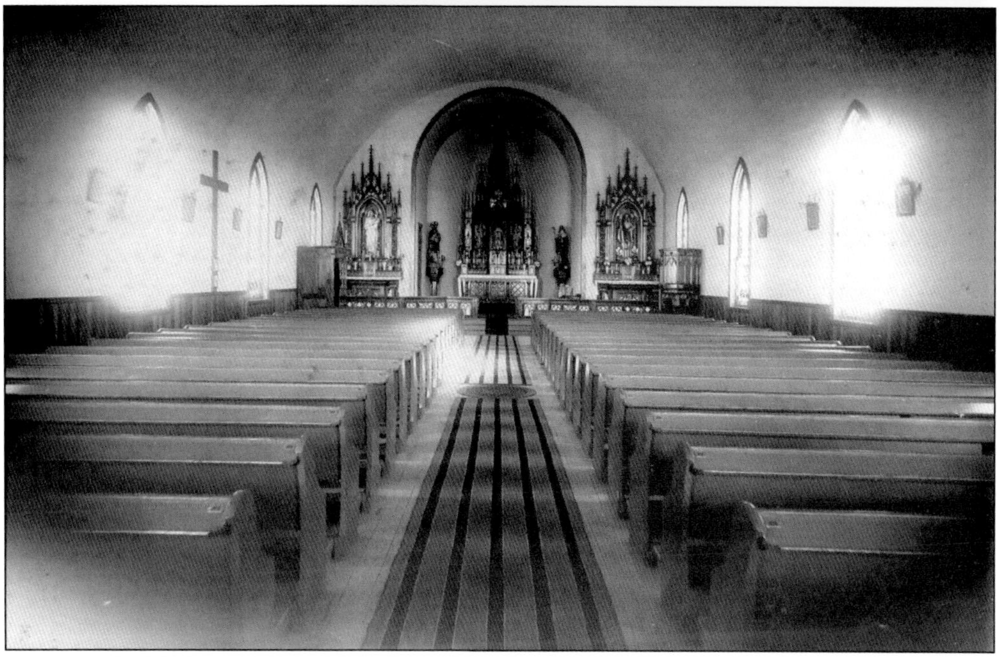

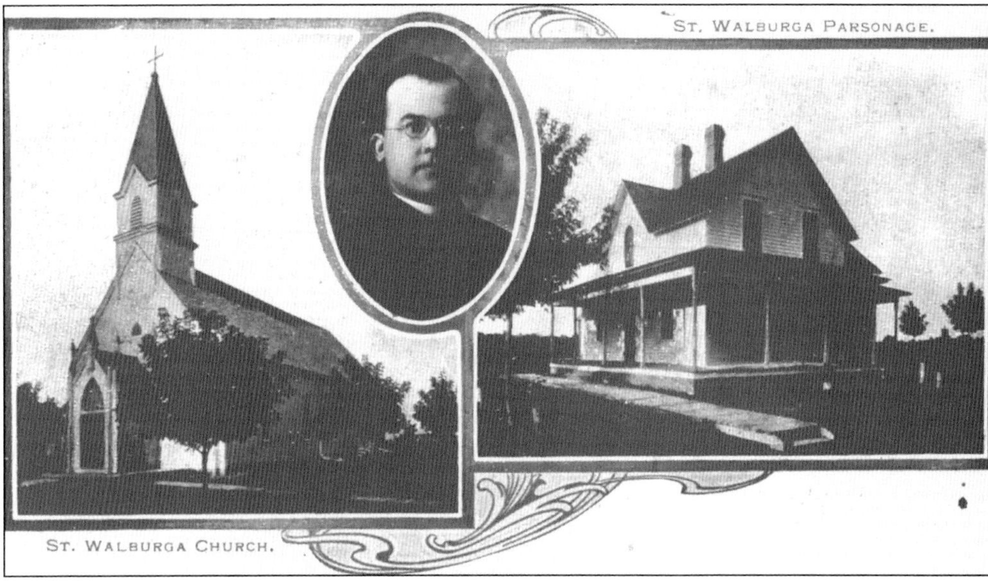

The beginning of the 20th century brought many changes. In 1906, Fr. William Eckl remodeled and frescoed the entire church as seen on this postcard. In 1912, another Catholic church, St. Martin of Tours, formed in Rogers Siding. Fr. Fedor Martin Doring served as pastor for both churches until 1915. In 1914, the joining of two oblate fathers exiled by British authorities and seeking German communities caused a divide in the congregation. At the onset of World War I, anti-German sentiments ran high; a small group of English-speaking parishioners requested permission to build their own chapel. Permission was granted, and a small wooden chapel was constructed; however, it burned down before the opening service. (Courtesy of Andrew Stueve.)

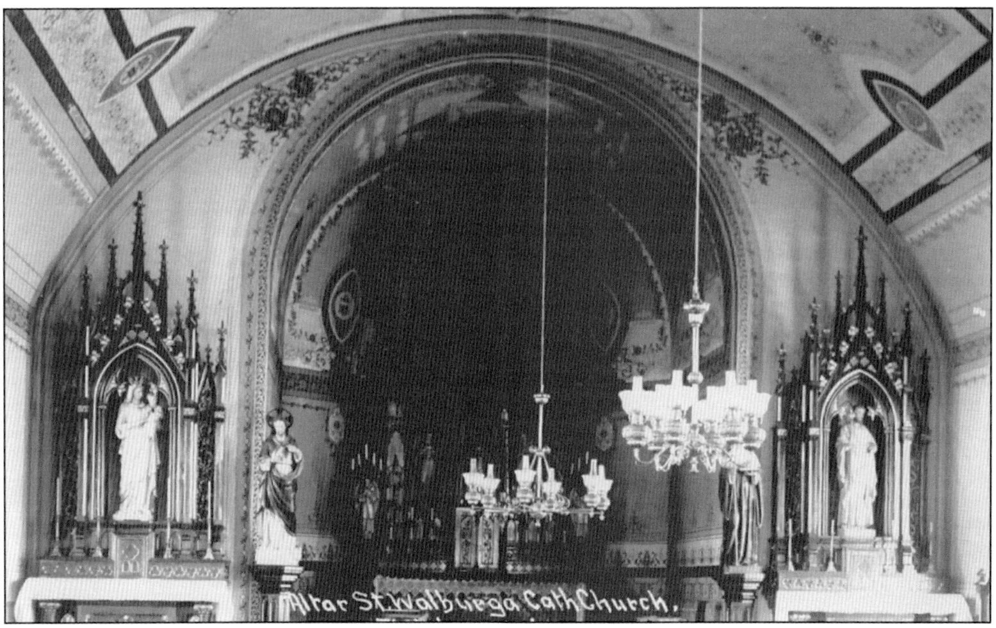

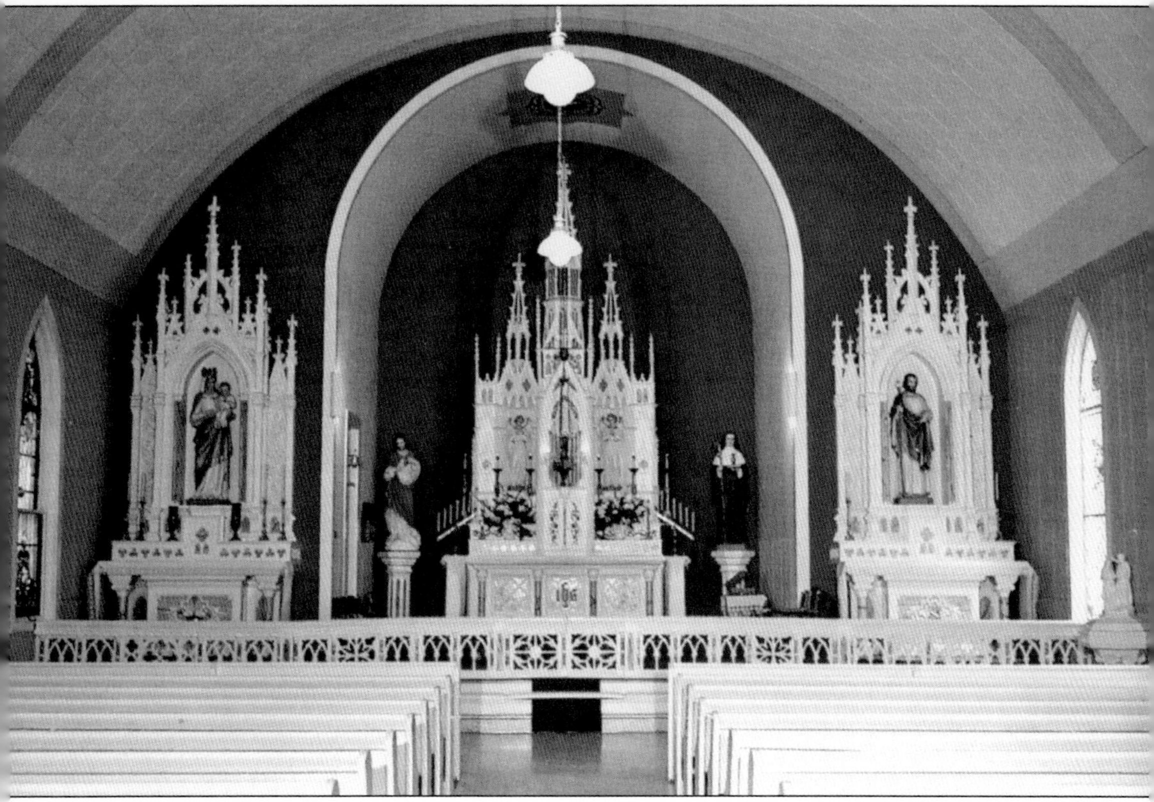

Fr. Russell J. Trembaly was appointed pastor in August 1959. In 1962, with assistance from Sr. M. Jamesine, the school's principal, he began remodeling and refurbishing St. Walburga Church. This task was completed with the help of many members of the parish. During the season of Lent, parishioners painted and remodeled the church. Members of the church assisted with the project to create a "thing of beauty and joy forever." The pews were painted white, which contrasted beautifully with the red carpet running the length of the middle aisle. The walls and ceiling were painted in soft pastel colors growing deeper as they approach the sanctuary, and the altars were painted devotional white. In addition, the beautiful sacred statues were artistically restored by the St. Paul Statuary Company. (Courtesy of Andrew Stueve.)

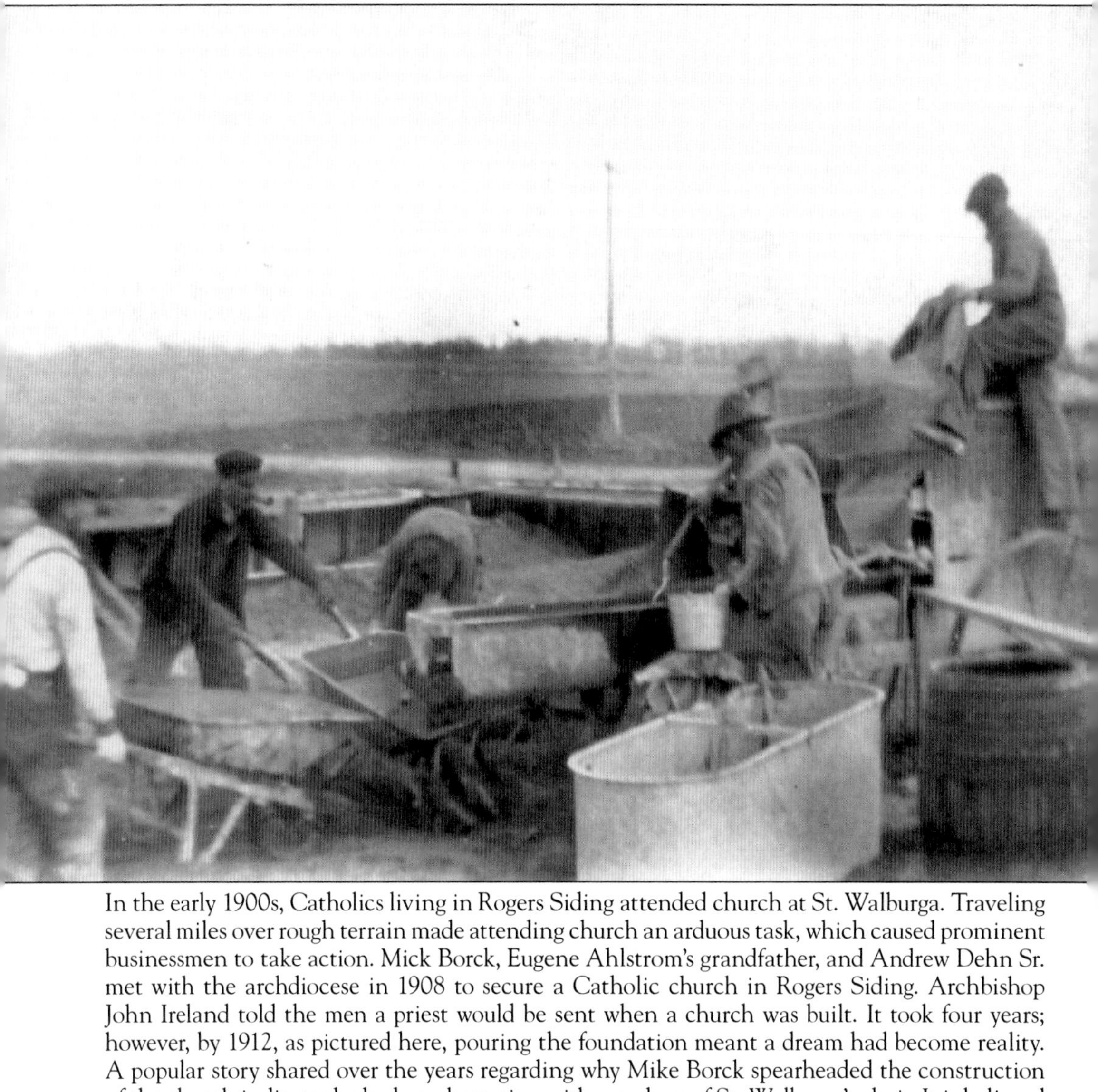

In the early 1900s, Catholics living in Rogers Siding attended church at St. Walburga. Traveling several miles over rough terrain made attending church an arduous task, which caused prominent businessmen to take action. Mick Borck, Eugene Ahlstrom's grandfather, and Andrew Dehn Sr. met with the archdiocese in 1908 to secure a Catholic church in Rogers Siding. Archbishop John Ireland told the men a priest would be sent when a church was built. It took four years; however, by 1912, as pictured here, pouring the foundation meant a dream had become reality. A popular story shared over the years regarding why Mike Borck spearheaded the construction of the church indicates he had an altercation with members of St. Walburga's choir. It is believed that Borck, who sang in the choir for many years, arrived at church to find a note on his chair. Although the content of the note is not known for sure, its message appeared to prevent him from participating in the choir any longer. This story cannot be substantiated; it is town folklore. (Courtesy of Leo Scharber.)

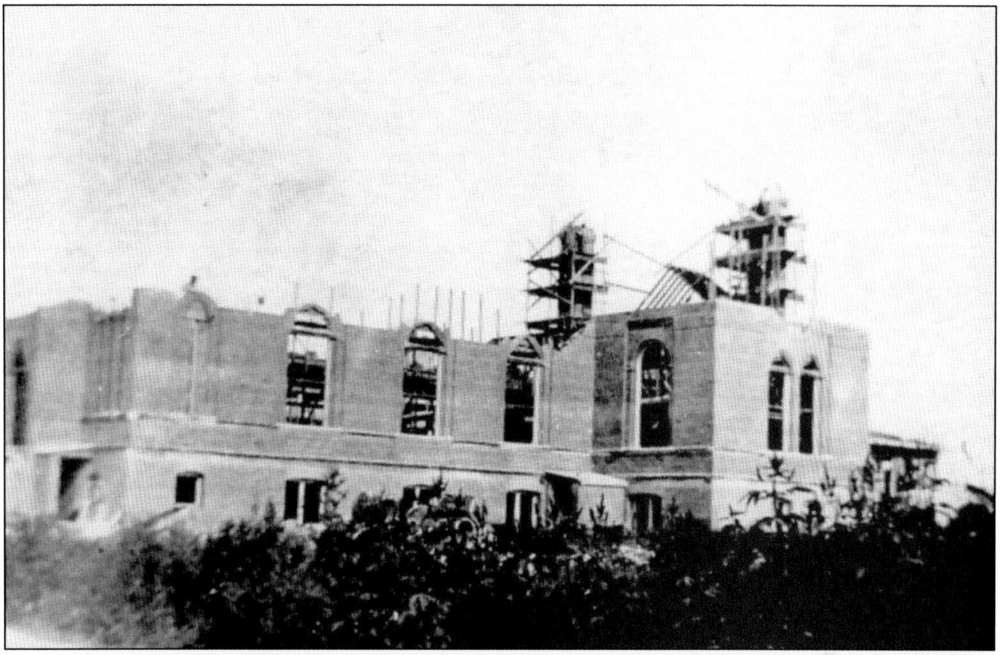

A meeting was held on January 18, 1912, forming two committees. The incorporating committee consisted of Mike Borck, Mathias Heuring, and Father Doring. The building committee included Father Doring, Andrew Dehn Sr., James Hynes, Joseph Klersy, and James Rogers. Supporters included the families of John Weber, Joseph Goth, John Scherber, James Weber, George Dahlheimer, Mike Riley, Henry Milless, Dan Janson, Mrs. Michael Jaeb, George Scherber Sr., Michael McManus, Philip Scherber, John Shelly, William McGinnis, Thomas Quinn, Henry Dehn, Anton Dehn, George Dehn, John McNeil, James Flynn, P. F. Ward, John M. Milless, William Greeninger, Hank Zahler, Prosper Scherber, John Beaswald, William Weber, Michael Curry, Peter Hagel, Thomas Demars Jr., Catherine Heinen, John Dehn, Paul Hagel, James Waddick, and Charles Miller. St. Martin of Tours awaits a roof in these pictures. (Courtesy of Leo Scharber.)

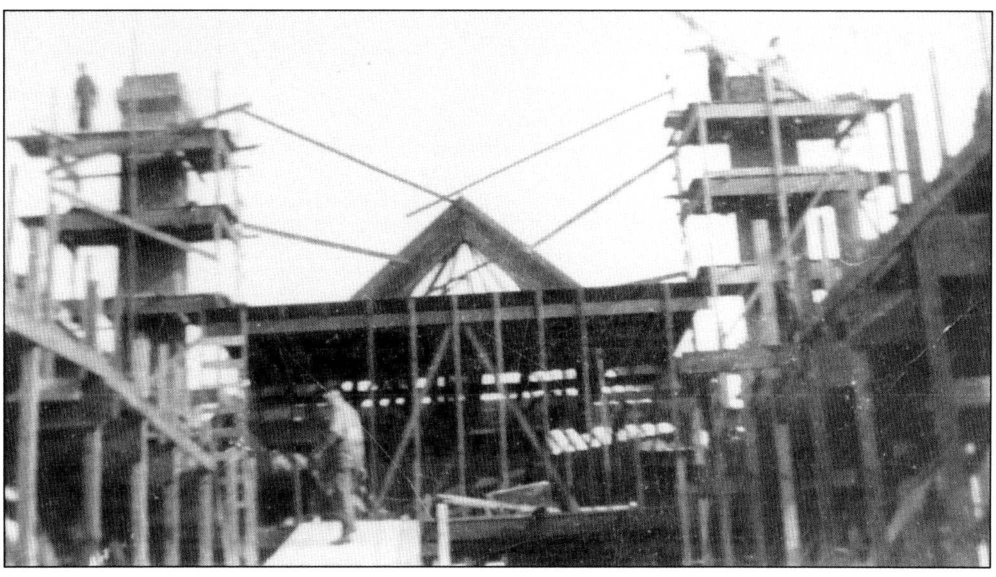

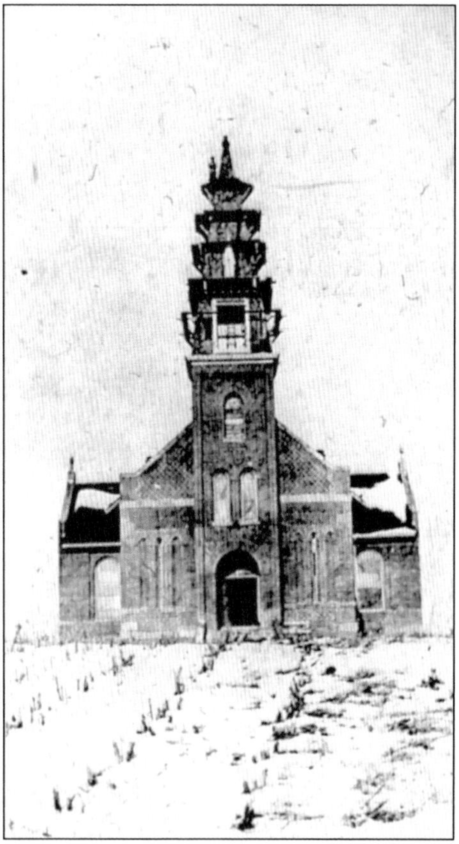

Articles of incorporation for St. Martin's of Rogers were filed on April 13, 1912. Families were committed to building the church; however, funds were tight, and construction was stalled after completing the basement. The first mass was celebrated on November 24, 1912. The first baptism, of Venereice Rose Klersy, was also celebrated. More firsts included the first burial on April 10, 1913, of Olivine Dargin (born in 1871); the first wedding on June 10, 1913, between Joseph Russell and Catherine Weber; and the first confirmation candidate, Edward Dahlheimer, confirmed on October 1, 1916. Doug Scharber shared that his parents, Otto Sharber and Hazel Rouillard, got married in the basement as well. In the fall of 1917, St. Martin of Tours was finished. Pictured is the construction of the bell tower and completed church. (Courtesy of Norb Zahler.)

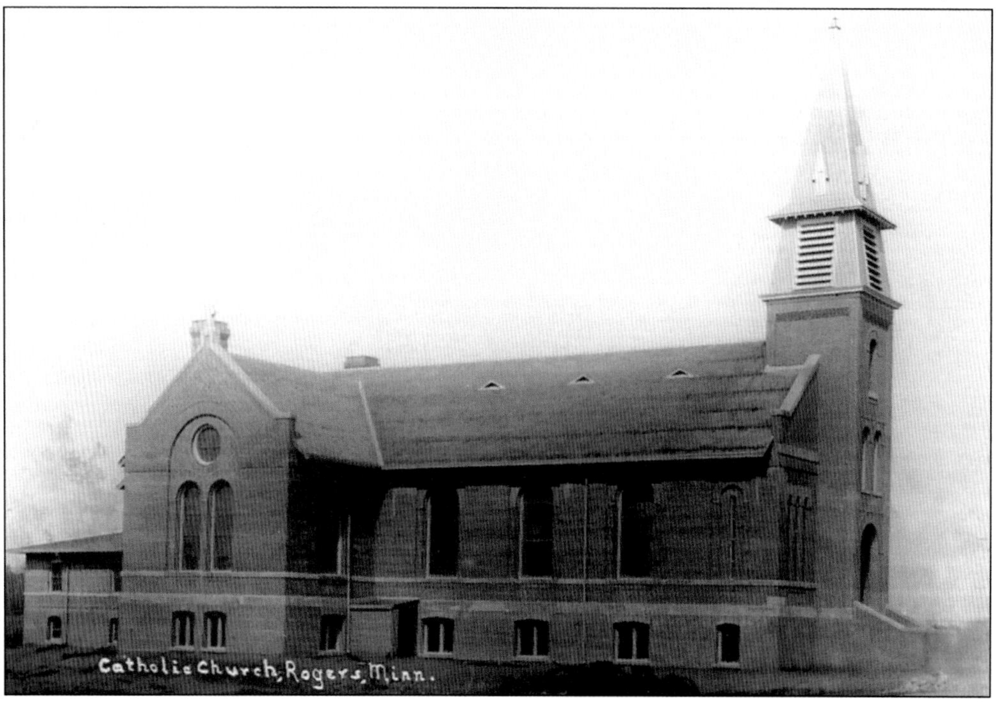

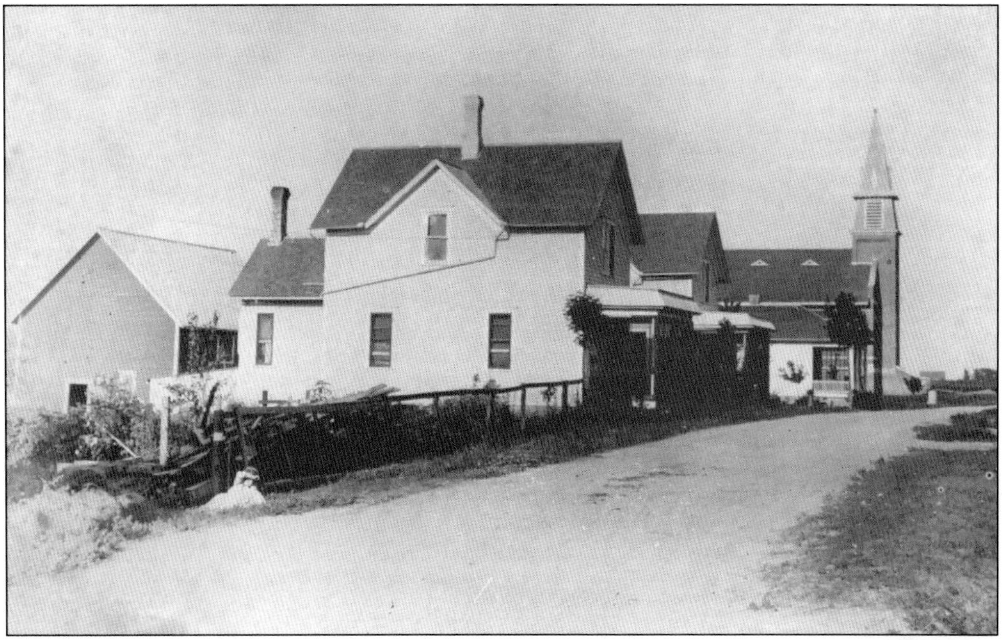

St. Martin's was built just east of Mathias Heuring's residence on what later became known as Church Street. When all the costs for completing the church were calculated, the total came to $40,885.17, which included $31,045.95 for building, $7,339.22 for furniture, and $2,500 calculated for "free labor." The parish list in 1918 included 113 households. Many Catholic families were excited to have a church close to home; however, some were disappointed in the division of the faith community. Hostility formed between the two congregations as each demonstrated loyalty to their respective church, but over time, the strong emotions subsided and tensions calmed, although many say the division has never gone away entirely. In 1922, the pictured parish house was built next to St. Martin's. (Above, courtesy of Danny, Janet, and Noreen Durant; below, courtesy of Leo Scharber.)

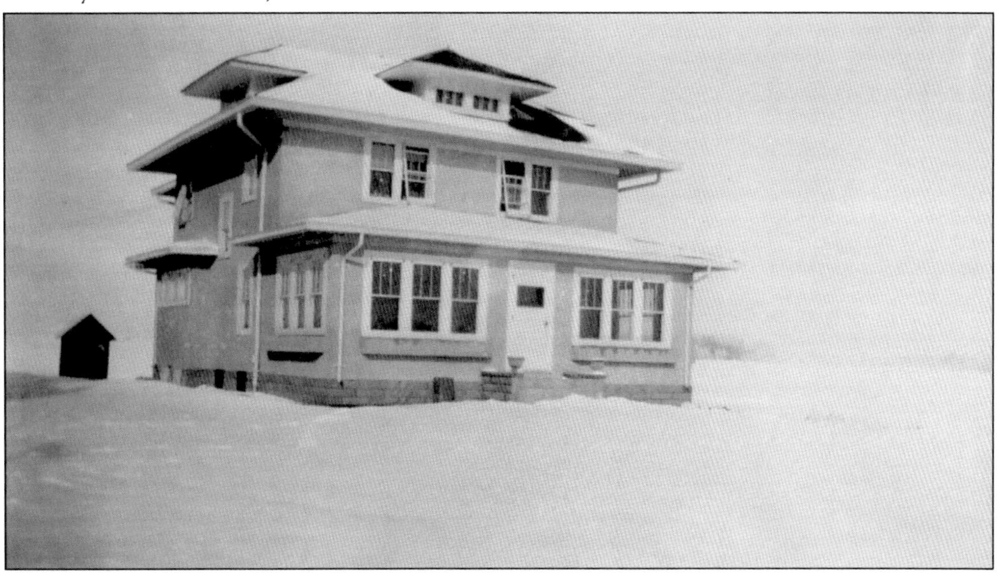

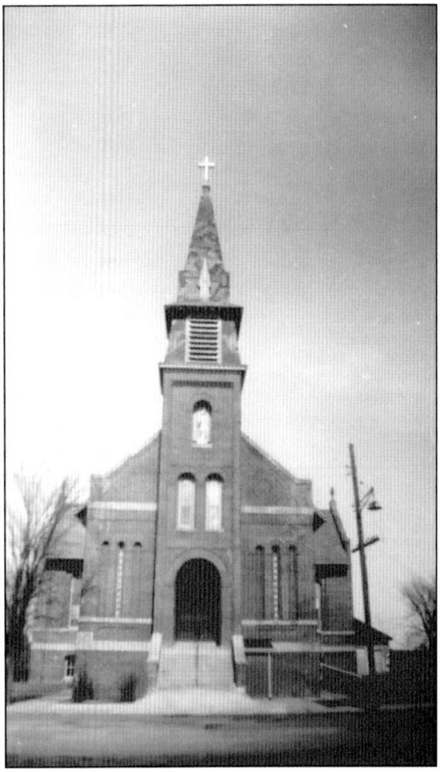

The entrance to St. Martin's, as pictured here, welcomes all in the early 1930s and 1940s as the people of Rogers sought innovative ways to stay entertained. This led to the creation of drama clubs. The St. Martin's Players put on a production of three one-act plays, and *The Light Eternal* was presented by the Rogers Dramatic Club. Also pictured are St. Martin's fourth- through ninth-grade children formed as a "living rosary" during an evening service on October 4, 1952. The event was in celebration of National Children's Day in honor of Our Lady of Fatima. The school nuns assisted with many special events involving the parish children. (Above, courtesy of Danny, Janet, and Noreen Durant; below, courtesy of Jack and Carol Hines.)

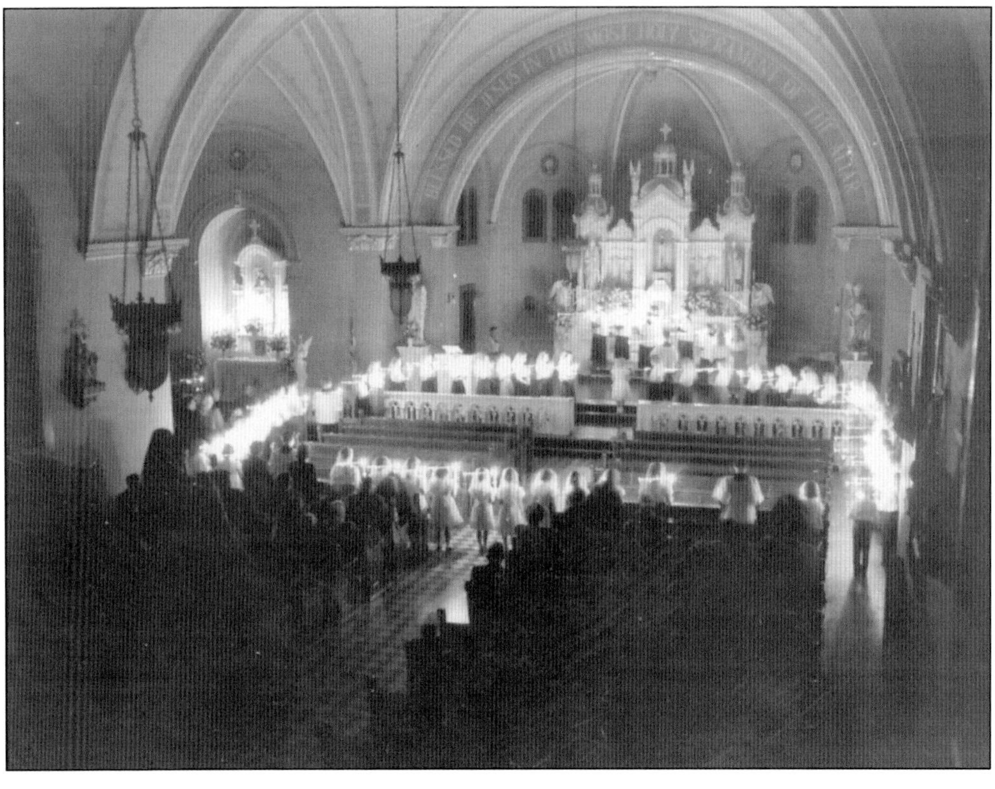

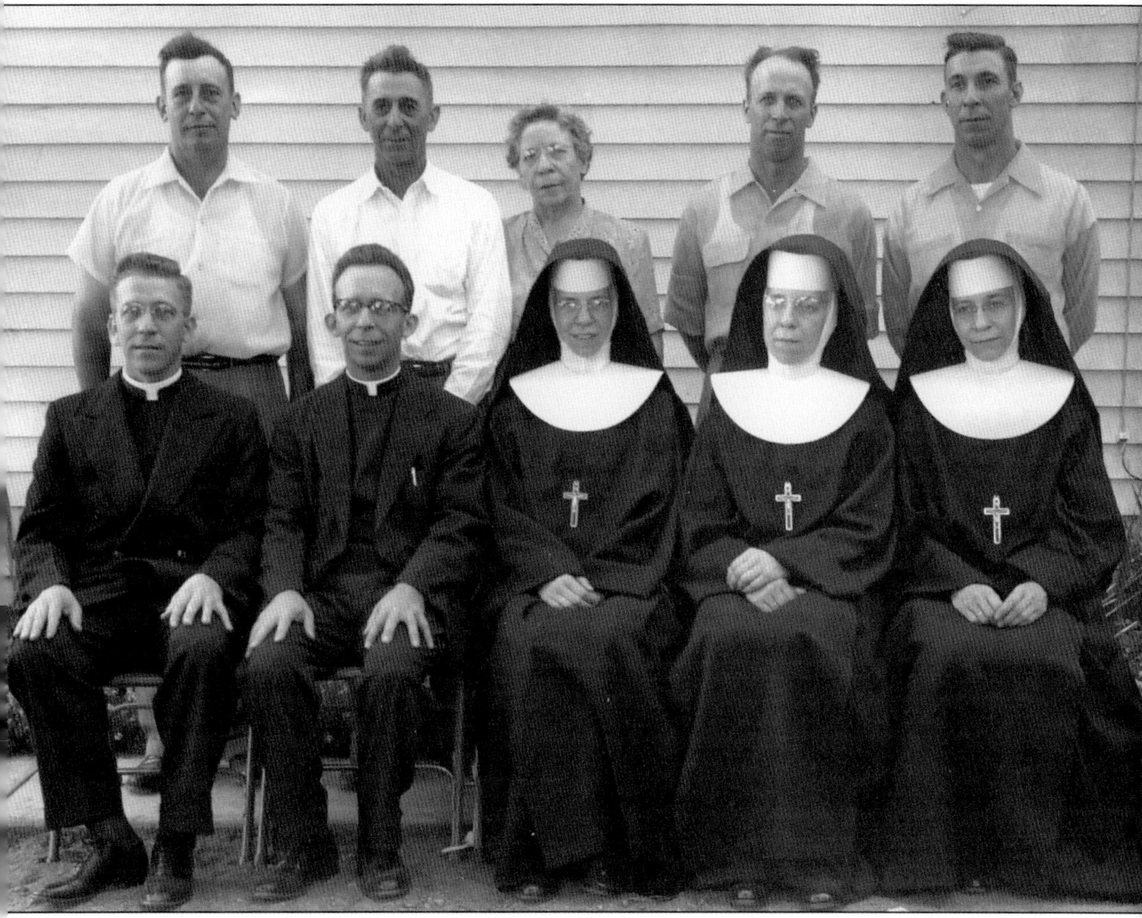

Mary Lou (Zachman) Dahlheimer shared that her grandfather Louis Zachman often commented, "I have eight children; three are sisters, two are brothers, and three are fathers." This picture illustrates his comment perfectly. Cecilia professed her vows on June 21, 1945, taking the name Sr. Mary Sylvan; Marcella made her profession on June 21, 1944, becoming Sr. Mary Genieve; and Rosalia became Sr. Mary Walburga on June 21, 1949. Clarence was ordained a Catholic priest on June 5, 1948, and Francis was ordained on August 24, 1951, both into the Order of Mary Immaculate. Mary Lou thought about becoming a nun but decided it was not the path for her. Her husband, Ray Dahlheimer, shared that his family thought he should be a priest or a brother because back then it was good to have a person of the cloth in the family. (Courtesy of Jack and Mary Lou Dahlheimer.)

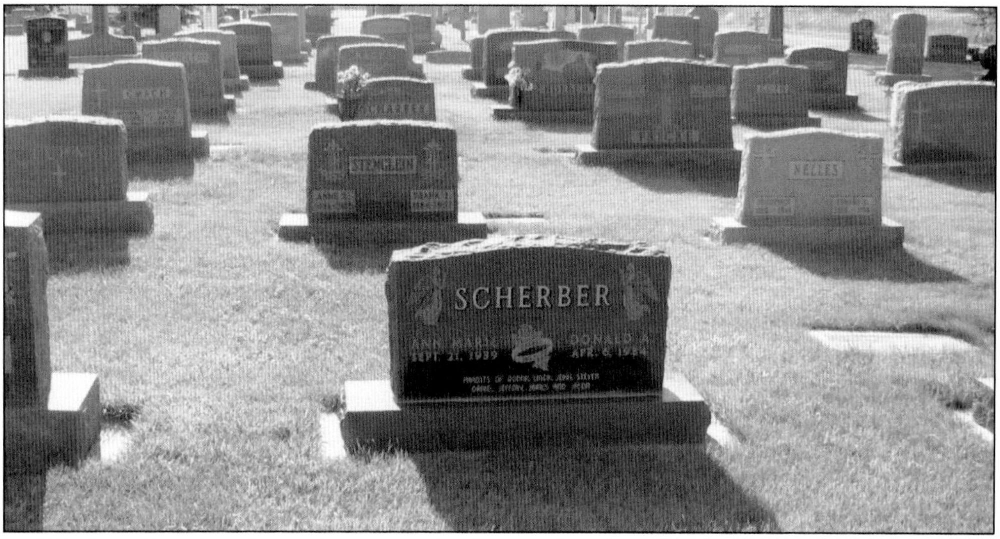

In 1883, John Stenglein donated two and a half acres of land across the road from the St. Walburga Church for the construction of a school and cemetery. As this picture illustrates, John's namesakes, along with many other founders of the community, have been laid there to rest. Also pictured is St. Martin's Cemetery. It was established when James Rogers, a church founder, donated one and a half acres of land north of town. The cemetery was expanded when a 16-foot strip was added in 1923 after the first survey was completed. In 1972, the church purchased one acre of land from Lillian Hines, and around 2000, an additional 16 feet were donated. By 2001, there had been 462 burials in St. Martin's Cemetery. (Courtesy of Rob Bell.)

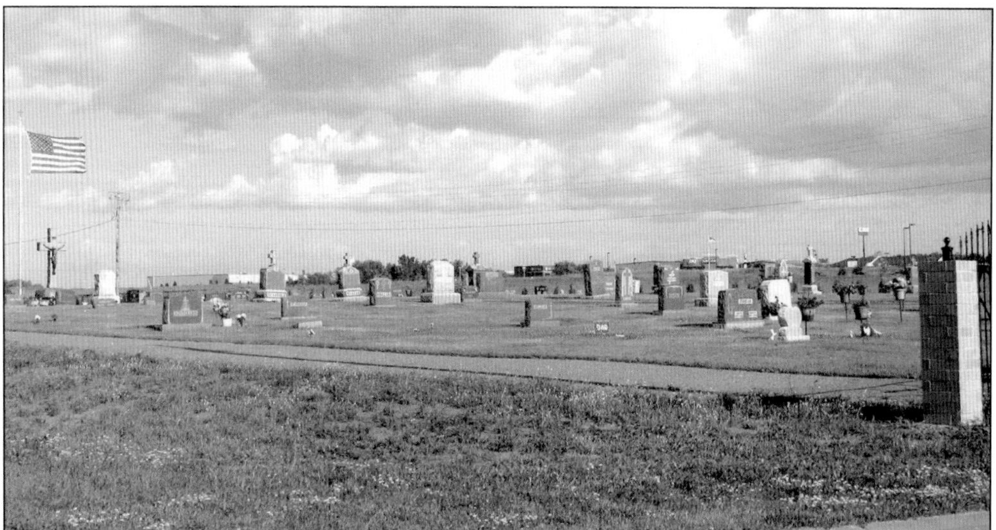

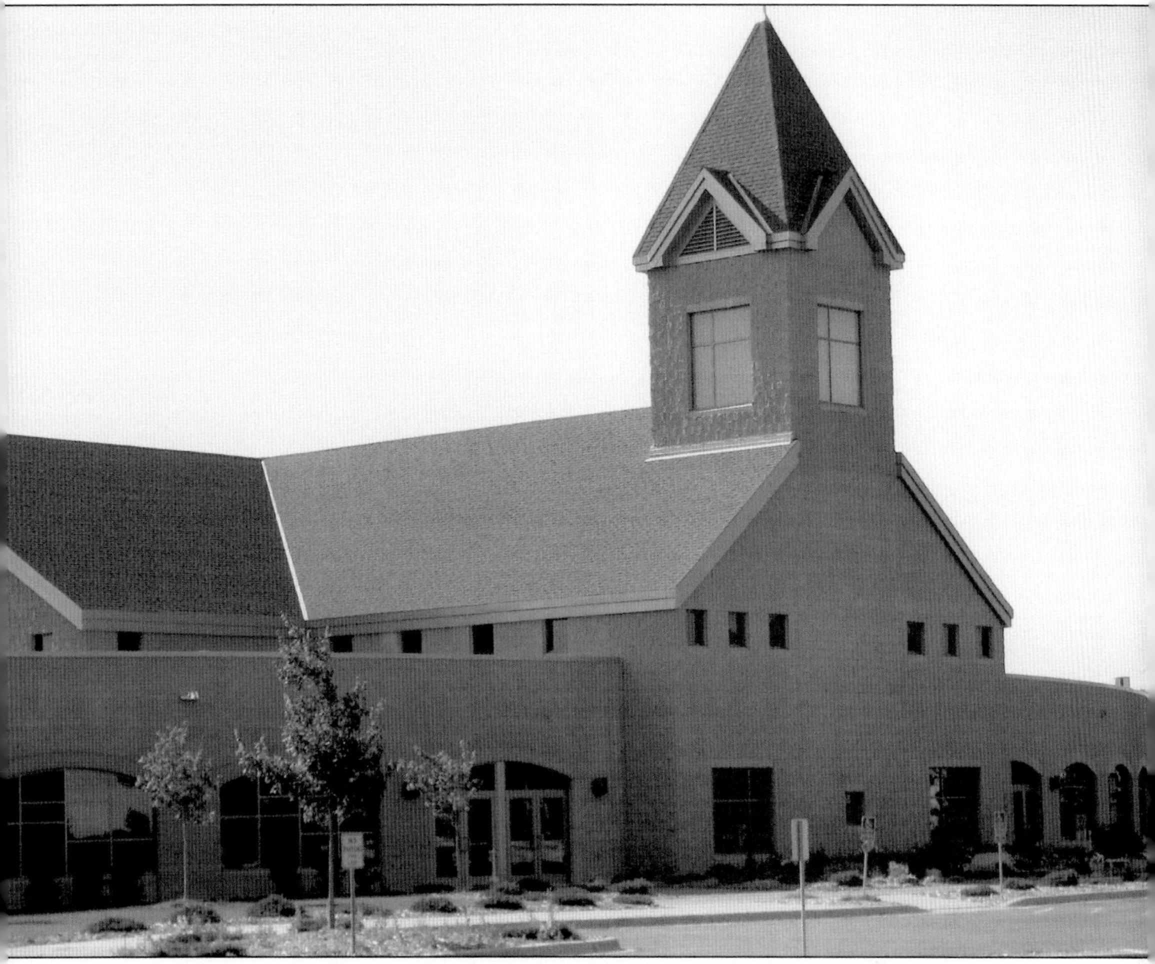

In 1973, the American Lutheran Church purchased land to establish a church in Rogers. An organizing meeting was held on June 22, 1974, at the Rogers Elementary School to determine support for a Lutheran church. The need was there, and a call went out to Pastor David Knutson of Jamestown, North Dakota. The first church service was held at the Rogers Elementary School on February 16, 1975, and the groundbreaking dedication was held on Palm Sunday. The Word of Peace Lutheran Church was welcomed into the American Lutheran Church on August 17, 1975, with 59 families. Judy and Norm Volkers reminisced when they were the third Protestant family living in the community; however, growth in the area created a need, and they became the founding mother and father of the Word of Peace Lutheran Church. Judy shared that when they started the Lutheran church their biggest supporters were the Catholics. (Courtesy of Rob Bell.)

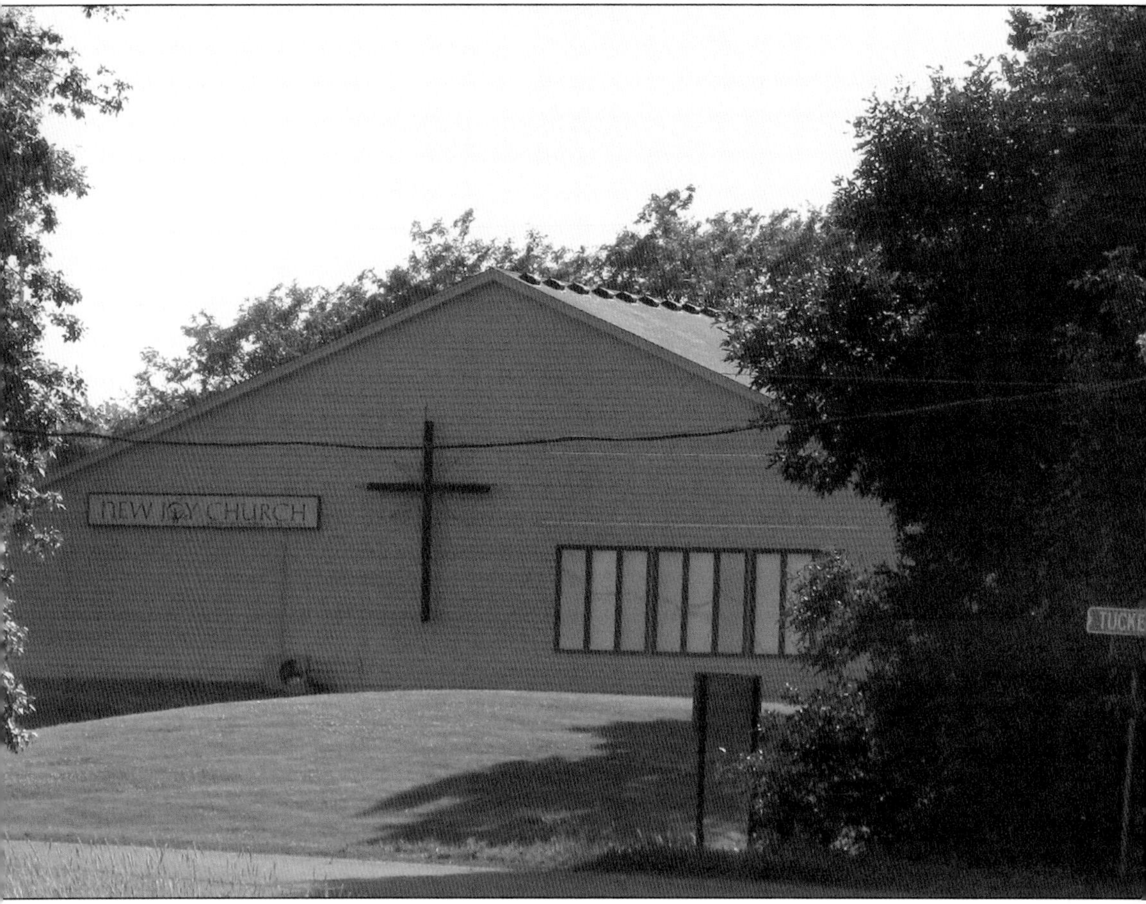

Four Evangelical Free Church, New Joy Church (Joy Free Church) families met in 1975 to consider establishing a new church. In January 1976, Rev. Ezra Budke began serving as part-time pastor. The new group shared church space with St. John's Episcopal Church; however, in 1978 the congregation of Joy Free Church decided it was time it build its own church and began searching for land in Hassan Township. The mission of the Joy Free Church is to glorify God by making disciples of Jesus Christ, who will love and glorify Him both individually and corporately by (1) celebrating in worshipping God, (2) cultivating spiritual growth, by grace and truth, in all believers, (3) caring for people in the name of Christ, and (4) communicating the Gospel locally and to the world. The church is located on Tucker Road. (Courtesy of Rob Bell.)

Three

BUILDING THE FOUNDATION

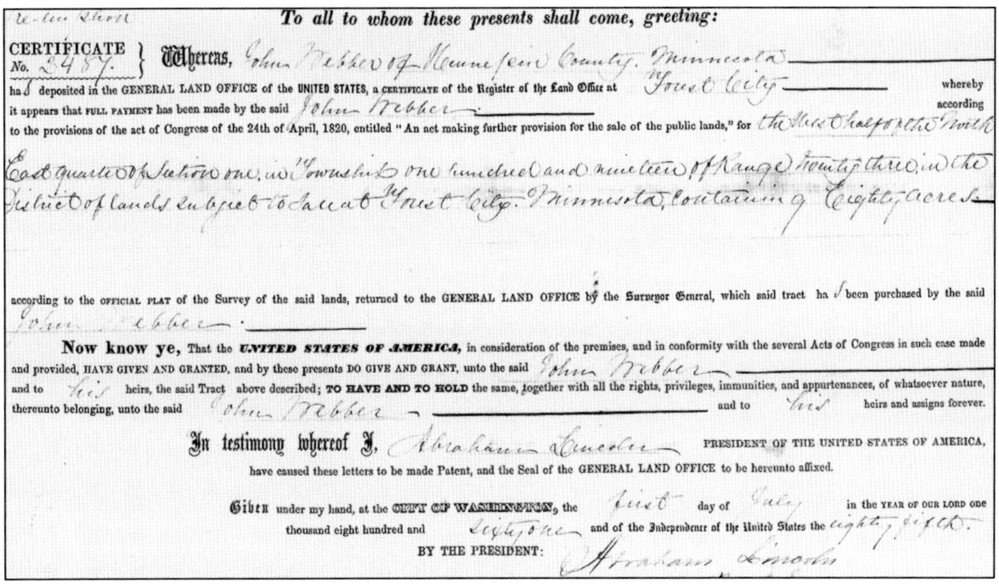
To all to whom these presents shall come, greeting:

CERTIFICATE No. 2487. } Whereas, John Webber of Hennepin County, Minnesota has deposited in the GENERAL LAND OFFICE of the UNITED STATES, a CERTIFICATE of the Register of the Land Office at Forest City whereby it appears that FULL PAYMENT has been made by the said John Webber according to the provisions of the act of Congress of the 24th of April, 1820, entitled "An act making further provision for the sale of the public lands," for the West half of the North East quarter of Section one, in Township one hundred and nineteen of Range twenty three, in the District of lands subject to sale at Forest City, Minnesota, containing Eighty acres

according to the OFFICIAL PLAT of the Survey of the said lands, returned to the GENERAL LAND OFFICE by the Surveyor General, which said tract has been purchased by the said John Webber.

Now know ye, That the *UNITED STATES OF AMERICA*, in consideration of the premises, and in conformity with the several Acts of Congress in such case made and provided, HAVE GIVEN AND GRANTED, and by these presents DO GIVE AND GRANT, unto the said John Webber and to his heirs, the said Tract above described; **TO HAVE AND TO HOLD** the same, together with all the rights, privileges, immunities, and appurtenances, of whatsoever nature, thereunto belonging, unto the said John Webber and to his heirs and assigns forever.

In testimony whereof I, Abraham Lincoln PRESIDENT OF THE UNITED STATES OF AMERICA, have caused these letters to be made Patent, and the Seal of the GENERAL LAND OFFICE to be hereunto affixed.

Given under my hand, at the CITY OF WASHINGTON, the first day of July, in the YEAR OF OUR LORD one thousand eight hundred and sixty one and of the Independence of the United States the eighty fifth.

BY THE PRESIDENT: Abraham Lincoln

The original John Webber homestead deed, signed by Pres. Abraham Lincoln on July 1, 1861, is now in the safekeeping of current landowner Denny Stieg. Denny is proud of the area in which he lives and is actively striving to preserve the heritage the founders established. At the dawn of the 20th century, quality was important; buildings were constructed to last. Current residents of the area shared they believe the following historical buildings still exist over 100 years later: the Fletcher store, the John and Margaret Nelles farm, the John and Catherine Nelles farm, the original St. Walburga Rectory, a residence at 11995 Fletcher Lane, the Andrew and Margaret Stenglein house, the Frank and Lenore Stenglein house, St. Walburga Church, St. Walburga Hagel Church mission house, St. Walburga Hagel School, and the St. Walburga Cemetery. Leroy Hegel, descendent of Helena and Peter Hegel who settled 160 acres in Hassan Township in 1858, stated eloquently, "Once it's gone, it's gone forever and it becomes society's loss." (Courtesy of Denny Stieg.)

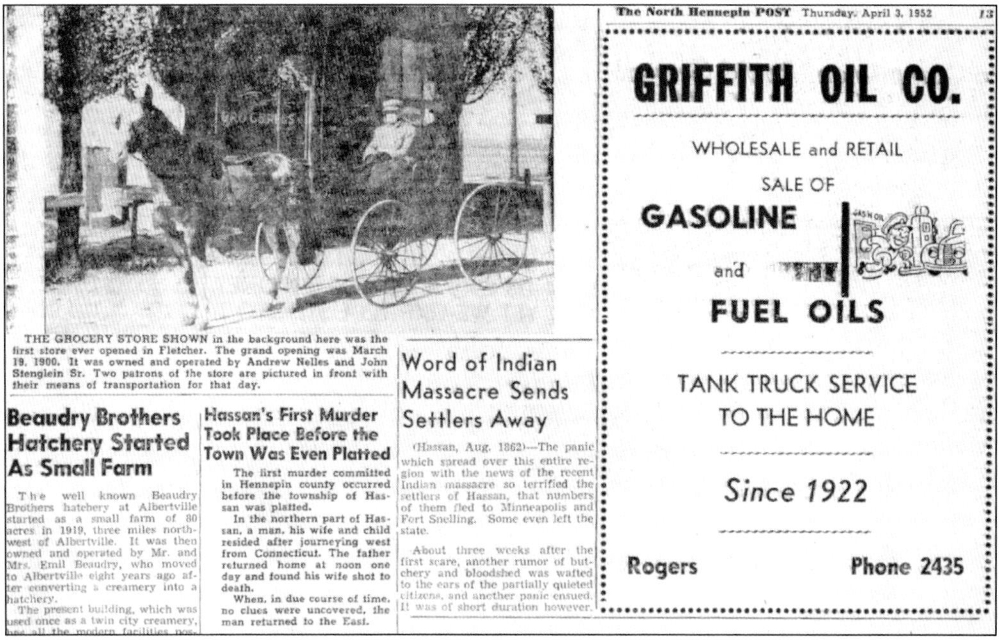

The North Hennepin POST Thursday, April 3, 1952 13

THE GROCERY STORE SHOWN in the background here was the first store ever opened in Fletcher. The grand opening was March 19, 1900. It was owned and operated by Andrew Nelles and John Stenglein Sr. Two patrons of the store are pictured in front with their means of transportation for that day.

Beaudry Brothers Hatchery Started As Small Farm

The well known Beaudry Brothers hatchery at Albertville started as a small farm of 80 acres in 1919, three miles northwest of Albertville. It was then owned and operated by Mr. and Mrs. Emil Beaudry, who moved to Albertville eight years ago after converting a creamery into a hatchery.

The present building, which was used once as a twin city creamery,

Hassan's First Murder Took Place Before the Town Was Even Platted

The first murder committed in Hennepin county occurred before the township of Hassan was platted.

In the northern part of Hassan, a man, his wife and child resided after journeying west from Connecticut. The father returned home at noon one day and found his wife shot to death.

When, in due course of time, no clues were uncovered, the man returned to the East.

Word of Indian Massacre Sends Settlers Away

(Hassan, Aug. 1862)—The panic which spread over this entire region with the news of the recent Indian massacre so terrified the settlers of Hassan, that numbers of them fled to Minneapolis and Fort Snelling. Some even left the state.

About three weeks after the first scare, another rumor of butchery and bloodshed was wafted to the ears of the partially quieted citizens, and another panic ensued. It was of short duration however.

This article, from the April 3, 1952, edition of the *North Hennepin Post*, highlights the grand opening of the Fletcher store on March 19, 1900. This store, located on the corner of Territorial Road and Corcoran-Dayton Road, was the first general store to service the hamlet. According to Denny Stieg, the front two-thirds of the Fletcher store served as a general store and the back one-third was a tavern; the areas were separated by saloon-style swinging doors. John Hagel shared the story of when his father, Leroy Hagel, and his father's friend Charles Vevea danced with chairs at the Fletcher tavern. Locals have enjoyed many memorable evenings in this establishment. The George Yankoupe family currently owns the building. (Above, courtesy of Crow River News; below, courtesy of Andrew Stueve.)

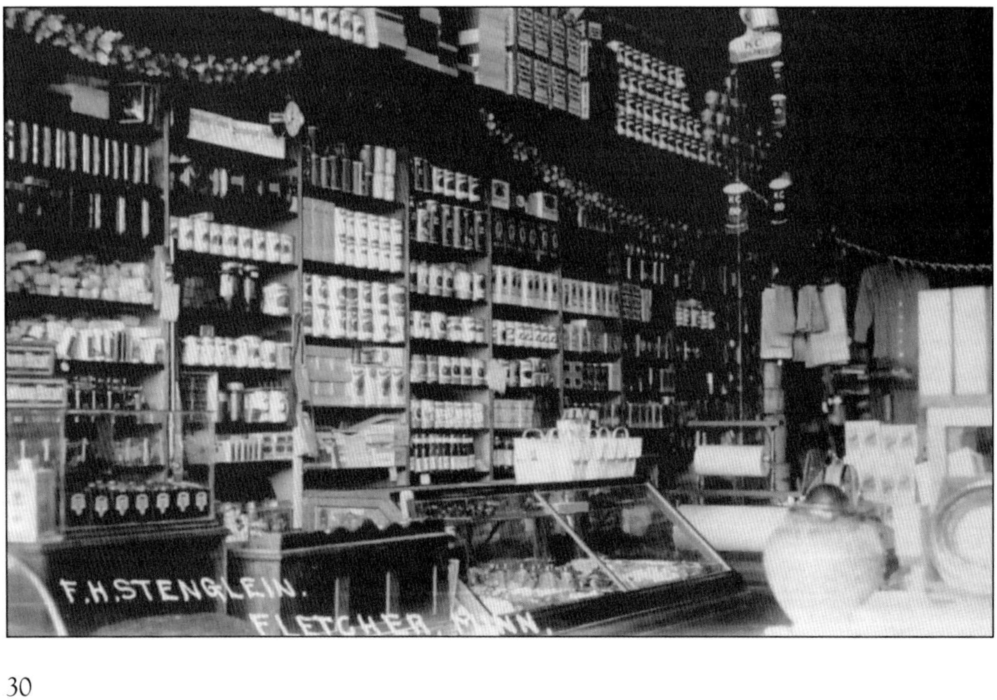

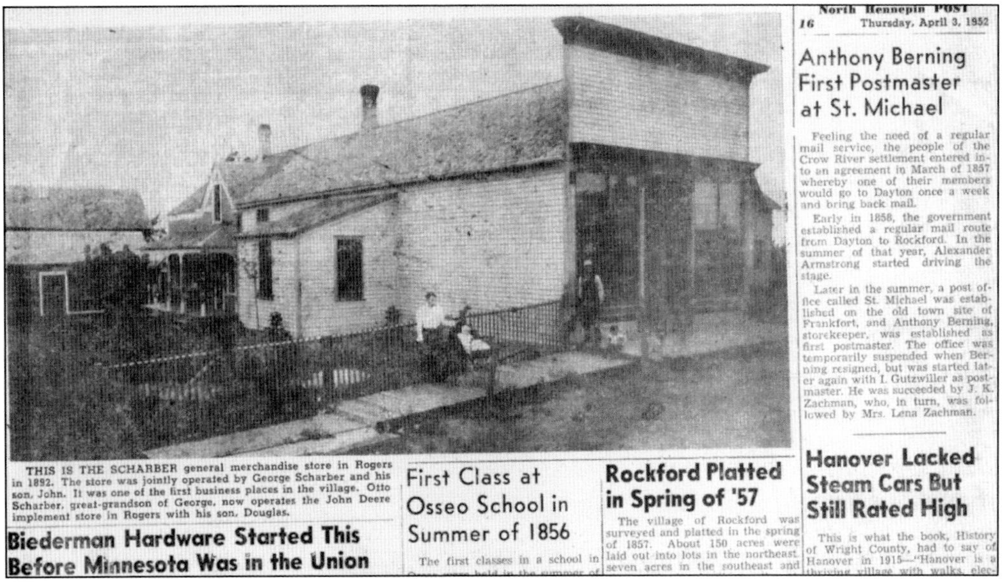

North Hennepin POST
16 Thursday, April 3, 1952

THIS IS THE SCHARBER general merchandise store in Rogers in 1892. The store was jointly operated by George Scharber and his son, John. It was one of the first business places in the village. Otto Scharber, great-grandson of George, now operates the John Deere implement store in Rogers with his son, Douglas.

Biederman Hardware Started This Before Minnesota Was in the Union

First Class at Osseo School in Summer of 1856

The first classes in a school in

Rockford Platted in Spring of '57

The village of Rockford was surveyed and platted in the spring of 1857. About 150 acres were laid out into lots in the northeast, seven acres in the southeast and

Anthony Berning First Postmaster at St. Michael

Feeling the need of a regular mail service, the people of the Crow River settlement entered into an agreement in March of 1857 whereby one of their members would go to Dayton once a week and bring back mail.

Early in 1858, the government established a regular mail route from Dayton to Rockford. In the summer of that year, Alexander Armstrong started driving the stage.

Later in the summer, a post office called St. Michael was established on the old town site of Frankfort, and Anthony Berning, storekeeper, was established as first postmaster. The office was temporarily suspended when Berning resigned, but was started later again with I. Gutzwiller as postmaster. He was succeeded by J. K. Zachman, who, in turn, was followed by Mrs. Lena Zachman.

Hanover Lacked Steam Cars But Still Rated High

This is what the book, History of Wright County, had to say of Hanover in 1915—"Hanover is a

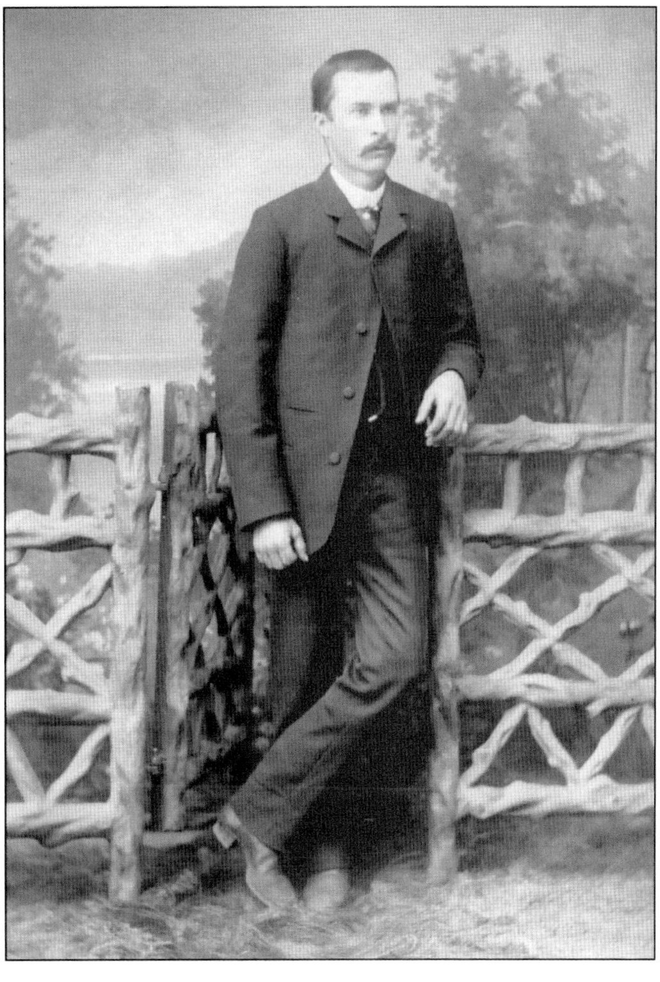

George Scharber was one of the early pioneers to the area. He and his son, John, jointly operated the Scharber general merchandise store in Rogers Siding as mentioned in this newspaper article. It was one of the first businesses in the community. Pictured in the buggy is Otto Scharber, one of the future owners and operators of the family business. This building burned down in 1903. John, pictured right, rebuilt the store and house, and later added an implement dealership. Scharber and Sons used to operate where USA Antiques resides today. Each building was constructed for $3,000. (Above, courtesy of Crow River News; below, courtesy of Leo Scharber.)

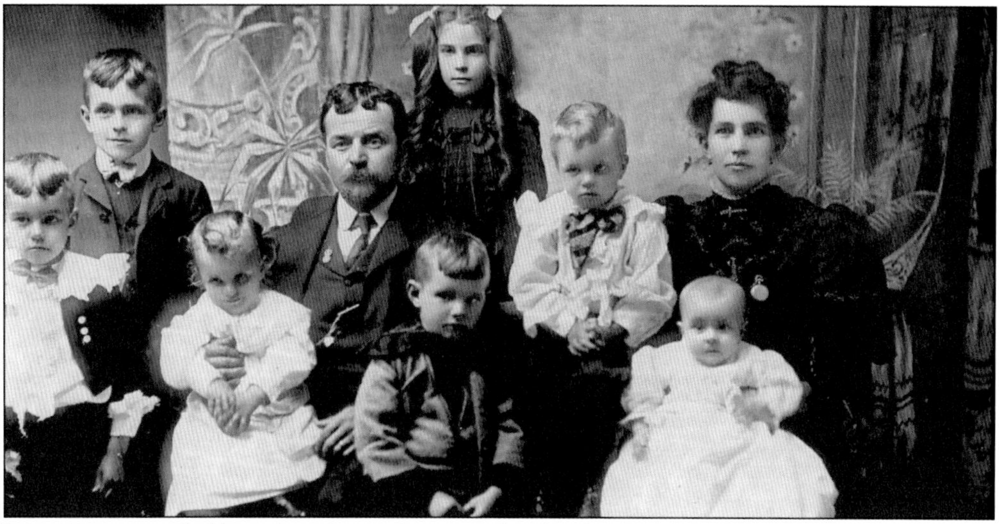

John Heinen settled here from Luxemburg. In this family picture are parents John Heinen and Katherine (Weber) Heinen, with children, shown from left to right, (first row) Rudy, Martin, John, Jacob, and Otto; (standing) Joe and Sarah. Not born at the time of this picture is Hubert. The first Heinen store was built in the late 1800s on Main Street where Church Avenue currently intersects. A new Heinen Mercantile was built in 1920. Dances were held upstairs for three years. The *North Hennepin Post* records the Rouillard-Zahler wedding dance was held on October 15, 1924, and Jack Hines stated his parent's wedding dance was held there as well. Melvin Rouillard shared that Heinen's had everything from safety pins to threshing machines. When his wife, Pearl, needed a chimney for her lantern Heinen asked "What size?" (Above, courtesy of Danny, Janet, and Noreen Durant; below, courtesy of Florian Heinen.)

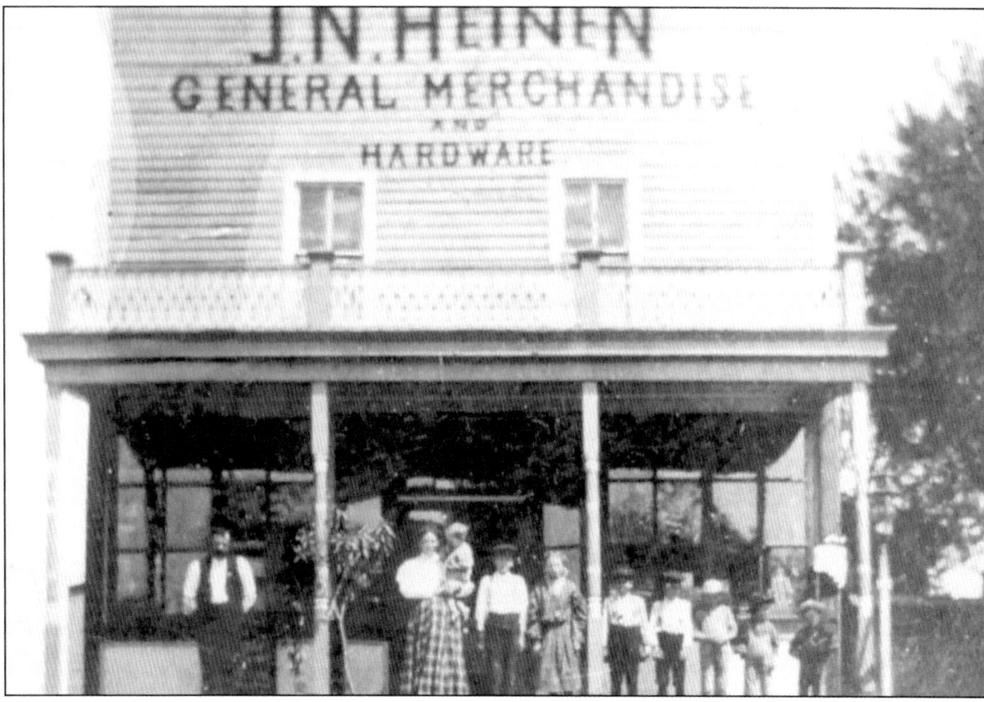

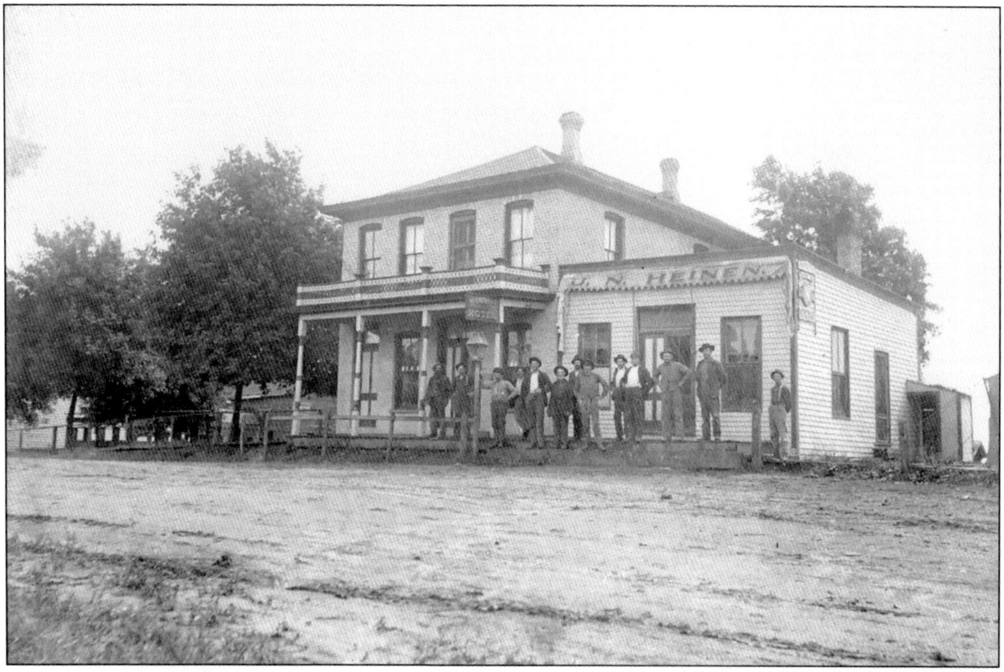

John Heinen and Katherine (Weber) Heinen also owned the Heinen Hotel at the end of Main Street by the railroad tracks in Rogers Siding. Florian Heinen remembers people coming from all around to stay at the hotel because it was close to the railroad tracks and depot. Behind the hotel was a shed where horses and buggies were kept. Businesspeople rented a horse and buggy and traveled to neighboring towns making sales calls. Leon LaVasseur shared that his grandparents lived in the hotel. The hotel stood where the public parking lot is now. Pictured below is a postcard of many of the early businesses in Rogers. (Courtesy of Florian Heinen.)

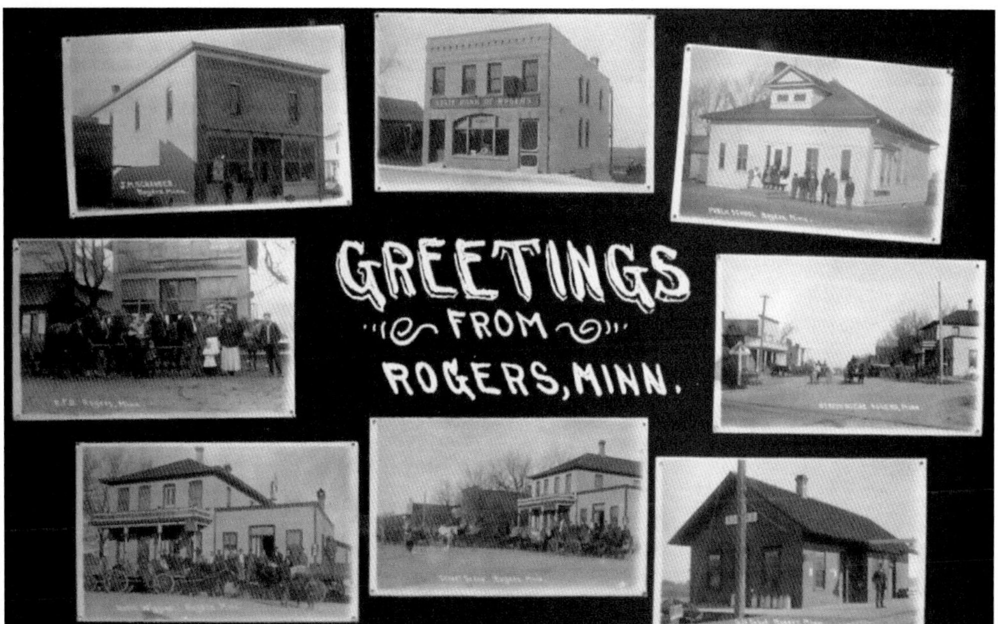

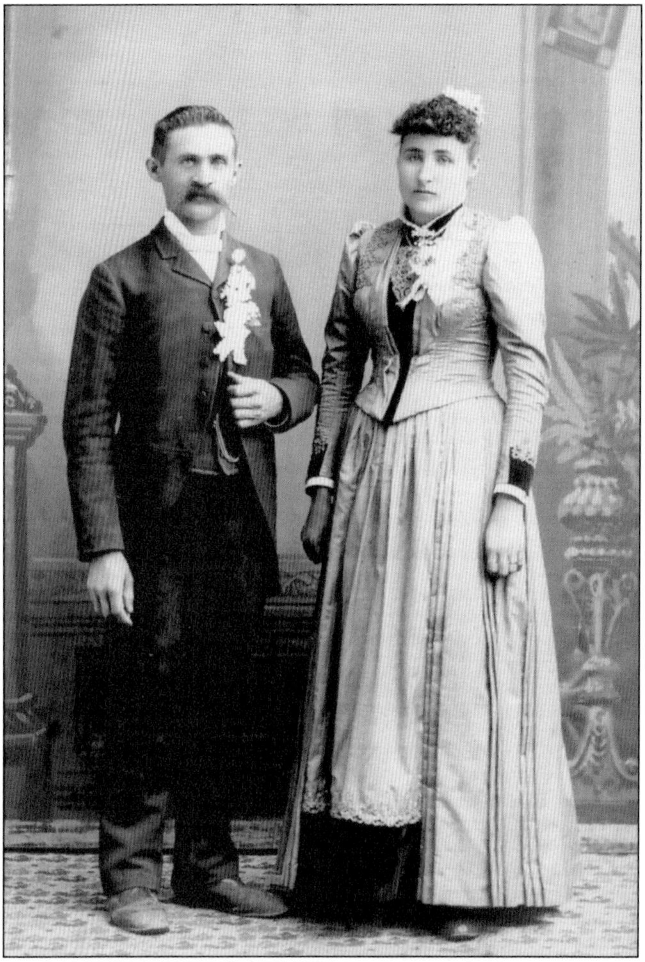

Orphaned at an early age in Luxemburg, Mike Borck joined his brother, Phillip, in St. Michael, Minnesota, when he was 21 years old. Mike became a prominent businessman in Rogers Siding and was instrumental in facilitating the incorporation of the Village of Rogers in 1914. On February 17, 1914, an election was held at Scharber's Hall to determine whether the territory described in the petition should incorporate as the Village of Rogers. The election outcome was 32 votes yes and 9 votes no. Mike served as the village's mayor from 1935 to 1937. He married Maria, who died at a young age; he then married Elizabeth and had two daughters, Emma and Elsie. Emma is Eugene Ahlstrom's mother. The other picture is an election in more recent years. (Above, courtesy of Norb Zahler; below, courtesy of Gordon Rouillard.)

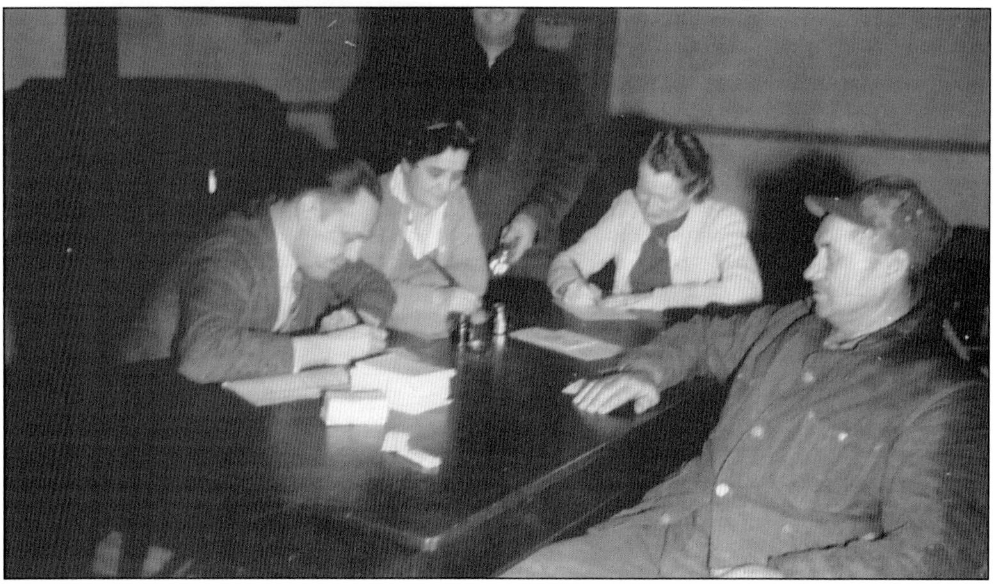

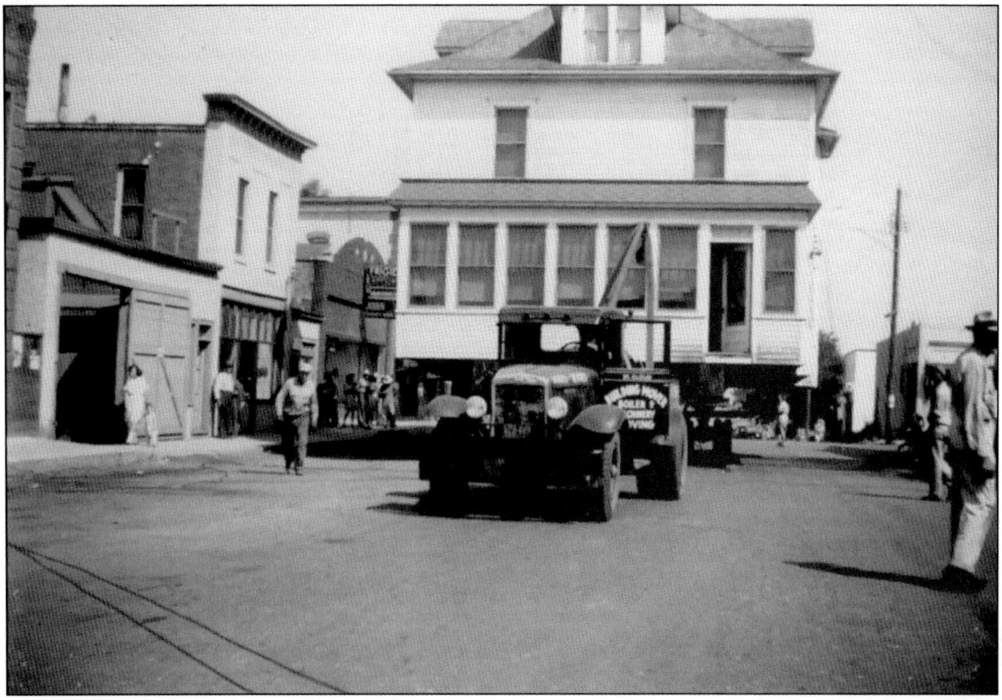

The day Doug and Rhea Scharber's house was moved, the town stood still, literally. There was a parade as the telephone lines were removed and the structure was slowly wheeled through Main Street taking care not to bump anything or anyone. Doug was mayor of Rogers for 22 years, and his son Steve was mayor for 15 years. When Norm and Judy Volkers bought their first home in Rogers, it was the first house on that block, and they still live there. Judy was on the city council for 11 years before she ran for mayor; she served as mayor from 1980 until 1984. The foundations that were laid by leaders of the community many years ago are still in place today. (Courtesy of Leo Scharber.)

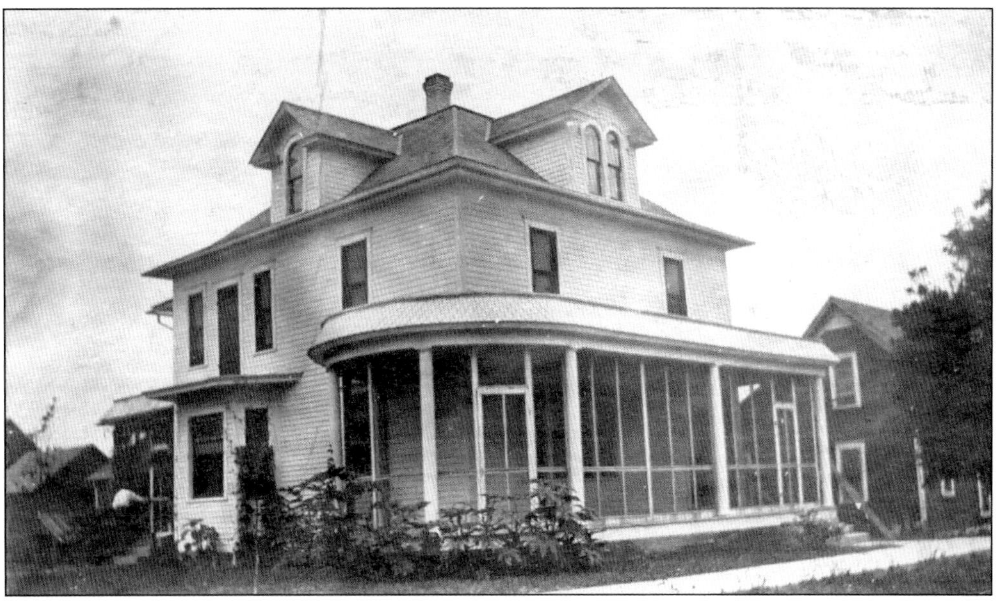

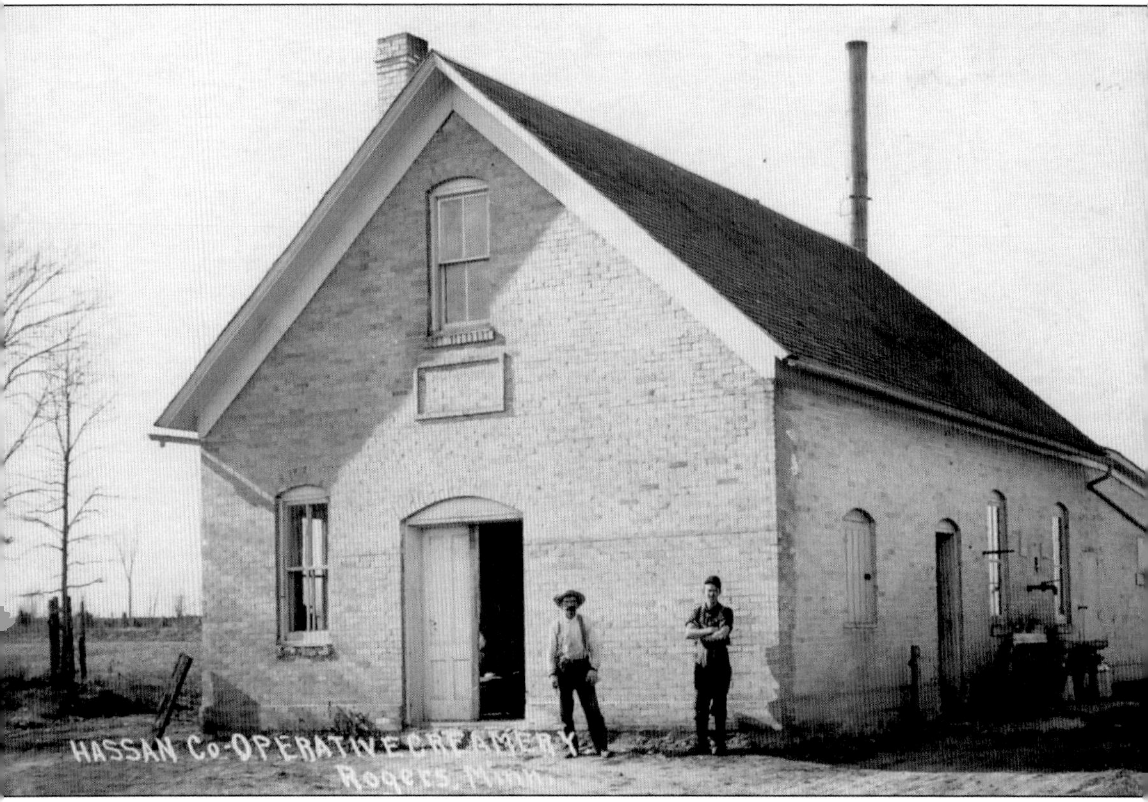

Pictured here is the local creamery; it burned down when Bob Milless was about 10 years old. JoAnn (Milless) Bourgeois remembered all the farmers having cows when she was growing up. She shared that two of the grocery stores brought cans to their farm so they could bottle their own milk. One local farmer milked 30 cows, then remodeled the barn and increased to 70 cows. His wife remembered checking on children between dumping milk pails; she had one in a cradle and one in a playpen. Chuck Christian stated that his dad had two full-time jobs: milking 30 cows twice a day and then his milk route. Christian recalled, "You better be up or dad would holler upstairs and the whole house shook. When he got home he expected to see chores being done." Jack Dahlheimer's theory on animal farming was that chickens generated money from eggs for buying clothes and groceries, pigs generated money for the taxes and mortgage, and cows took care of the feed bill. (Courtesy of Danny, Janet, and Noreen Durant.)

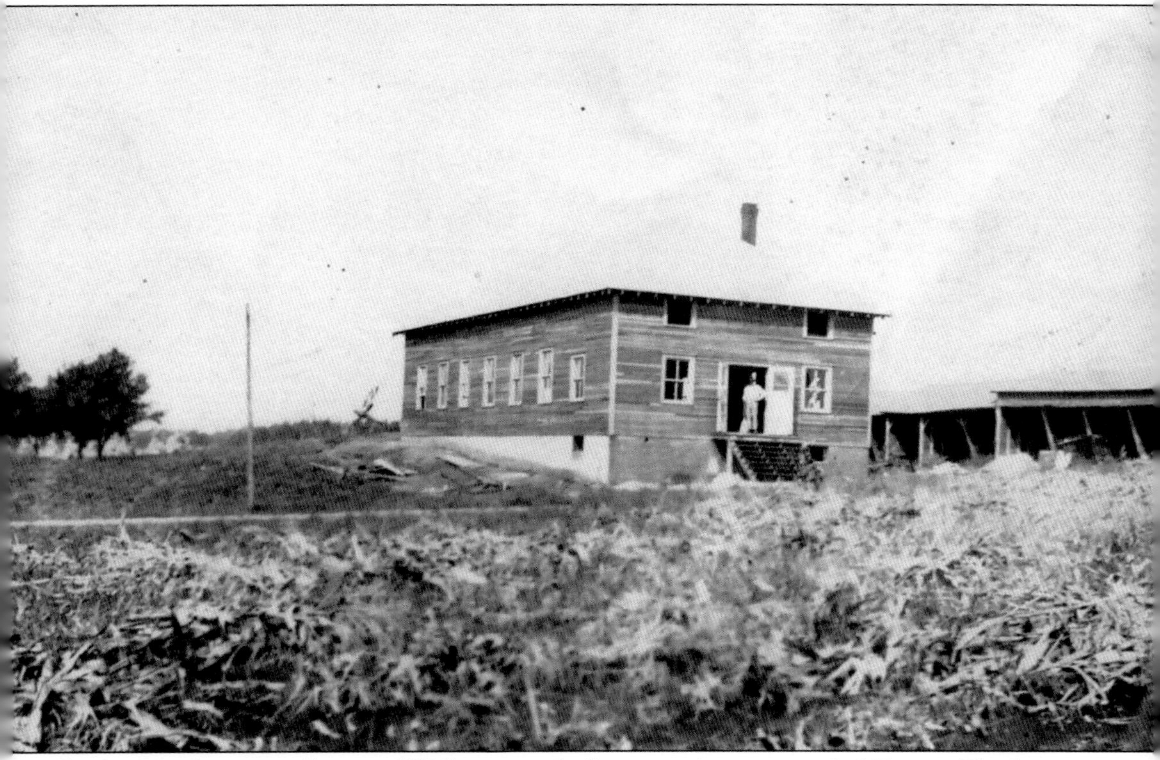

Fletcher Hamlet, originally named Walburga, gradually emerged over a period of 25 years. The first settlers, Andrew and Margaret Stenglein, emigrated with their children from Bavaria, Germany, around 1855 and homesteaded at the crossroads of Territorial Road and Corcoran-Dayton Road. Two years after they arrived, the Stengleins helped organize St. Walburga Church. Within a short time, there was a rectory, cemetery, and school. By 1895, a blacksmith shop stood at this major intersection. A butcher shop opened next. In 1900, a post office was established and Walburga was renamed Fletcher in honor of U.S. congressman Loren Fletcher; the post office closed in 1906. In about 1914, the Fletcher Hall Association was formed and the building pictured was constructed. Lenny and Lila Schlegel, among others in the community, remember having their wedding dance in this building. It was also used for plays, social gatherings, and fall festivals. (Courtesy of Lenny and Lila Schlegel.)

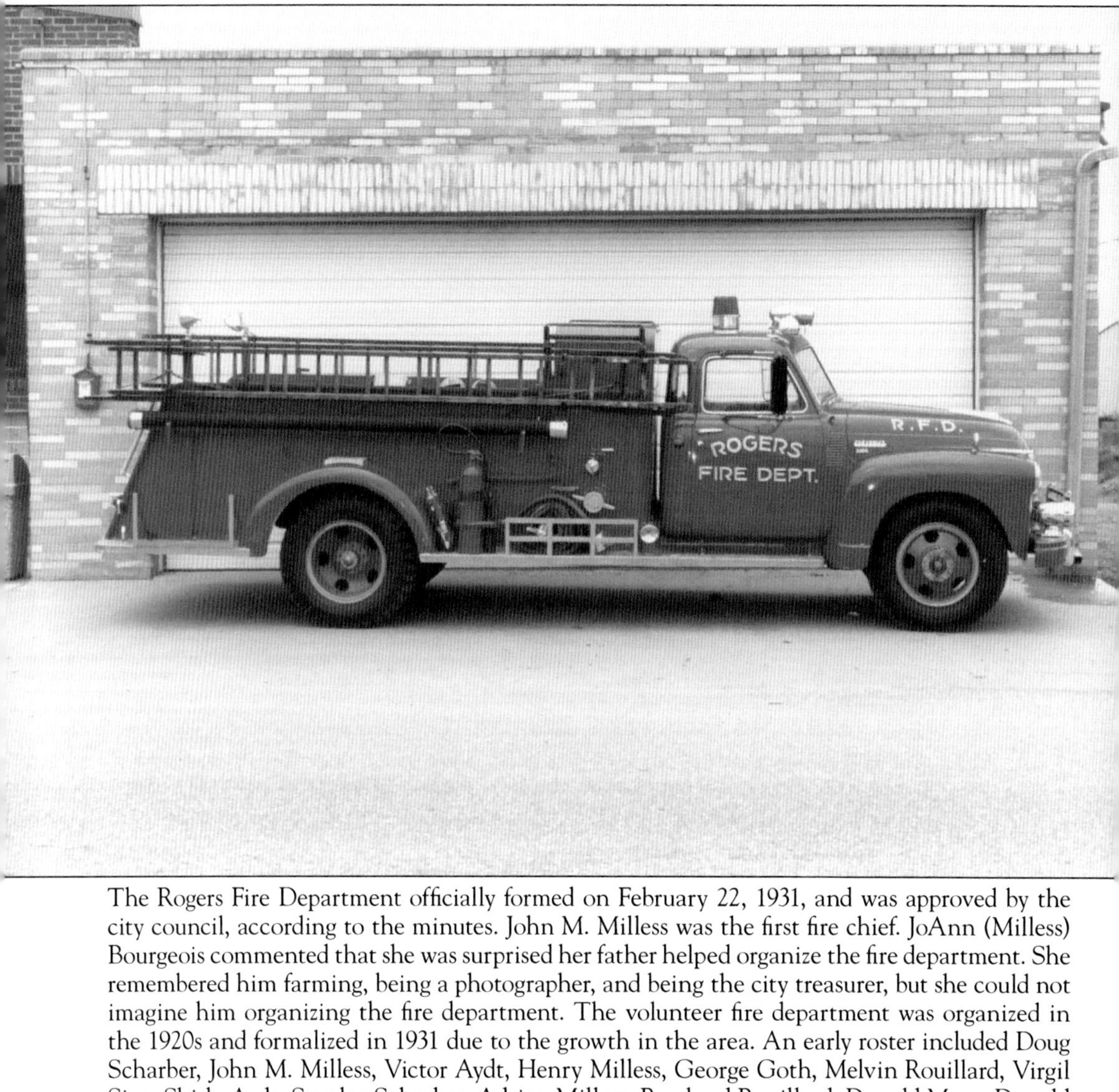

The Rogers Fire Department officially formed on February 22, 1931, and was approved by the city council, according to the minutes. John M. Milless was the first fire chief. JoAnn (Milless) Bourgeois commented that she was surprised her father helped organize the fire department. She remembered him farming, being a photographer, and being the city treasurer, but she could not imagine him organizing the fire department. The volunteer fire department was organized in the 1920s and formalized in 1931 due to the growth in the area. An early roster included Doug Scharber, John M. Milless, Victor Aydt, Henry Milless, George Goth, Melvin Rouillard, Virgil Sipe, Shirly Aydt, Stanley Scharber, Adrian Milless, Rowland Rouillard, Donald Marx, Donald Weber, Bob Raudenbush, Jim Dahlheimer, Gorden Marx, Mirandus Milless, Carl Ahstrom, Ben Macke, Coon Farrian, Jerome Gmach, Dude Milless, Bob Milless, Merle Heinen, and Gene Ahlstrom. Between 1954 and 1957, there were over 40 volunteers. The year 2006 marks the 75th anniversary of the Rogers Fire Department. (Courtesy of Fire Chief Brad Feist.)

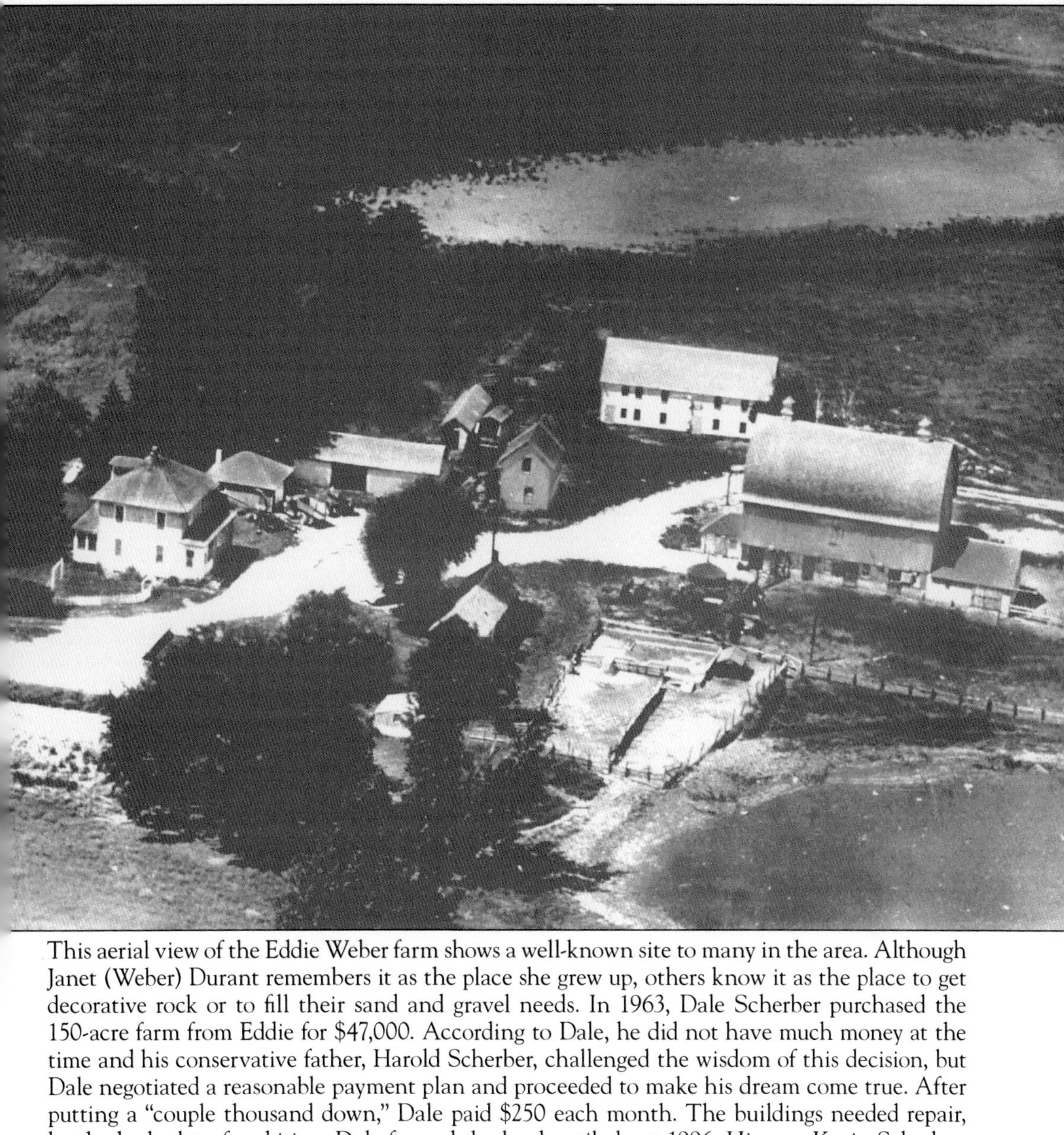

This aerial view of the Eddie Weber farm shows a well-known site to many in the area. Although Janet (Weber) Durant remembers it as the place she grew up, others know it as the place to get decorative rock or to fill their sand and gravel needs. In 1963, Dale Scherber purchased the 150-acre farm from Eddie for $47,000. According to Dale, he did not have much money at the time and his conservative father, Harold Scherber, challenged the wisdom of this decision, but Dale negotiated a reasonable payment plan and proceeded to make his dream come true. After putting a "couple thousand down," Dale paid $250 each month. The buildings needed repair, but he had a lot of ambition. Dale farmed the land until about 1996. His son, Kevin Scherber, shared that they started the family-operated business Hassan Sand and Gravel in about 1973. This family business has helped build the foundations of many homes and businesses in the community. (Courtesy of Danny and Janet Durant.)

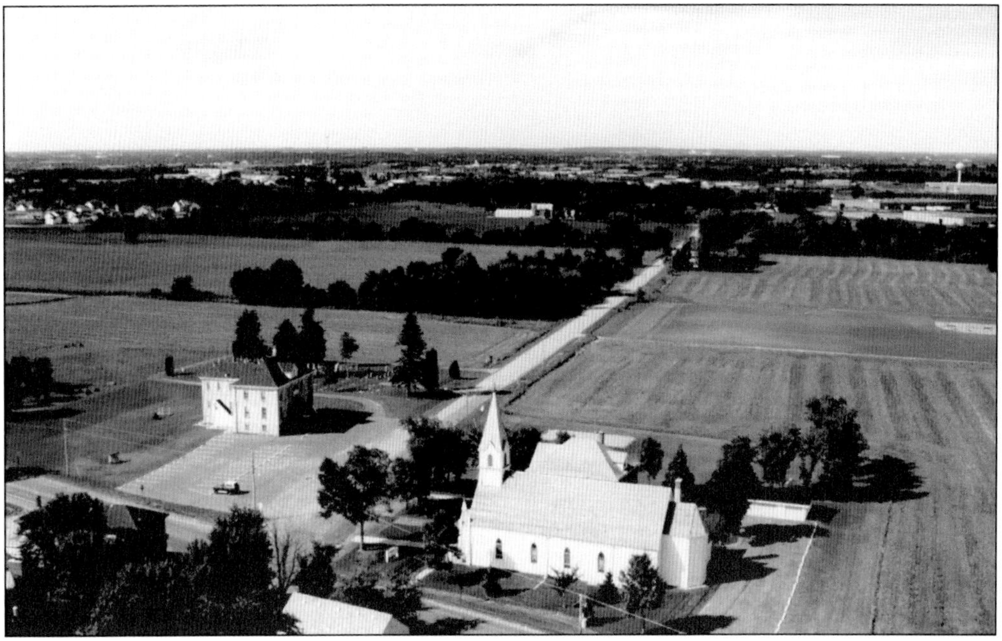

Just 30 miles northwest of downtown Minneapolis lays the quiet and still unincorporated hamlet of Fletcher. The area was founded in 1854 and gradually developed a trade center over 25 years. Fletcher boasted the only passage between Minneapolis and the northwestern communities until Highway 152, later known as County Road 81, was built in 1953. The community's founders were ambitious businessmen; however, it is speculated that the railroad crossing through neighboring Rogers Siding and bypassing Fletcher may have impeded the hamlet's ability to thrive. On the other hand, many people enjoy the peaceful scenery in Fletcher, one of the few areas in Hennepin County where one can still find farmland. These are aerial pictures over Fletcher and Rogers. (Courtesy of Chuck Christian.)

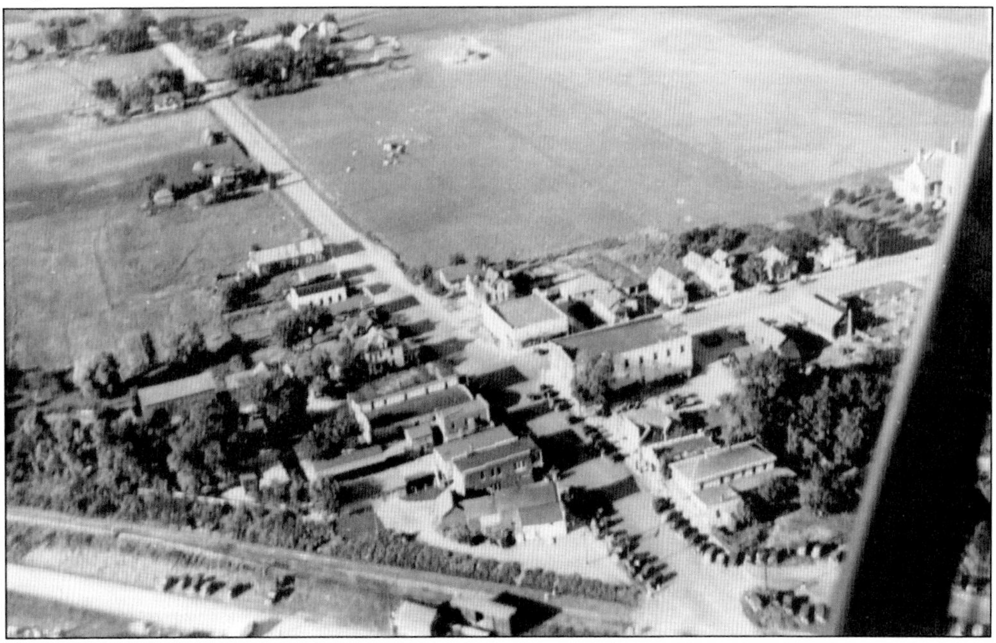

Four

School Days

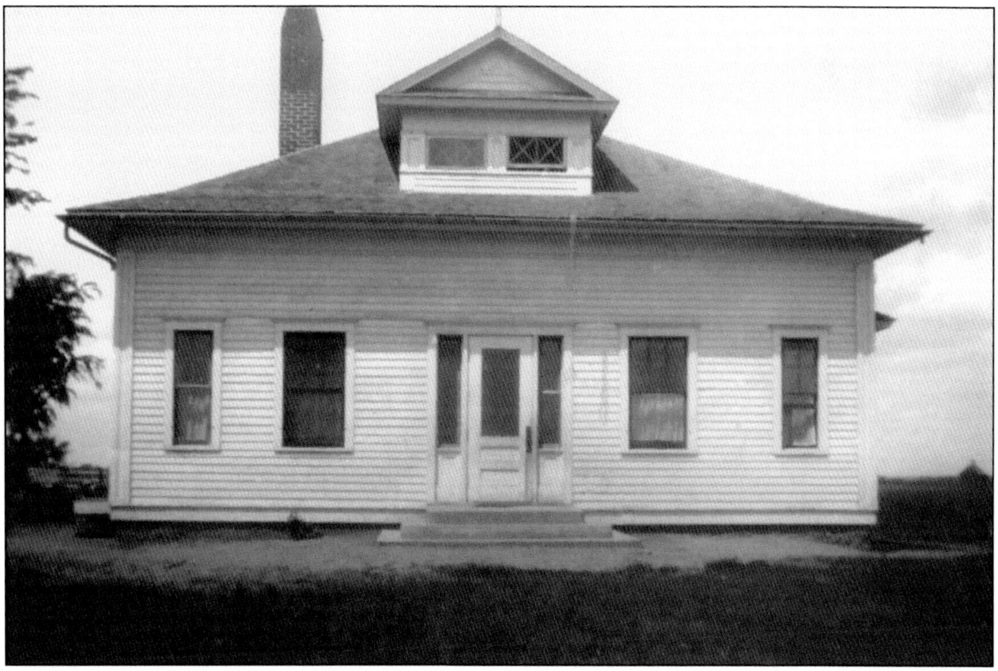

Rogers, Hassan Township, and Fletcher were peppered with several one-room schoolhouses; however, it seems most remaining residents attended the Hassan School, District 69, District 70, or St. Walburga prior to 1950. This picture was taken of the District 69 building in its prime. These schools usually had one teacher who instructed first through eighth grades. Students generally attended class from 8:30 or 9:00 a.m. until 4:00 p.m. and often only received, what seemed to be, about 10 minutes a day with their teacher. The first teacher in town was paid about $60 or $70 per month. When the children got to school they would do their "chores" before school began. Eugene Ahlstrom remembered going across the road to pump water for the class and building a fire to keep the school warm. Students had one hour for lunch and 15 minutes for recess. They played baseball or enjoyed swinging during that time. (Courtesy of Leo Scharber.)

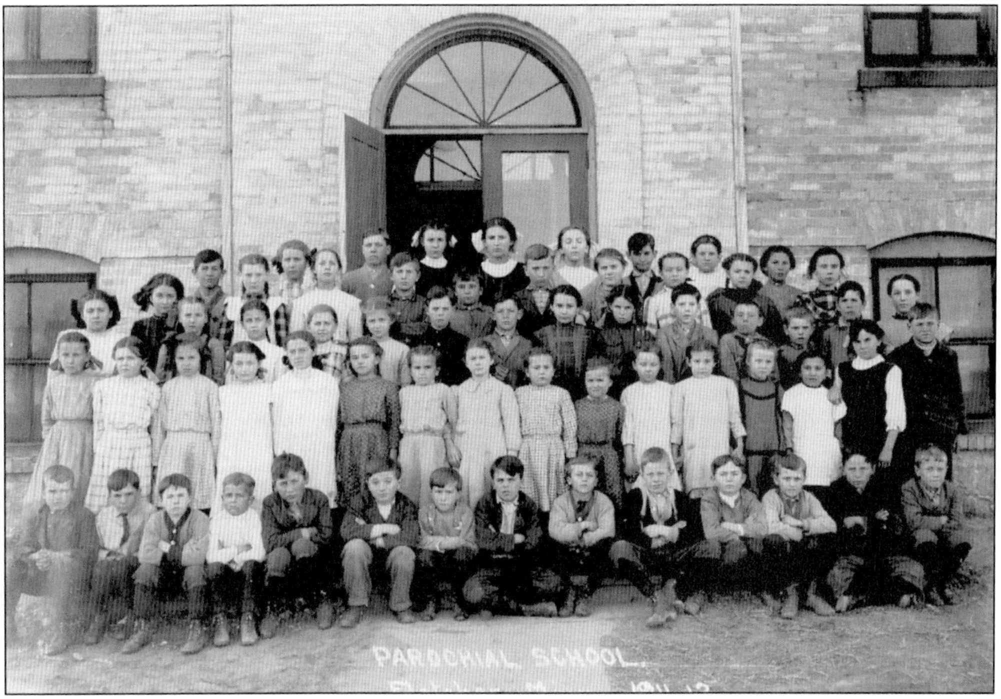

The first parochial school in the area was erected in 1865, across the road from the original St. Walburga Church on County Road 117. In 1886, after the church was moved down the road to Walburga (later known as Fletcher), a new school was built north of the rectory. It was a one-room schoolhouse, which quickly reached its capacity of 60 students. In 1902, it was moved across the street and incorporated into a new three-story, brick-veneered school. In the fall of 1904, three Sisters of St. Francis joined the school and operated it for 63 years. These first- through eighth-grade class pictures were taken around 1911. (Courtesy of Andrew Stueve.)

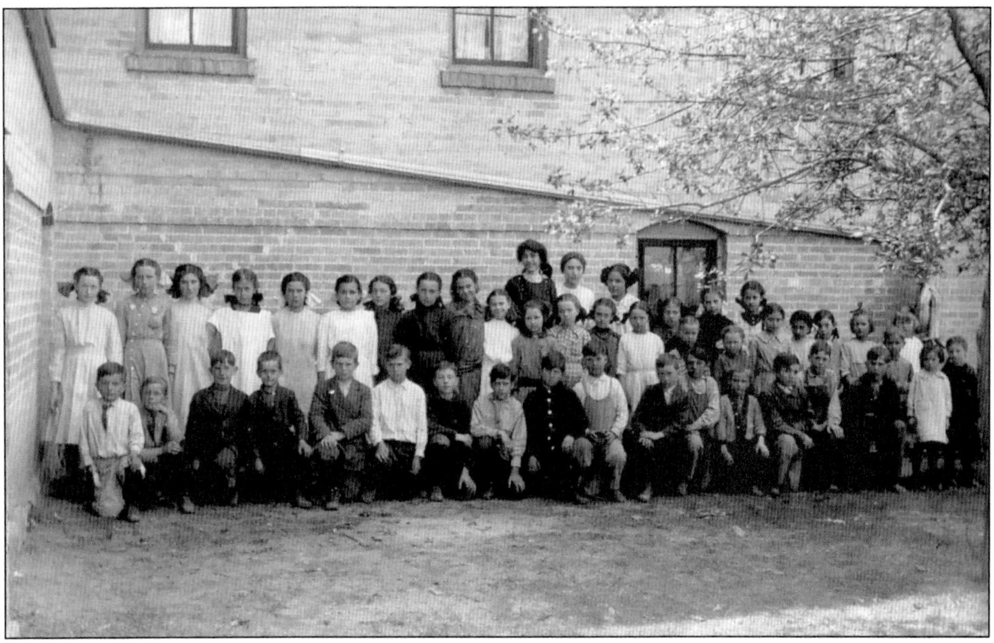

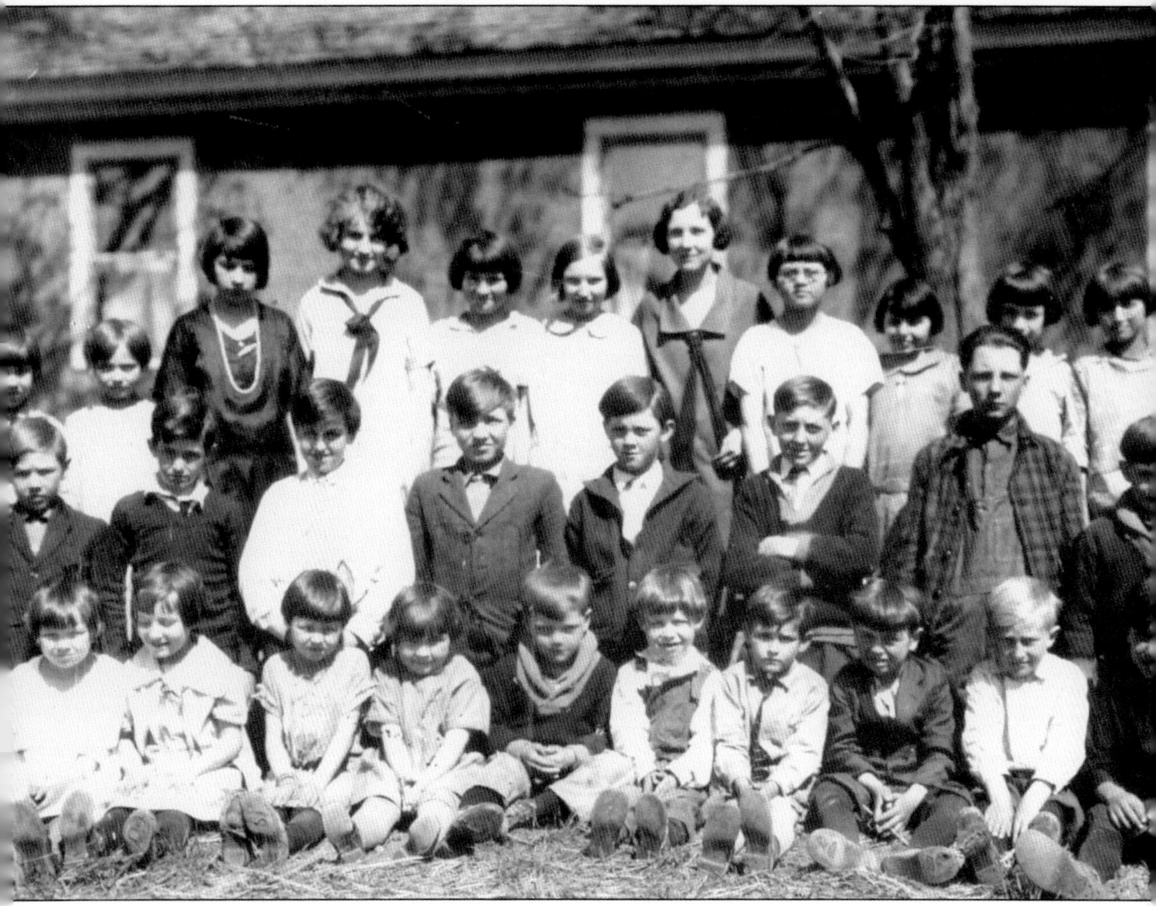

Several students in this 1924 picture from District 70, which was located on the current County Road 144, are still active in the community. Leo Scharber attended the school for only six months but remembered a teacher who brought her dog to school. She also brought her shotgun and kept it in the cloakroom; on her way home, she would hunt pheasant. At lunch, the teacher would pass a basin for scraps. The dog ate like a king. A tradition, remembered by Carmen Hawkins, was the annual Christmas program. There was a scene where it was supposed to get dark, so someone climbed a ladder and took the kerosene lantern down to turn the light out. If the lantern would have ever fallen, the place would have burned down. Ferdella (Rouillard) Gmach shared there were 51 students in eight grades with one teacher. (Courtesy of Melvin Rouillard.)

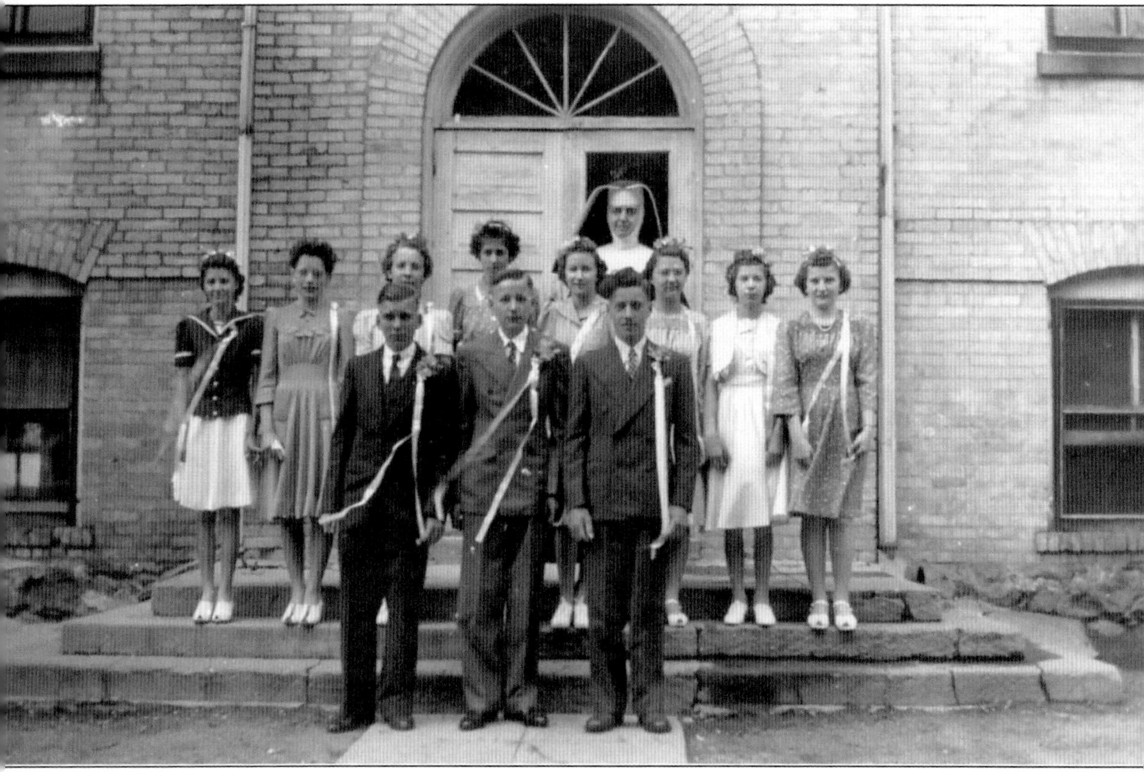

Lenny Schlegel was a member of this eighth-grade graduating class of St. Walburga. Because Schlegel was conscientious, the nuns made him a janitor; he filled the coal in the school, priest house, and church every day. Doug Scharber, on the other hand, shared that he was mischievous. He never did anything destructive, but he got into a lot of trouble because he laughed at inappropriate times or talked out of turn or simply had his mouth open when it should not be open. A nun told him, "Master Douglas, you are going to bump your horns one of these days." Then there was the group of guys who decided to play hooky from school and went to Poate's barn to swing in the hay. A nun found out and went to fetch them. She made them walk in front of the car all the way back to the school. Although most of the teachers at St. Walburga were nuns, Florence Lenz remembers teaching there. (Courtesy of Lenny and Lila Schlegel.)

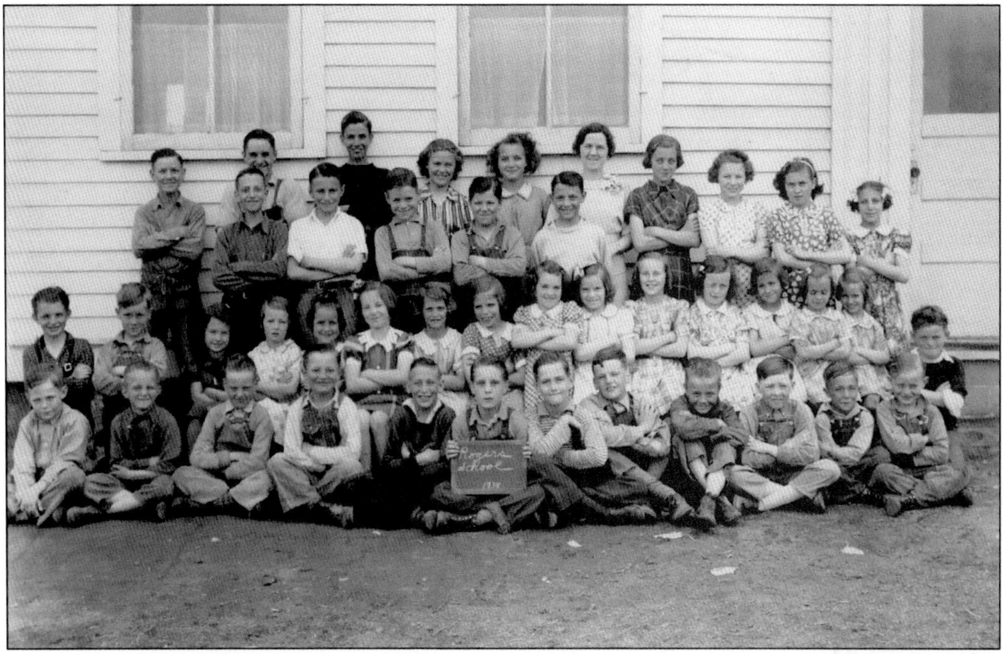

Leo Scharber shared that District 69 was one of the best schools in the area because it had a teaching area, library, girls' and boys' cloakrooms, and eating area. There were around 45 students enrolled in first through eighth grades each year. Although this may seem like a lot of students for one teacher, everyone interviewed agreed they liked having eight grades together because they learned from the older grades. JoAnn (Milless) Bourgeois shared that she walked to school each day. Leo Scharber recalled that Merle Heinen drove a truck, and their teacher, a Mr. Campbell, would send them into town to get him a "special candy bar with cherries on top" and his mail, and he did not care how long they were gone providing they had his candy bar and mail when they returned. Pictured are the 1938 and 1940 classes. (Courtesy of Leo Scharber.)

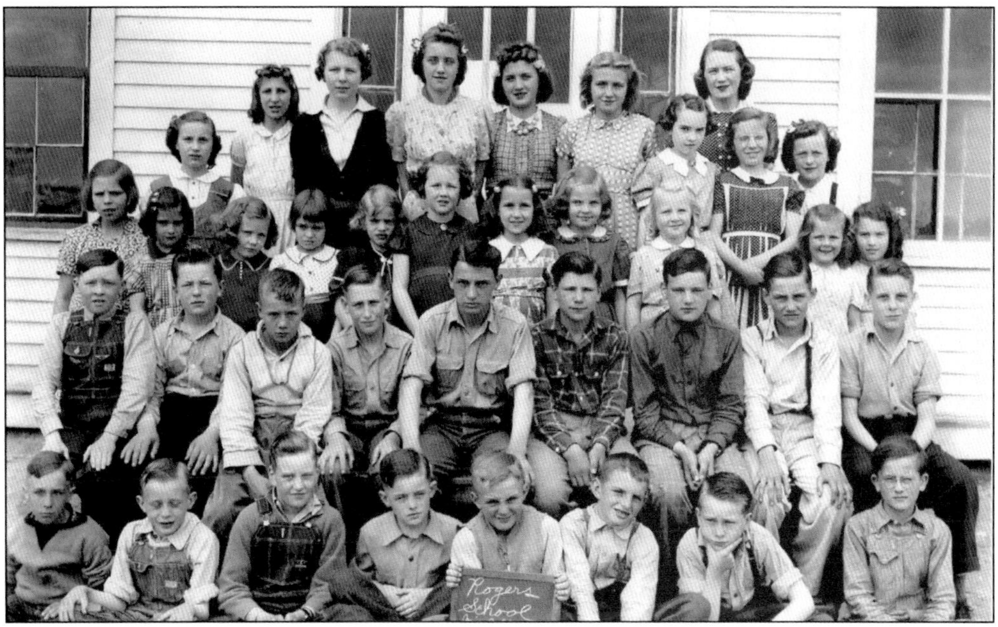

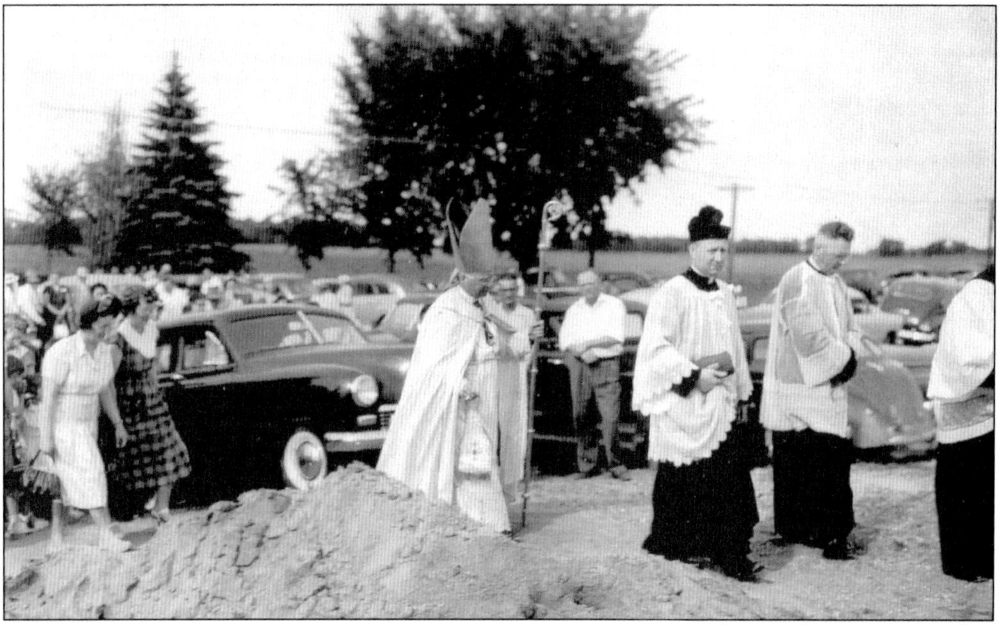

St. Martin's Catholic Church received approval on March 29, 1950, to construct a school and convent. Norb Zahler, a lifelong parishioner, was thrilled because he was hired by Walter Butler Construction Company to work on the project. Pictured here is St. Paul archbishop John Murray when he visited the construction site of the new St. Martin's school and convent during the summer of 1950 for a dedication ceremony. Also shown are St. Martin's parishioners gathered around the archbishop to witness the dedication. Construction of the school building was well underway, but it was not complete when school began, so students used alternate spaces. The facility was finished on November 26, 1950. Mary Lou (Zachman) Dahlheimer remembers the day the school opened; they picked up their books and walked across the street while a nun played the accordion. (Courtesy of Norb Zahler.)

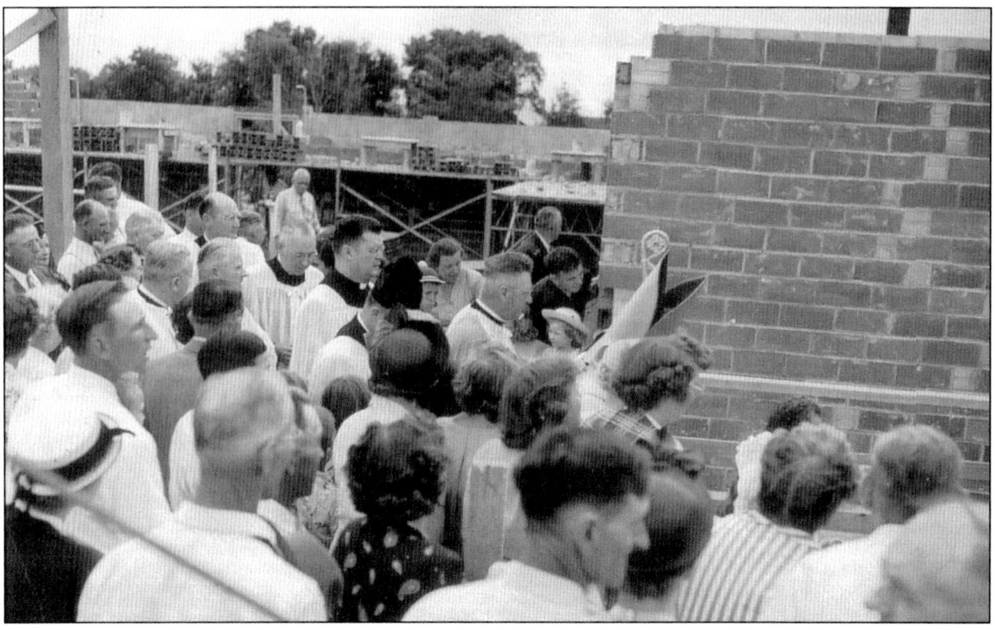

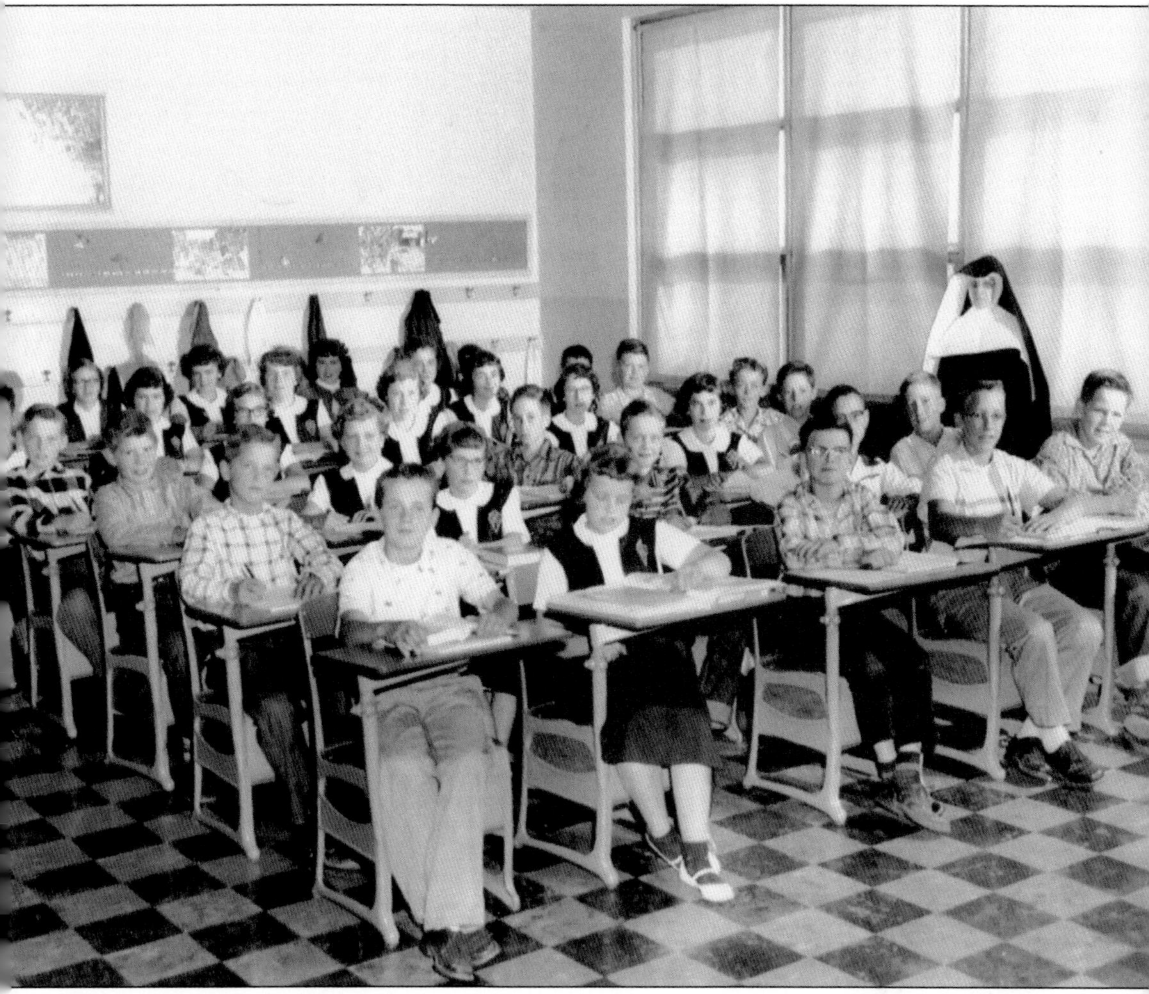

Once St. Martin's Catholic School opened, the one-room schoolhouses closed. Chuck and Dave Christian both remember switching from St. Walburga to St. Martin's Catholic School. Several people shared that even the non-Catholic families went to St. Martin's Catholic School; they simply did not attend religion classes. Students, such as Chuck Christian, often went to St. Michael to attend high school. Mary Lou (Zachman) Dahlheimer attended high school in Mankato, Minnesota, to become a nun. Although she changed her mind about becoming a nun, she liked the school, so she completed her education there. Dahlheimer commented that she made many close friends while attending St. Martin's and she still gets together with them. One of these friends is Jack Hines, who is pictured in this classroom photograph taken about 1952. (Courtesy of Jack and Carol Hines.)

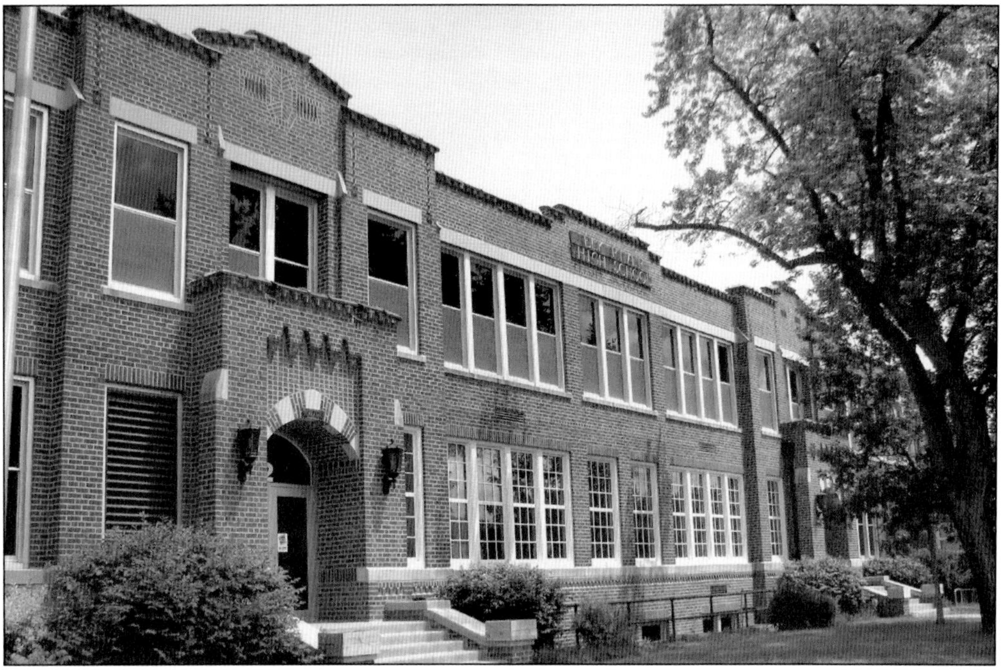

After completing eighth grade at District 69, Bob Milless attended high school in Elk River. Milless remembered when he and three buddies skipped school and went to Anoka High School to "check things out." They were greeted by the superintendent, who called the Elk River High School and explained the situation. A few days later, the boys were summoned into the superintendent's office one at a time. He had a piece of rubber hose and said, "Hold out your hands." Afterward he said, "Okay Bob, let's forget it." Milless thought he was nice. Milless played football in high school, and he really enjoyed playing in the stadium pictured below. According to Peggy Dahlheimer, it was the best stadium in Minnesota at the time. Leo Scharber's daughter was one of the double homecoming queens (there was a tie) in 1982. (Courtesy of Rob Bell.)

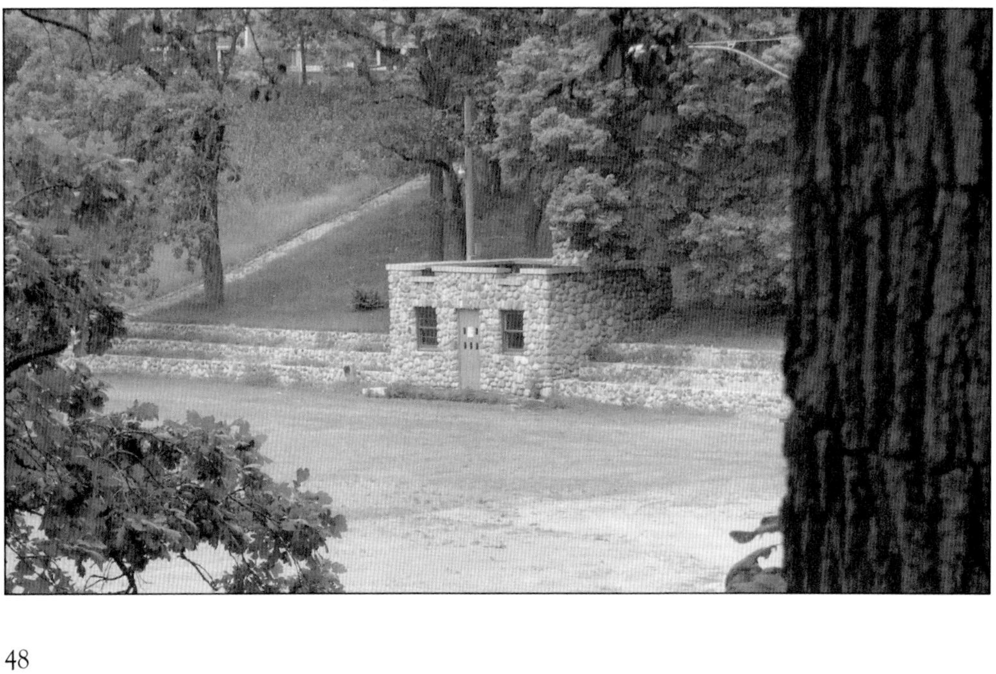

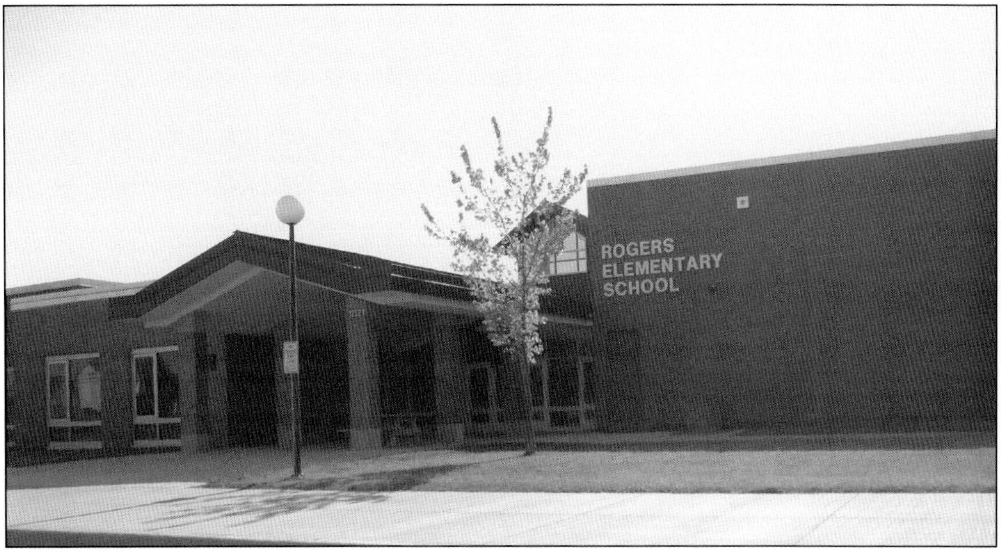

In the 1960s, Minnesota consolidated school districts throughout the state, eliminating the one-room schoolhouse altogether. Due to the consolidation and rapid growth in the area, Independent School District 728, located in Elk River, began experiencing overcrowding. As reported by the *Crow River News* on August 31, 1966, an estimated high enrollment of 1,846 students were expected to attend school on September 6, 1966. The article goes on to state, "There will be one section of kindergarten at Rogers to accommodate Rogers' residents and relieve the space load in Elk River. . . . All of the buildings will be filled to overflowing capacity." The Rogers Elementary School was finished in June 1970. A second elementary school, Hassan Elementary, opened its doors in 2005; both schools are pictured. (Courtesy of Rob Bell.)

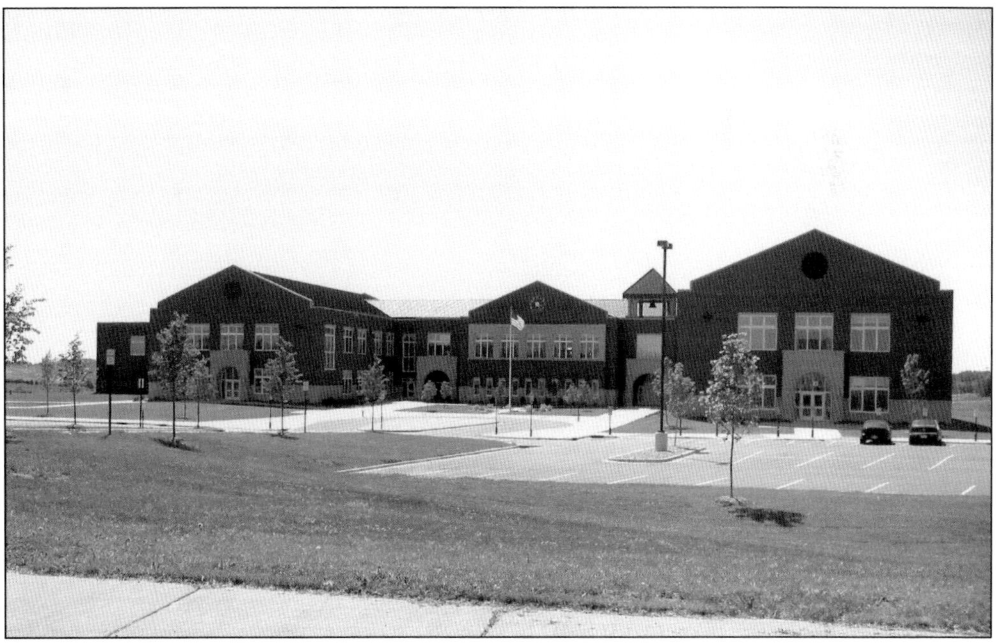

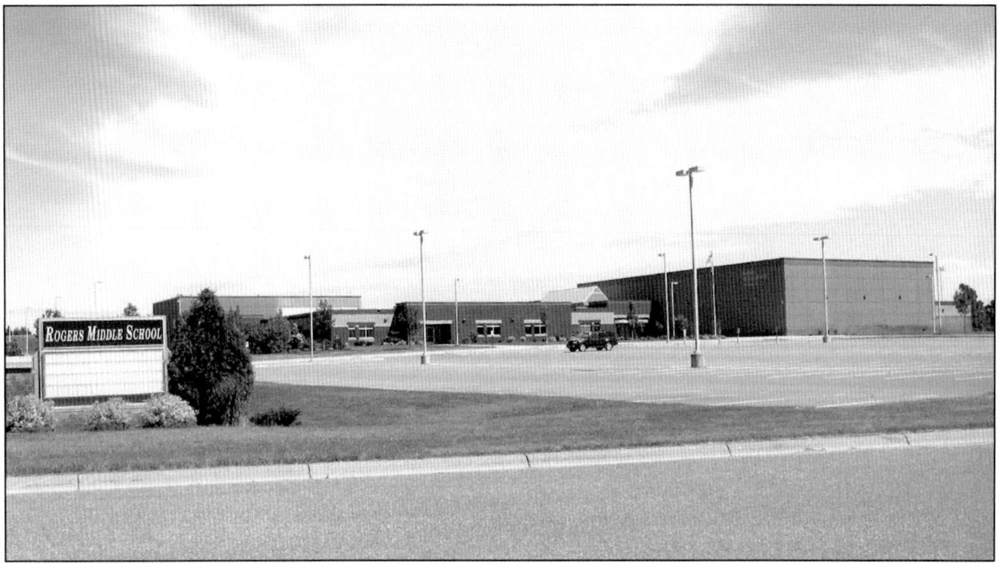

In 1934, Margaret Plude offered the convenience of paid student transportation when she began the first bus route to Elk River using a Model A Chevrolet. Within two short months, she was able to purchase an actual bus. Melvin Rouillard remembers being the first person on the bus each morning; he went to the Dayton school. Norb Zahler took the bus to Elk River and remembered when government funding started in about 1948; the Plude Bus Company grew. JoAnn (Milless) Bourgeois remembered feeling overwhelmed going from a school of 45 students with only 4 in her grade to a school with three or four homerooms for each grade, but she loved it. The community has worked together to bring the Rogers Middle School and Rogers High School, pictured here, to the area. (Courtesy of Rob Bell.)

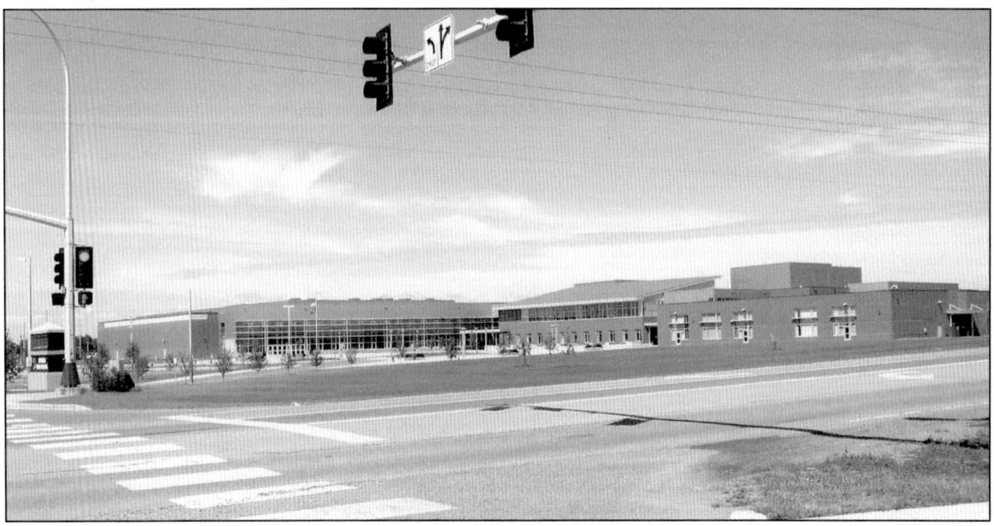

Five

The American Dream

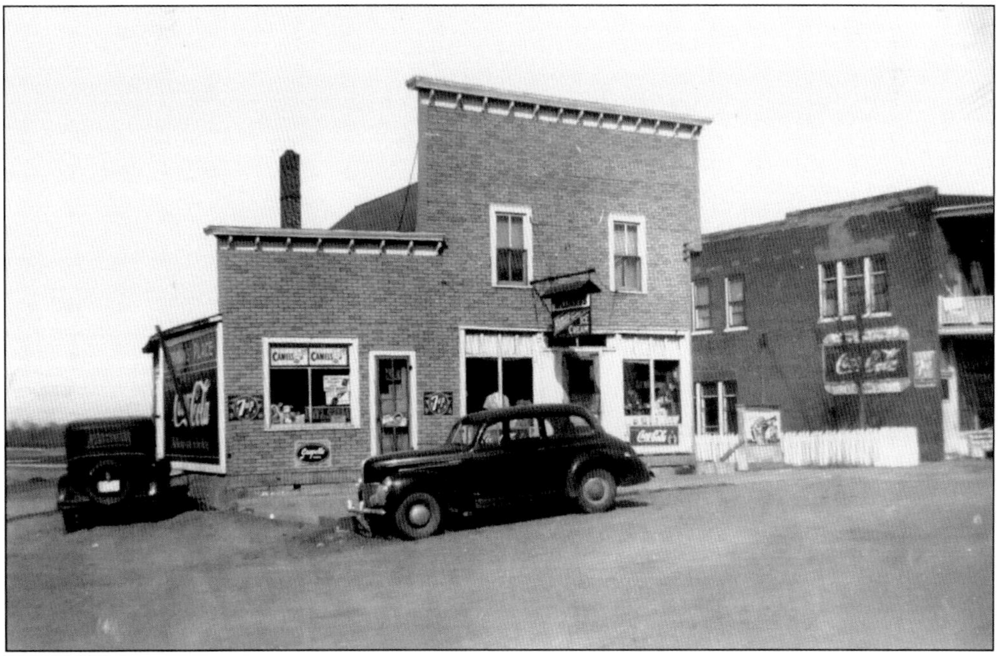

The Harveses owned this building before it was sold to Andy Wishy, who converted it into a pool hall that sold 3.2 beer and offered barber services; Aime Moren was the barber. Katie Farrian later became the owner. Locals remember Farrian's as a "tavern and malt shop" that served delicious food. The town scale was in front of Farrian's, which made it a local gathering spot. Dave and Jeff Christian remember being paid for the weekly newspaper in ice cream; they are pretty sure they owed her by the end of the week. Dave recalled that Katie always knew when you were having a bad day; she said ice cream fixed everything. Mary Lou (Zachman) Dahlheimer enjoyed when she and her siblings saw their dad's car sitting outside Farrian's because they knew he would buy them some pop. That was a big treat! Her dad would say they were lucky he was still in town; now Mary Lou realizes he planned it that way. The building now houses two businesses, a dog groomer and a bead shop. (Courtesy of Leo Scharber.)

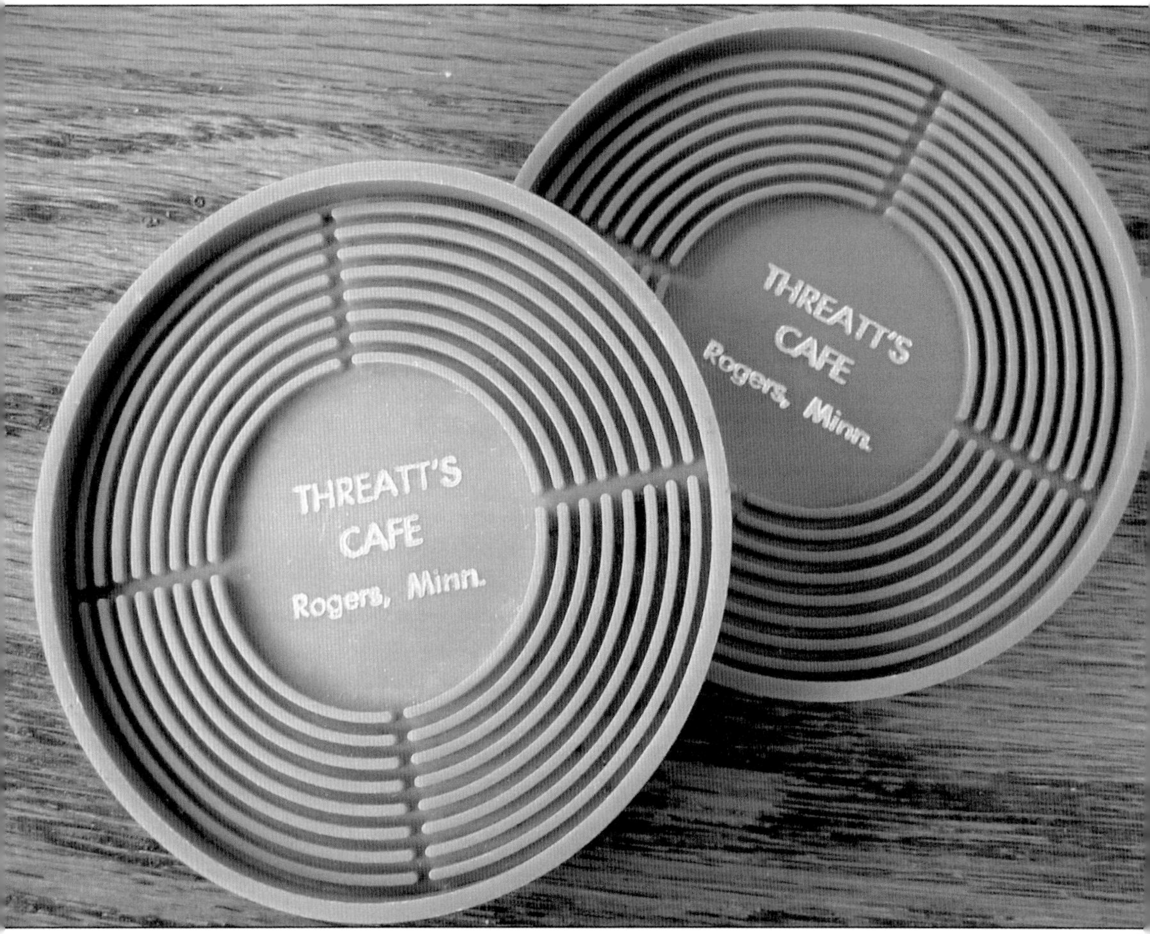

Frank and Elizabeth Threatt made everyone feel welcome at Threatt's Bar B Que. They offered a limited menu, but everything they made was wonderful. People still rave about the barbecue ribs that fell off the bone and the creamy cole slaw. Locals shared Frank and Elizabeth were the first African American people to live in Rogers. Although there was speculation they were invited to open their restaurant to help a past business owner "get even with the town," everyone was very happy they became members of the community. Frank was the baseball coach for two or three years and played catcher on the team. Leo Scharber shared that his wife, Marion, worked for Threatt's. Chuck Christian and Jack Hines visited Frank a few years before he died and asked if he still made the barbecue sauce and cole slaw. Frank's response was, "No, Elizabeth took the recipes to the grave with her." The building is still on Main Street. (Courtesy of Antique Mall of Rogers.)

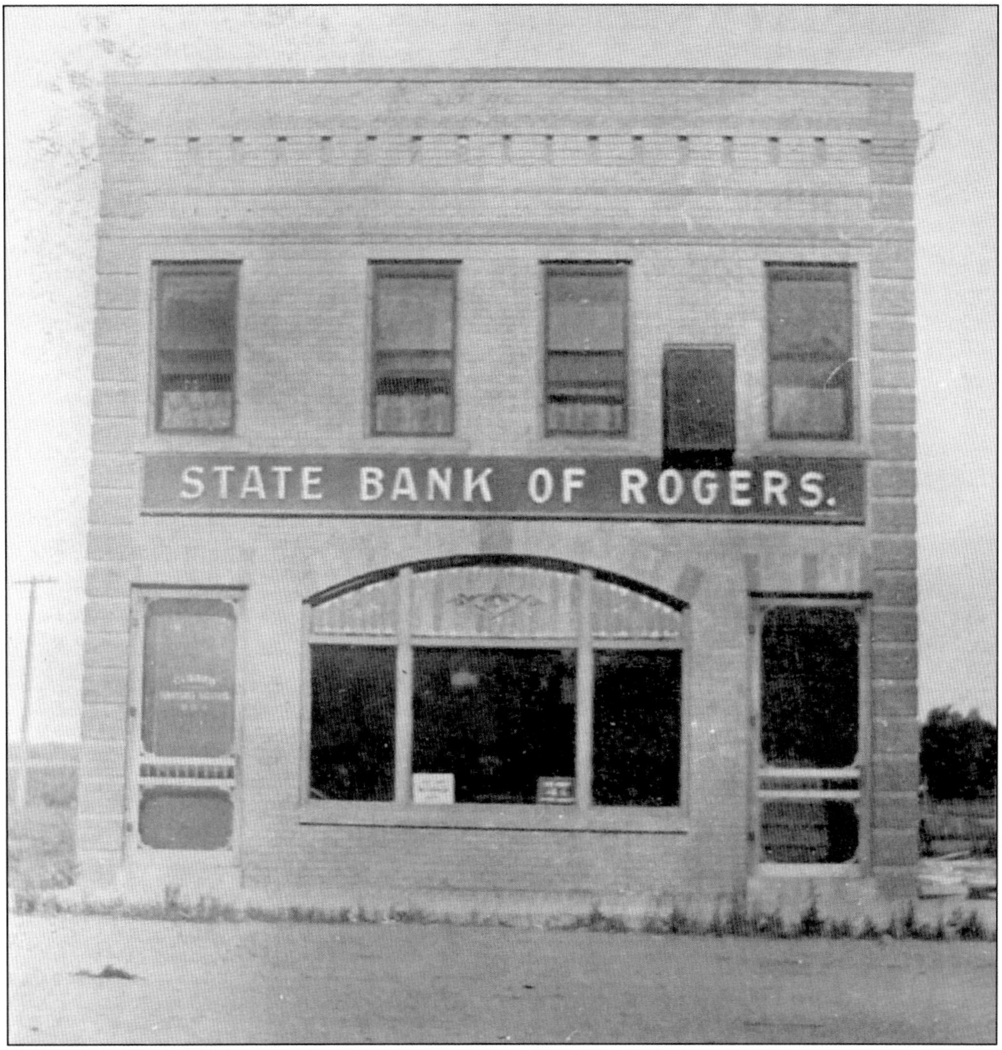

The State Bank of Rogers was built in 1909. Leo Scharber shared a story about when the bank was being built. Evidently there was a group of Irishmen building the bank and they got into a brick fight, so they had to stop construction until they could find a crew that got along. Mike Borck worked as assistant cashier and later became president of the bank. Oliver Kapsner and Jim Peterson later worked at the bank. Peterson was the owner, but Kapsner was known for understanding people and empathizing with their situation. Scharber reminisced about the Depression; he had money in the State Bank of Rogers when it went broke. JoAnn (Milless) Bourgeois worked at the State Bank of Rogers after she graduated from high school. The bank was located where Lefty Schaber's insurance agency is now; he even uses the vault for safekeeping. (Courtesy of Leo Scharber.)

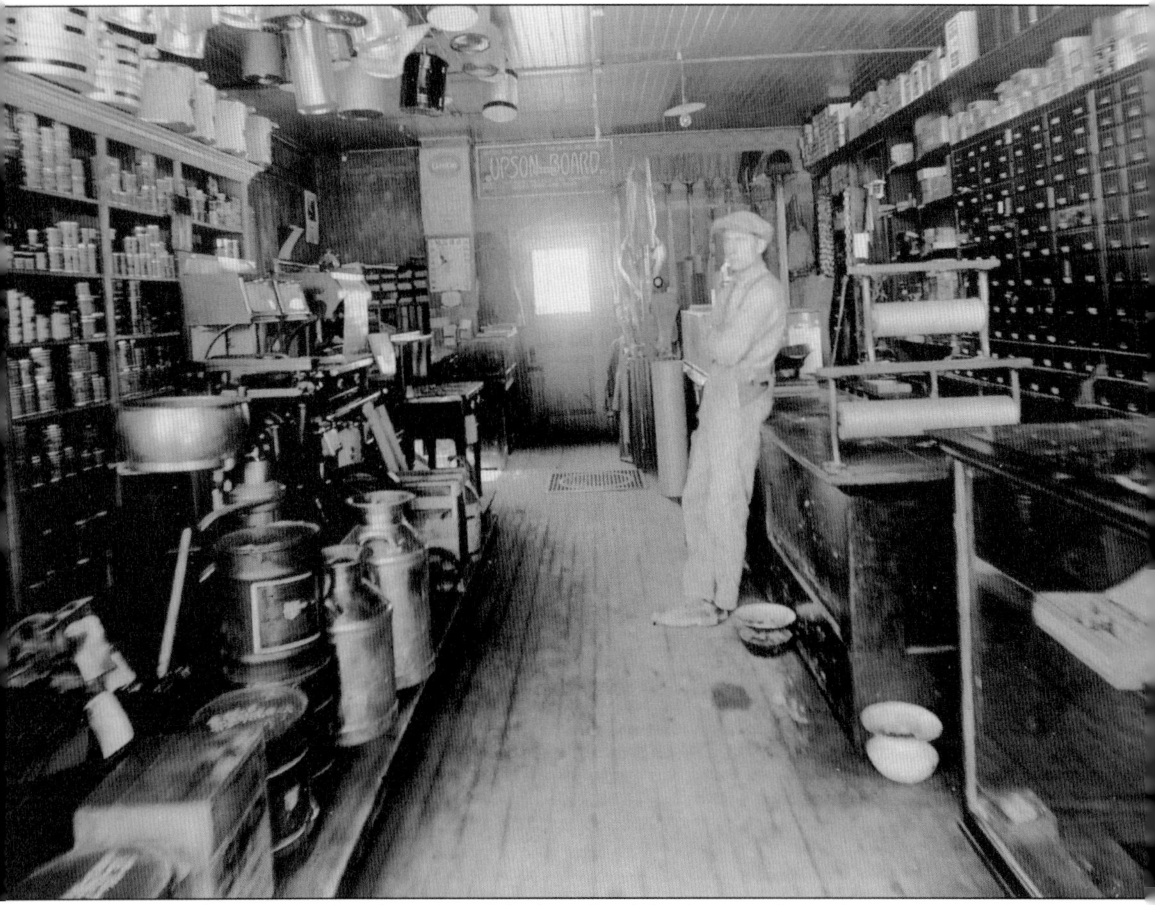

Pictured here is Ben Macke, who worked at the Scharber Hardware Store; he was married to Melida Scharber. The store was home to the local post office; Hazel (Rouillard) Scharber served as acting postmaster for a short period of time before Otto Scharber became the official postmaster. Eugene and Dorothy "Dot" Ahlstrom purchased the hardware store from the Scharbers and bought a small inventory. The post office remained in the hardware store, and Eugene became the postmaster. Eugene ran the business efficiently for about 11 years. Eugene shared that it only cost about $3 a month for utilities. He sold the building about the time he retired. In the early days, Dot had one shelf in the hardware store that she used for Hennepin County Library books. People from the community borrowed books until Hennepin County reclaimed the books one Thursday morning. As mayor, Judy Volkers championed the Rogers Library project, which was brought to the community under her leadership. Red Rooster Auto Parts is now in this original building. (Courtesy of Leo Scharber.)

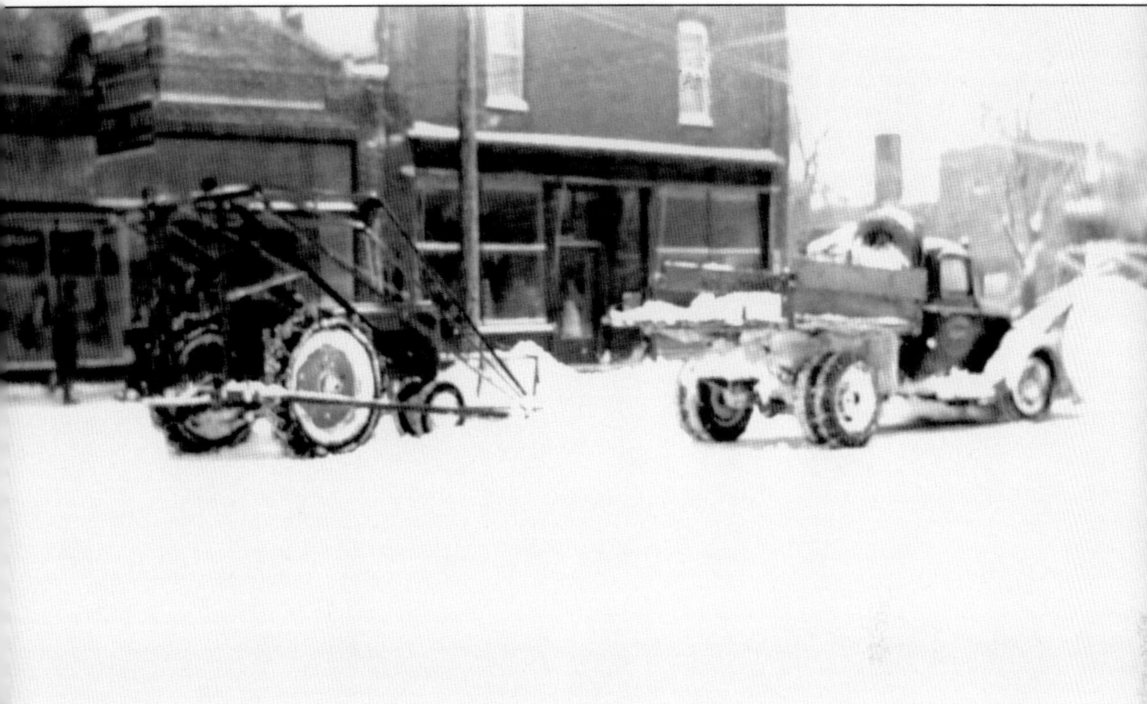

Snowstorms packed a powerful punch in 1940 as remembered by Carmen (Rouillard) Hawkins and Ferdella (Rouillard) Gmach. Both girls attended District 70. Their teacher, a Miss Johnson, decided to send the children home during a snowstorm. The girls and their teacher set out for the nearest farm place but lost their direction. They finally reached the Hines' residence and stayed there for three days. The Rouillards did not know where their daughters were because they did not have a telephone; eventually, they got home. According to Ferdella, they could have stayed in the school because there was food and heat, but the teacher thought they should leave. Howard Dahlheimer shared he was home with scarlet fever but remembers the snowbank in front of the farm was about as high as the power line. Bob Milless explained he was in Elk River when school closed, and the children were sent home on the bus; it was a scary experience for him. This image was taken in front of the Red and White grocery store. (Courtesy of Lenny and Lila Schlegel.)

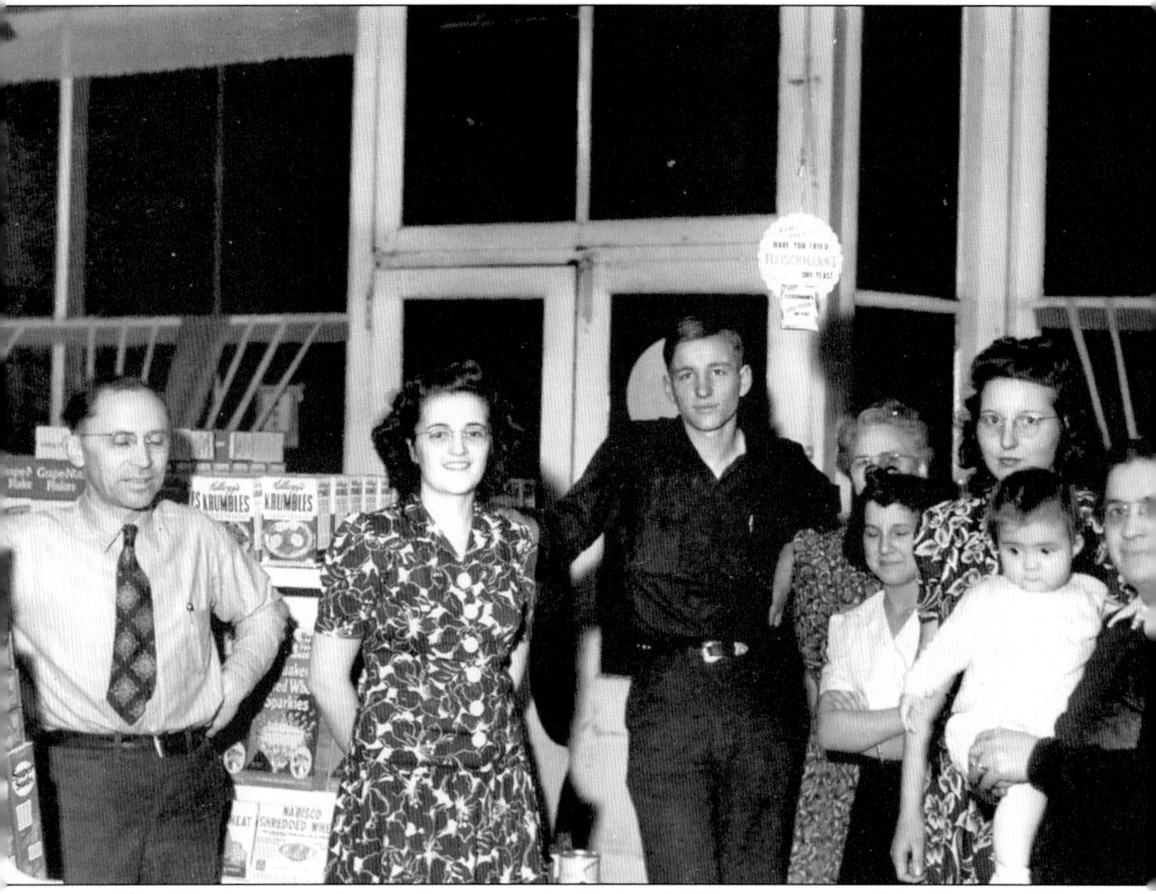

The Scharber general store, known as the Red and White, was owned by Otto and Hazel Scharber. Pictured here, from left to right, are Otto Scharber, Rhea Scharber, Lenny Schelgel, Rosie Hagel, JoAnn (Milless) Bourgeois, Germain Schlegel, Suzanne Scharber, and Hazel (Rouillard) Scharber. Bourgeois mentioned she was about 12 in this picture. The grocery store was between the John Deere implement and the hardware store. Lenny rode his bike to work from Fletcher to Rogers each day. Doug Scharber and his cousin Leo Scharber would go to Minneapolis to get machinery and groceries. Leo remembers Doug saying, "Com' on Leo, let's go to the city." He drove a 1937 truck with a straight stick. It was loaded so heavy they could barely get up Fricke's Hill. When they returned, Leo would work until 7:00 p.m. putting everything away. Leo reflected when Gerhart Scherber, Otto Scharber, and John Heinen all had grocery stores, they were on all three corners on Main Street, and everyone seemed to make a living. This building currently houses an insurance company. (Courtesy of Lenny Schlegel.)

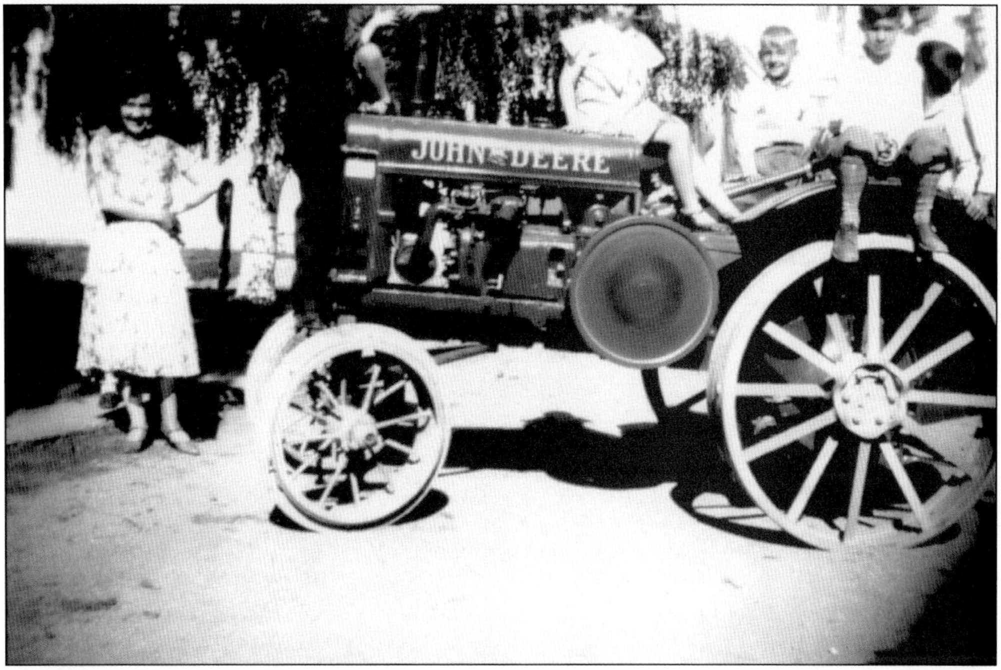

In 1906, two years before the original building burned down, John Scharber entered the implement business. Otto Scharber took over the joint business in 1928. Otto continued as the implement dealer along with his sons, Stanley and Doug. The John Deere implement was located at the center of town. This is one of the tractors with Scharber family members posing in 1929. John Deere Days were celebrated once a year in Rogers. This photograph was taken during the February 4, 1948, celebration at the local dance hall. John Deere Days were a big deal in town. Lunch was provided to everyone attending, and then a free movie was shown. Due to growth, the implement moved outside of town, and an antiques store moved into its space. (Above, courtesy of Leo Scharber; below, courtesy of Lenny and Lila Schlegel.)

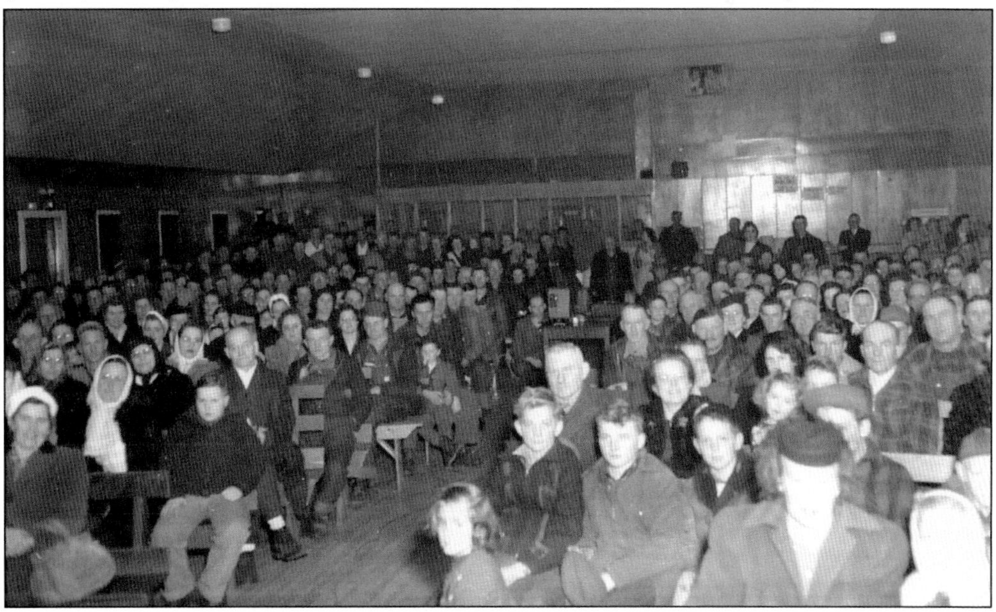

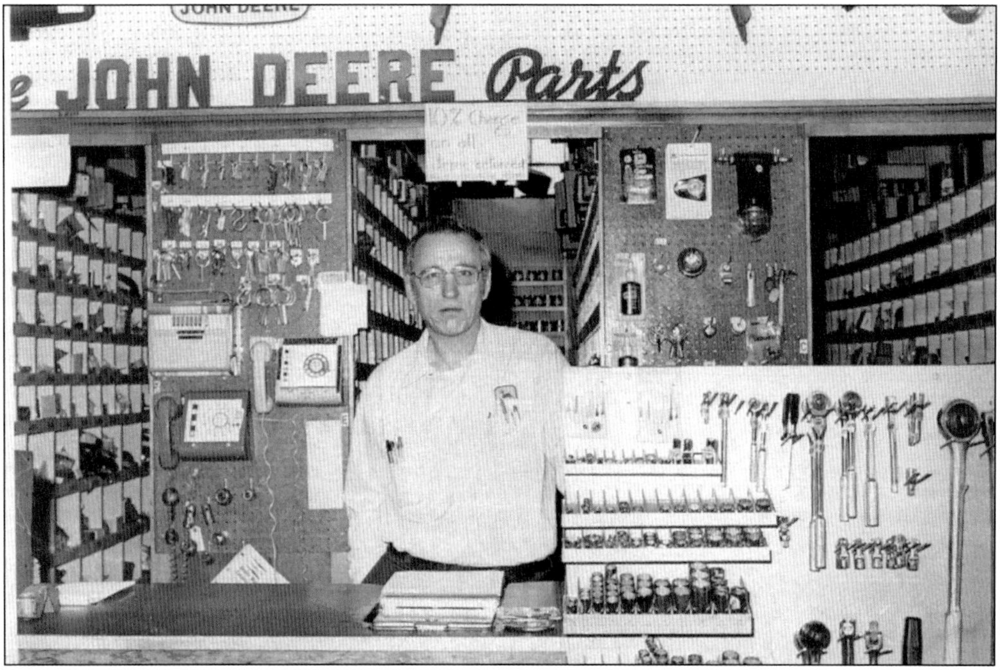

Lenny Schlegel was a faithful employee to the Scharbers for 62 years. Here he is working at Scharber and Sons implement dealership sometime during the 1970s. Schlegel worked at the implement after the hardware and grocery stores were sold. Also depicted is a 1944 John Deere tractor being delivered by Scharber and Sons. (Courtesy of Lenny and Lila Schlegel.)

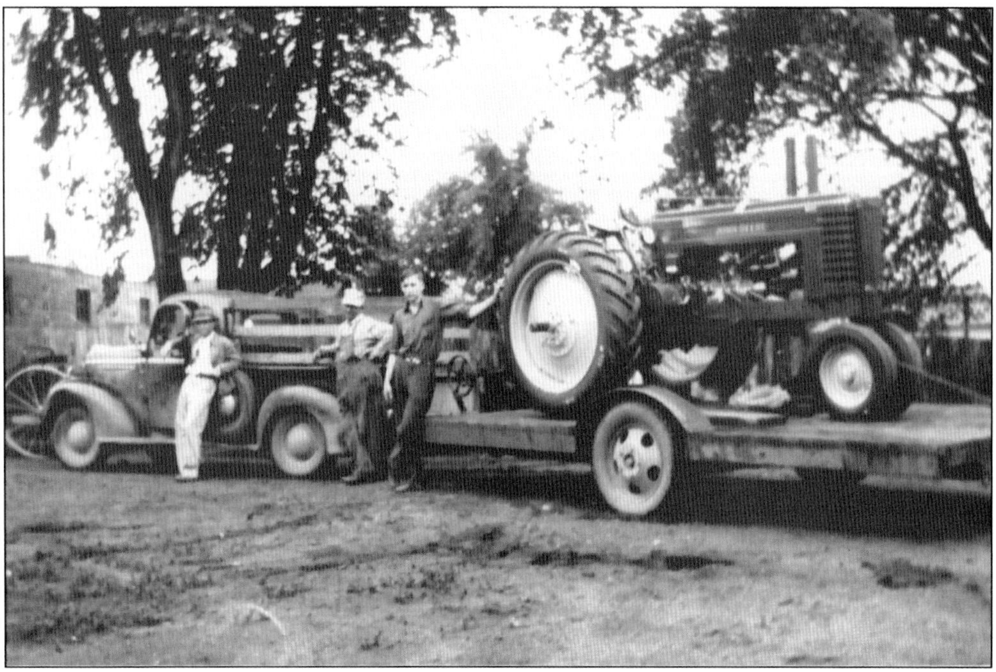

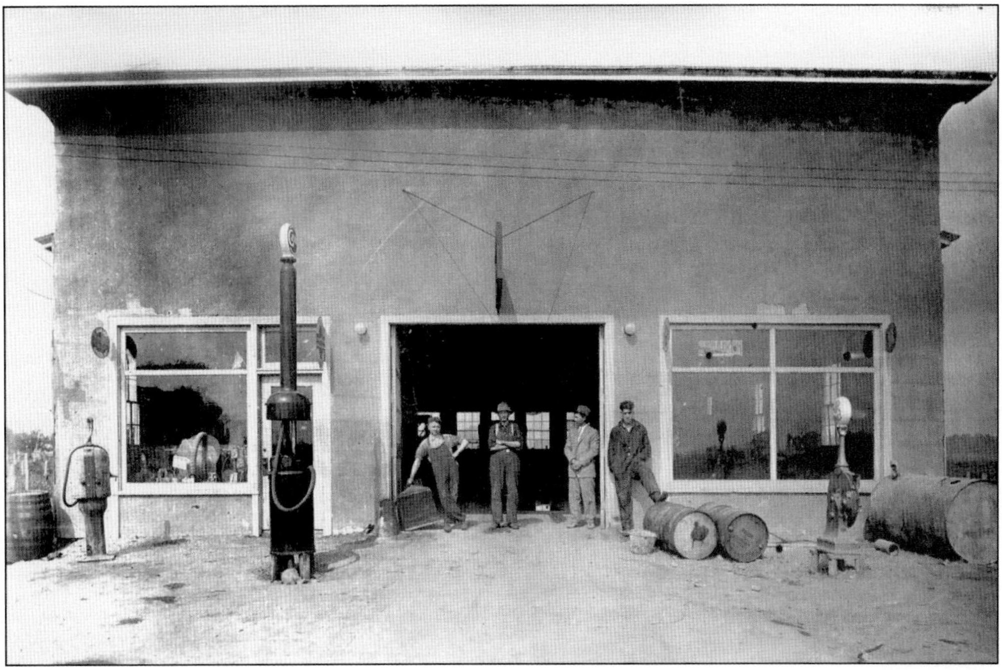

As the automobile entered the scene, so did the need for automobile repair shops. Sadly, speed, poor road conditions, and mechanical malfunctions caused many deaths in the early days. Denny Stieg shared that while researching the family lineage, his wife found a tragic article about a six-year-old girl and eight-year-old boy who walked from Berning's Bridge to St. Michael in the dark because their car ran into a telegraph pole and their father died. The car had been seen earlier by a mechanic. It was reported the lights could not be repaired, and the gentleman was advised not to drive, but he chose to make the trek. This story was from November 27, 1922. Pictured here is the first garage in Rogers, owned by Lawrence and Otto Scharber, as it appeared in 1926. (Courtesy of Leo Scharber.)

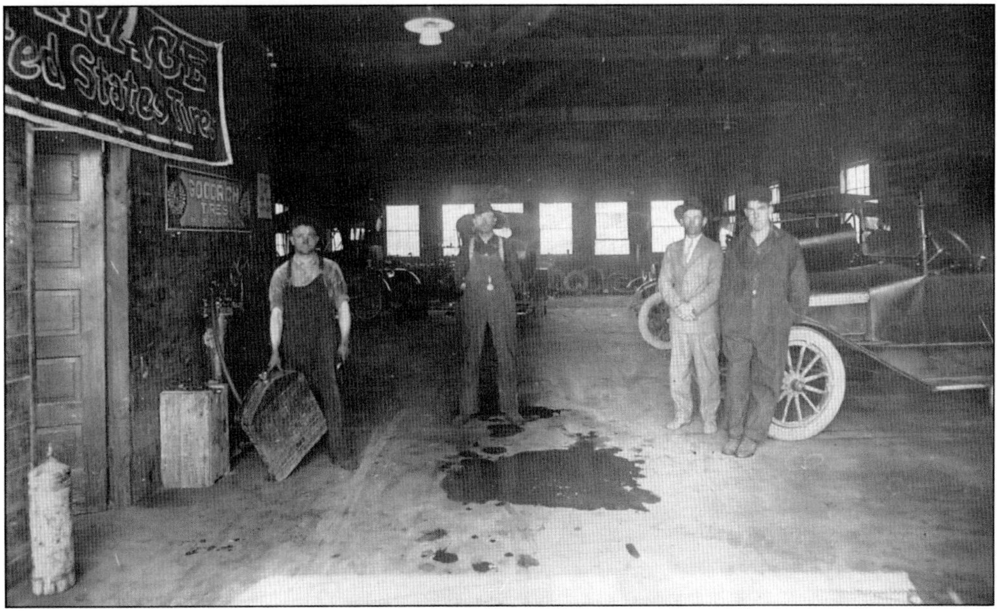

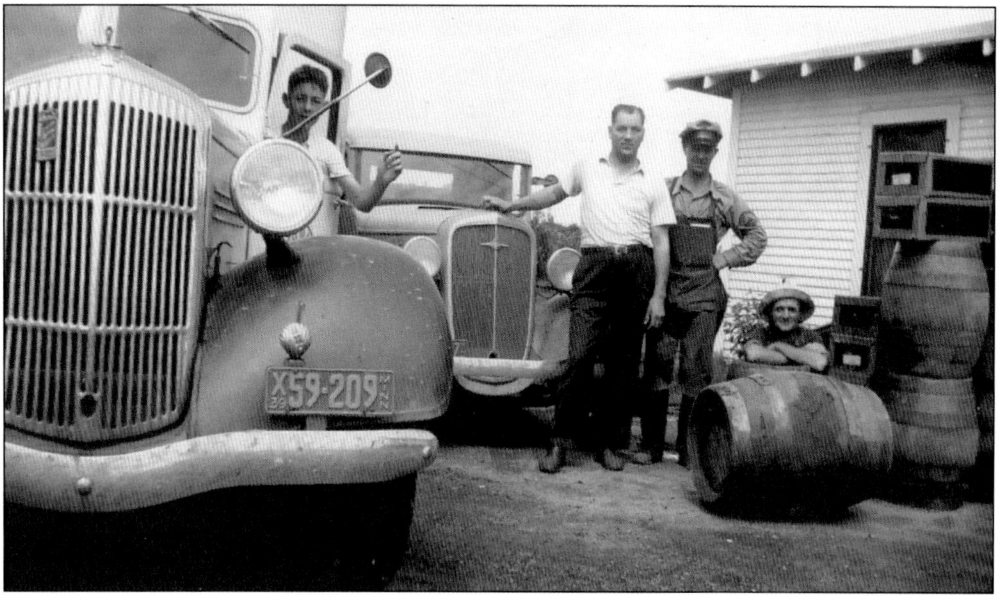

Joe Rouillard, Gordon Rouillard's dad, was the beer man in Rogers. He distributed for Grain Belt. Joe had a milk route before he had the beer route. In 1933, Joe emptied milk cans at the creamery in Minneapolis and, during Prohibition, dried some and filled them with sugar for the bootleggers. Gordon told of when Norb Zahler asked if he was missing any beer. Gordon asked Joe, who said he was questioning the drivers, because 20 12 packs of Hamm's beer were missing. They discovered some boys could raise the overhead door a little without sounding the alarm. They sent the smallest one in to unlock a door and then stashed beer across the tracks for a future date. Gordon left the beer and warned the sheriff's department; they caught the boys. (Courtesy of Gordon Rouillard.)

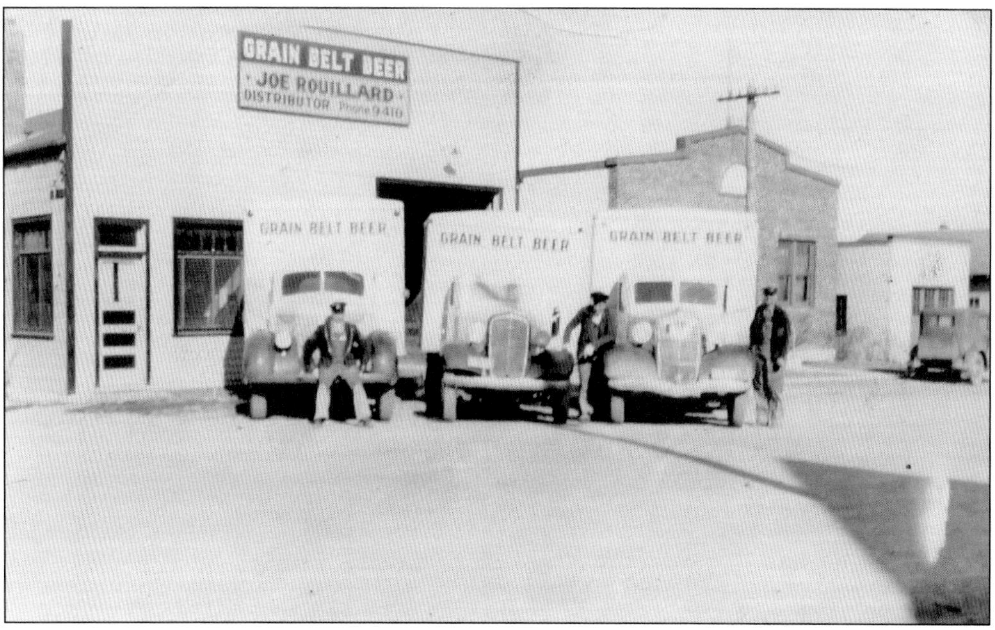

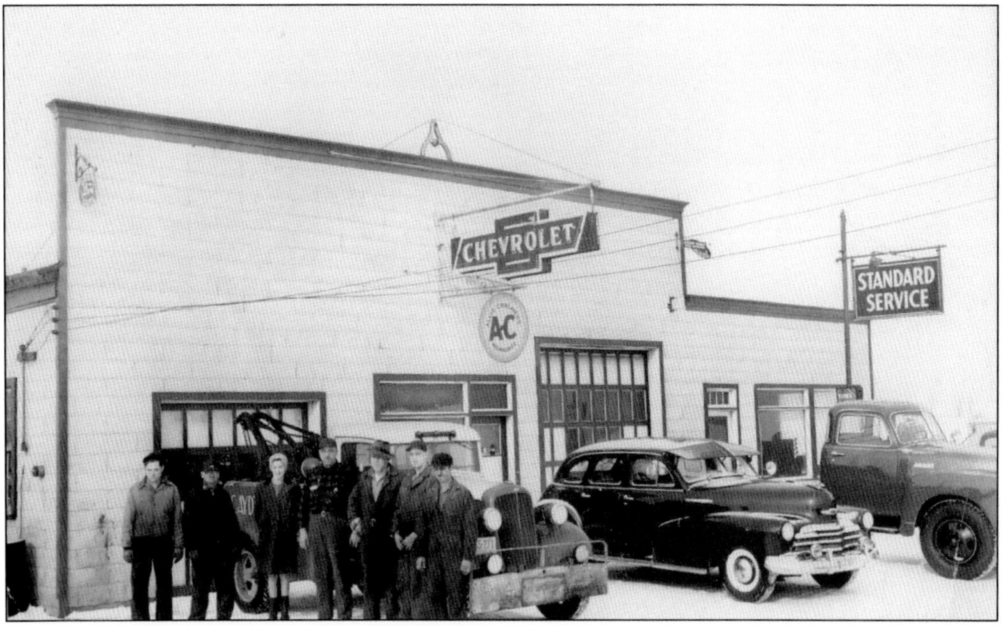

Betty (Aydt) Beck, Victor Aydt, Shirley "Abby" Aydt, and Jack Anselment are among those included in this 1949 picture of Aydt Chevrolet car dealer on Main Street in Rogers. Victor gave patrons gifts, such as metal ashtrays and thermometers. These items are on display at the Antique Mall of Rogers. The original dealership stood where the Asian restaurant is currently located. Aydt Chevrolet was purchased by the Miller family, and in 1955, Miller Chevrolet relocated to its current site on John Milless Drive. Also pictured here are Abby Aydt, Bobby Holland, and Gordon Rouillard in the back of a Chevrolet truck. (Above, courtesy of Leo Scharber; below, courtesy of Gordon Rouillard.)

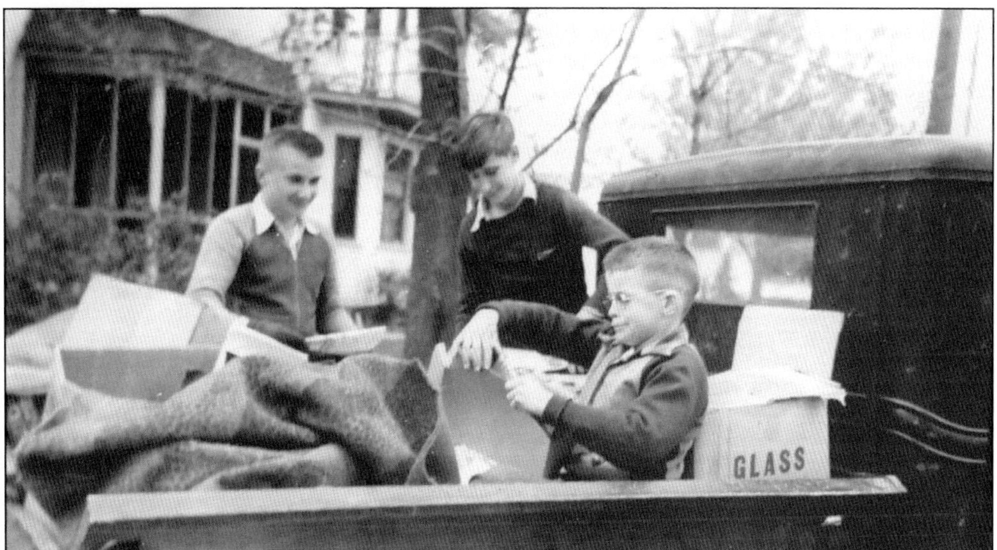

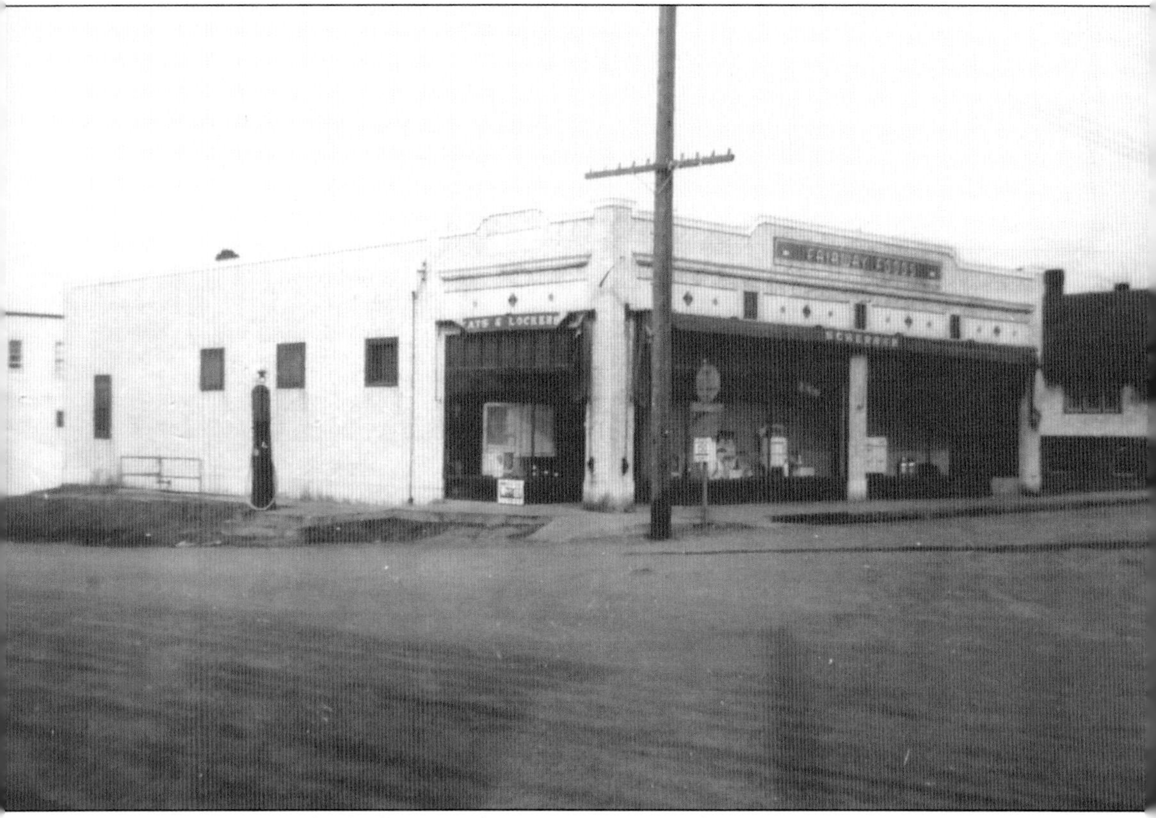

Gerhart Scherber also had a general store on a corner of Main Street. Eventually the business moved a half block down the street to incorporate a meat locker; animals were slaughtered on site. When city sewer was installed, there were problems disposing of the blood; however, they could still store customers' meat. Scherber conducted business using the barter system. When Jack Dahlheimer was young, he remembered his mother, Alice, taking eggs to the grocery store because "they were worth credit" there. Scherber would candle the eggs to see if they were good. When Alice wanted to go shopping with Emma Ahlstrom in the cities, she would go to the grocery store to get money; they liked Thomas' in Minneapolis. Gerhart Scherber also carried Minnesota machinery. Bob Milless worked there for one winter before he went into the service. His brother, Henry Milless, took over the store when Scherber retired in the 1950s. Henry sold the building in the 1980s. Both buildings that had been occupied by Gerhart Scherber still exist on Main Street. (Courtesy of Leo Scharber.)

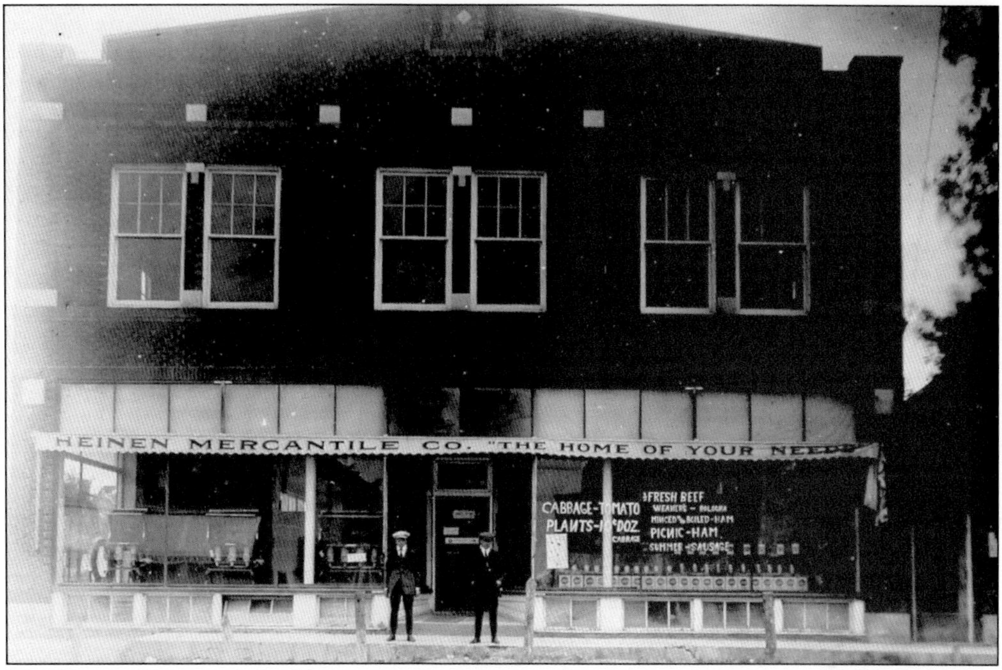

The Heinen Mercantile building as it was constructed in 1920 and then remodeled are pictured here. In 1923, Heinen started selling FarmAll and International Harvester implements. In 1946, the business decision was made to stop selling groceries and move the parts into bins downstairs. In 1955, Ford was seeking a dealer in Rogers. They asked the bank for a recommendation and were told Heinen would be the best dealership. According to Florian Heinen, Ford was not an easy company to deal with, and in the end, Florian had a frank conversation with the representative, a resignation letter was signed, and the inventory was withdrawn. Although it was a difficult six years, many people harbor fond memories surrounding the unveiling of new cars each year. This building is now known as the Antique Mall of Rogers. (Courtesy of Florian Heinen.)

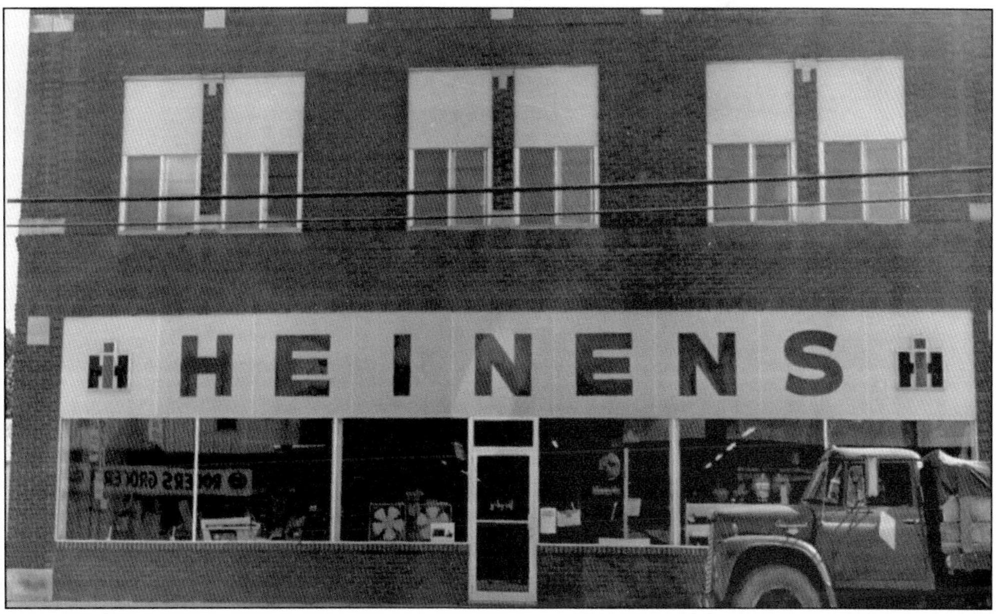

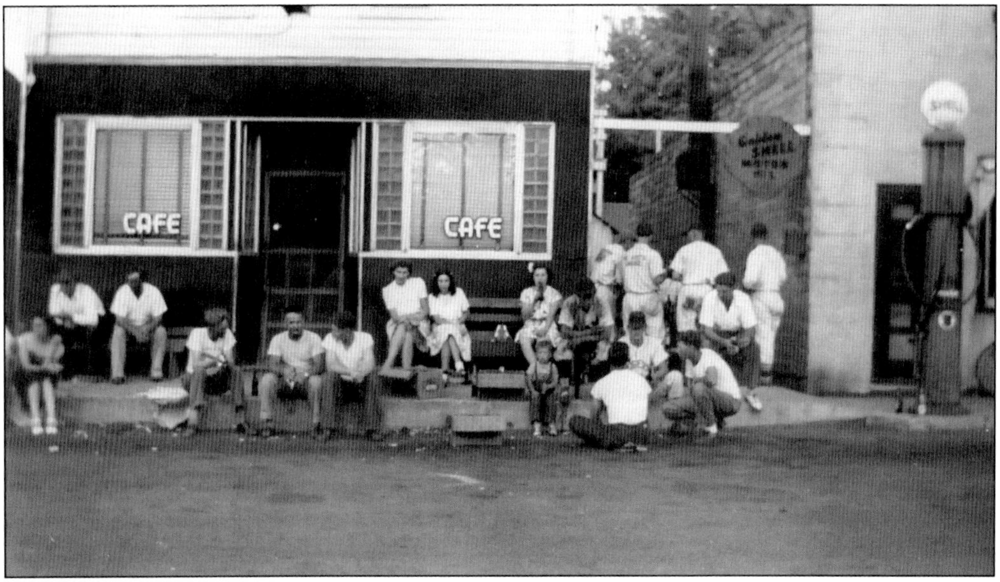

Carol (Berg) Hines's father, Cliff Berg, owned and operated Rogers Café on Main Street. Hines remembered serving customers hamburgers and 3.2 beers. Everyone came to the café after the baseball game on Sunday afternoon. She pointed out that bars serving 3.2 beers could be open on Sunday, but other businesses were not allowed to operate. Henry Rouillard purchased the café from Berg in 1941. Lester Rouillard purchased the café in 1947 and renamed it Rouillard Café; the Rouillard family lived upstairs during this time. The John Beriou Oil Company Co-Operative gas station stood next to the café; these buildings can still be found on Main Street. (Above, courtesy of Lenny and Lila Schlegel; below, courtesy of Leo Scharber.)

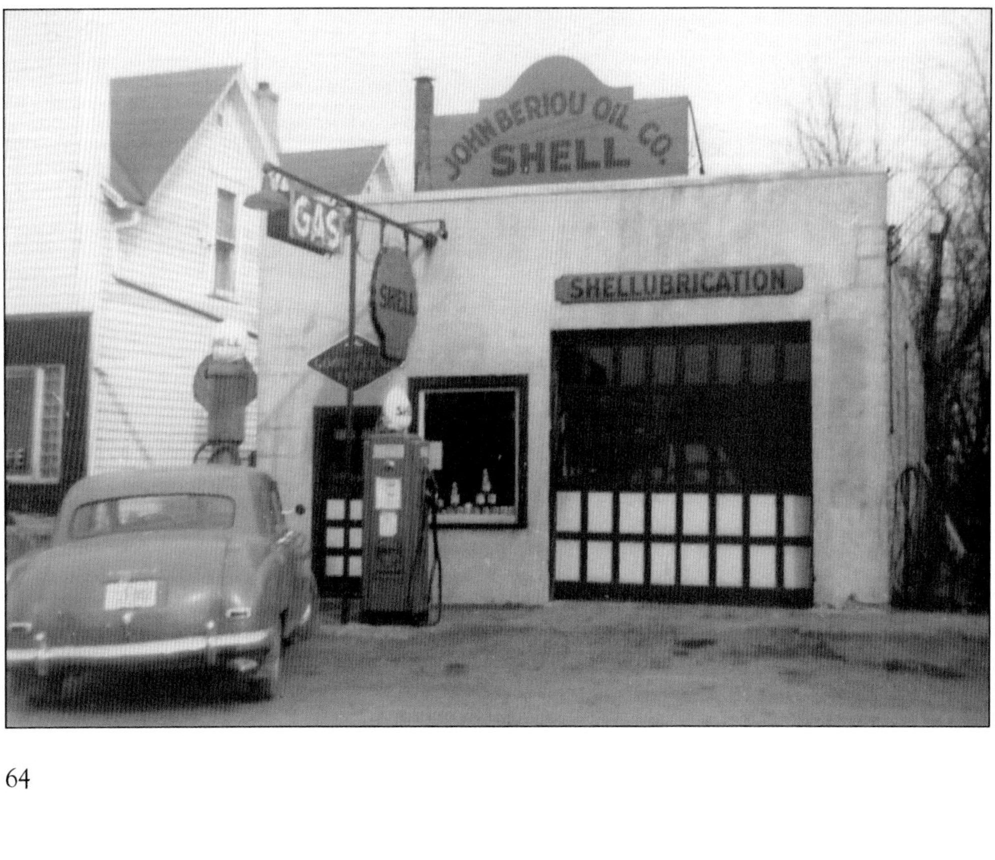

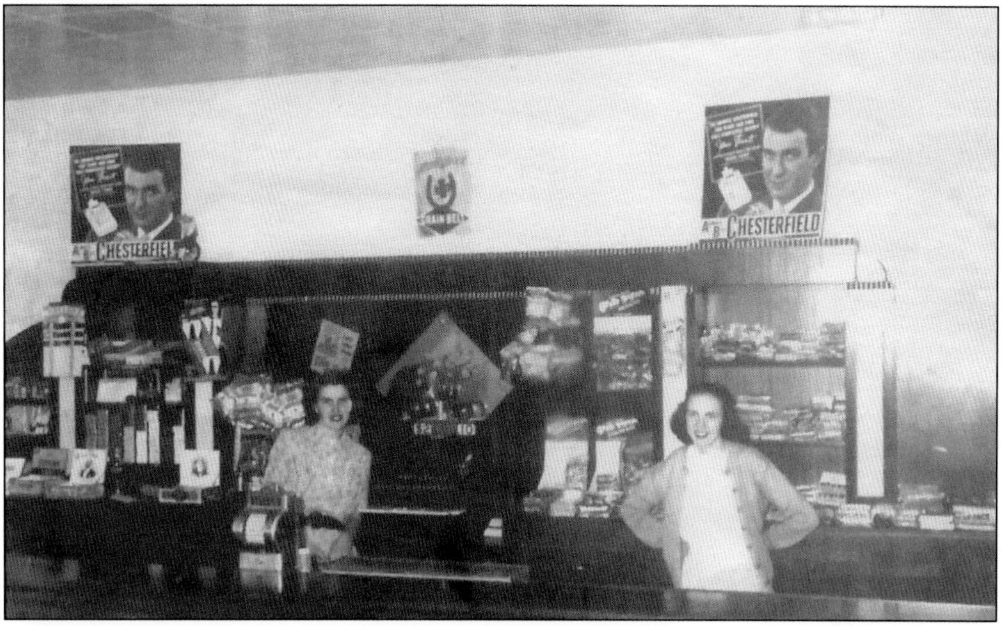

Ferdella (Rouillard) Gmach and her friend Marie (Rueter) LaVasseur ran the Rouillard Café for three years; Ferdella's father, Lester, owned it. They served lunches and 3.2 beers. One of Ferdella's strongest memories was when the military men left for World War II. Ferdella and Marie hung their pictures on the walls of the café so the community could honor them. Ferdella also remembers the café brawls. When men started a fight in the café, Ferdella opened the door and Marie pushed them out; they would fall down and continue fighting. In about 1959, Rogers converted to a municipal liquor store. The café was purchased by the city and became the Municipal Liquor Store. According to several people, creating a municipal liquor store almost tore the town apart. (Above, courtesy of Jerome and Ferdella Gmach; below, courtesy of Norb Zahler.)

6 WEEK WAIT EXPECTED BEFORE FATE OF ROGERS STORE IS KNOWN

A wait of from four to six weeks is expected before the fate of the Rogers municipal liquor store issue is decided by Judge Harold Rogers of the Hennepin county district court.

At the hearing Tuesday, April 1, the judge told all attorneys involved in the matter to submit their argumens in written briefs.

George Hedlund, attorney for the village of Rogers, contended that the lawsuit should be dismissed because the evidence presented by the attorney for two former private bar owners—Gene Fissette and Leo Arenz—did not constitute a lawsuit.

The bond companies, a state organization of all managers of municipal liquor stores and the attorney general's office agreed with Hedlund.

Arenz and Fissette claimed in their lawsuit that municipal liquor stores were unconstitutional.

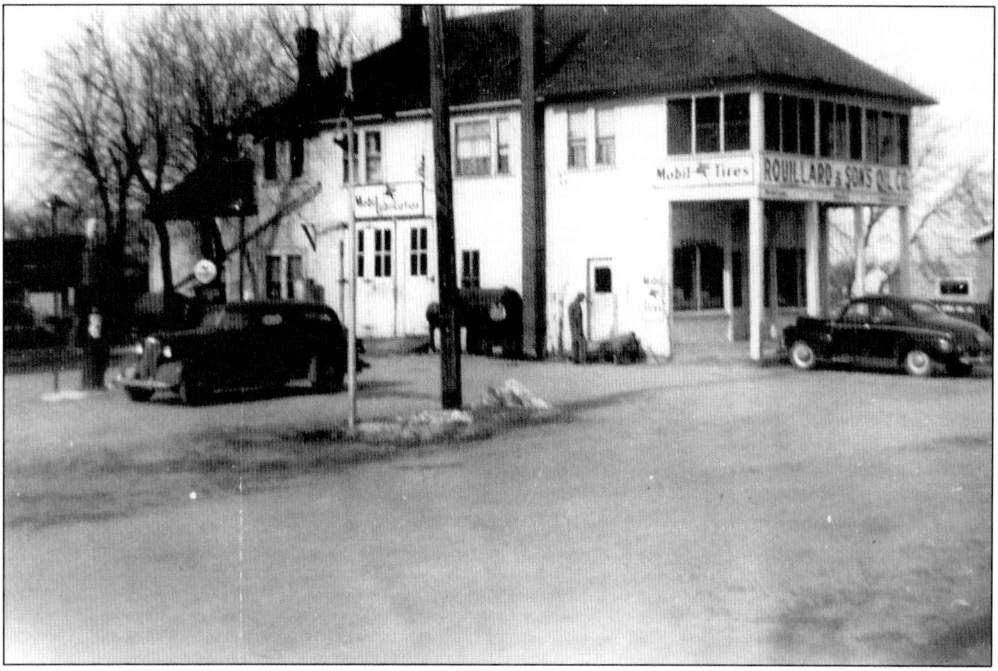

When he returned from World War II, Melvin Rouillard married Ethel Malone, a nurse from Kansas City. After having their first child, Melvin decided to invest in a Mobil gas station in Rogers. It was located on the southwest side of Main Street by the railroad tracks. Melvin explained that a group hand-dug the holes for the gas tanks. Melvin's family lived upstairs and worked downstairs; that was common during that era. After building the business, Melvin sold the gas station and moved on to his next venture. Melvin shared he was always working, and at the age of 88, he still makes the crowds smile by selling homemade popcorn and 1919 root beer with his children and grandchildren from his Popcorn Papa popcorn wagon at community events. (Above courtesy of Leo Scharber; below, courtesy of Lenny and Lila Schlegel.)

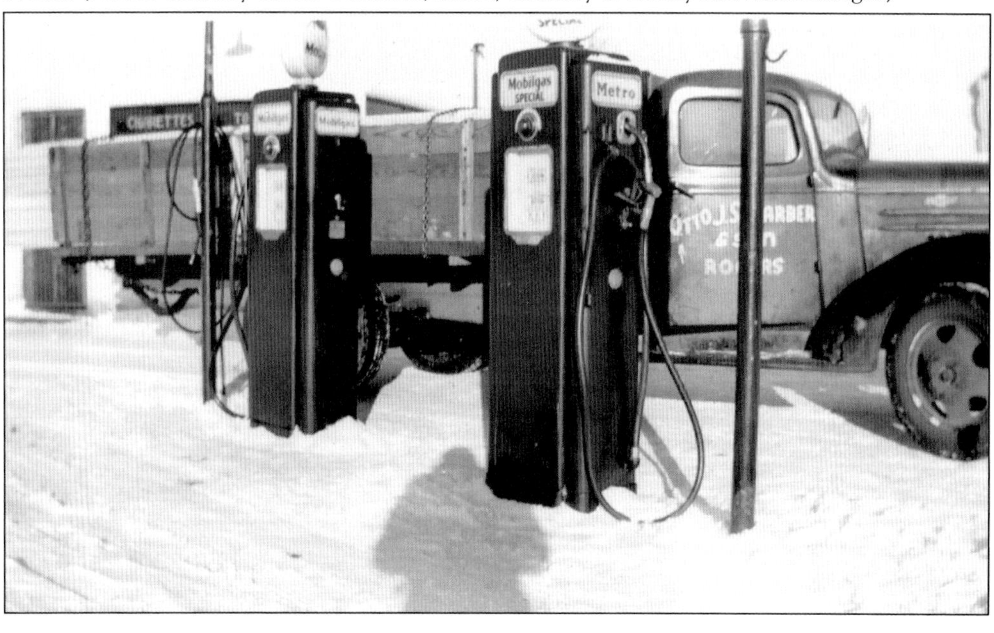

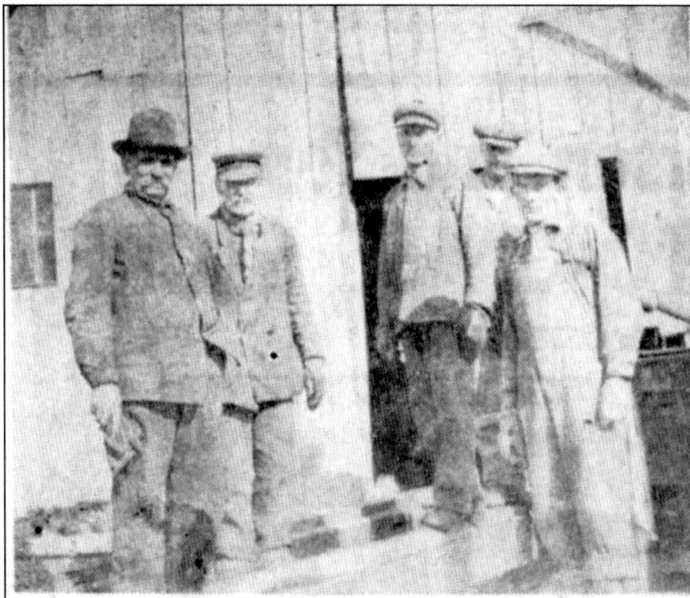

PRIOR TO 1920, farmers from Rogers and surrounding areas relied upon the Rogers sawmill (below) to get their logs sawed. Farmers traveled from such distant points as Dayton, Maple Grove and Champlin to get the work done. The five men (above) worked at the mill for years. Included are Ferdinand Guers, George Eisen, John M. Nelles, Ed Nelles and Joseph H. Nelles. Guers and Eisten were the owners. There was a feed mill next to the saw mill, which was a busy place on Saturday—feed grinding day. Farmers fed grain to their horses instead of to their cows then. There are several beautiful homes located now where the saw mill used to be, including the home of Vic Aydt.

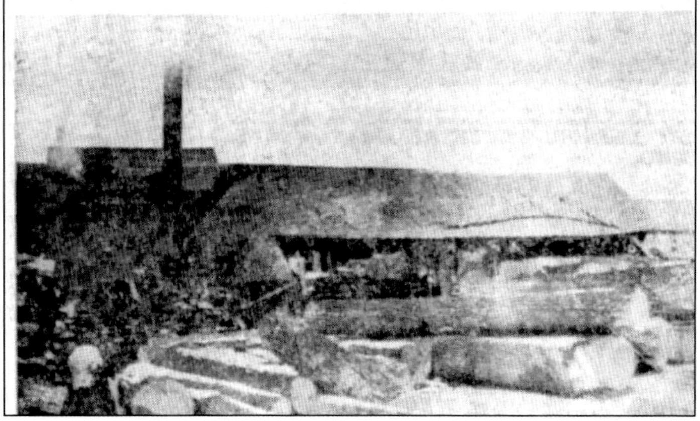

Being part of the "Big Woods" meant Hassan Township was heavily wooded with maple, oak, ash, basswood, and other deciduous trees. It took several years and many backbreaking hours of labor to clear an area of land for farming. "Probably they had the 'valor of ignorance' and if they had realized what was involved would not have attempted it. However, into the forest they plunged," was a passage sited in the *Ghostley Chronicles*. Wood was used to sustain family living early on; however, eventually sawmills were built in neighboring communities and then locally. Settlers came from miles around during the winter to have their logs processed by local sawmill workers. Farmers were cutting trees to clear their land, and everybody had loads of logs that were hauled to Rogers. George Eiser owned the sawmill for about 13 years. Homes have been constructed in its place. (Courtesy of Crow River News.)

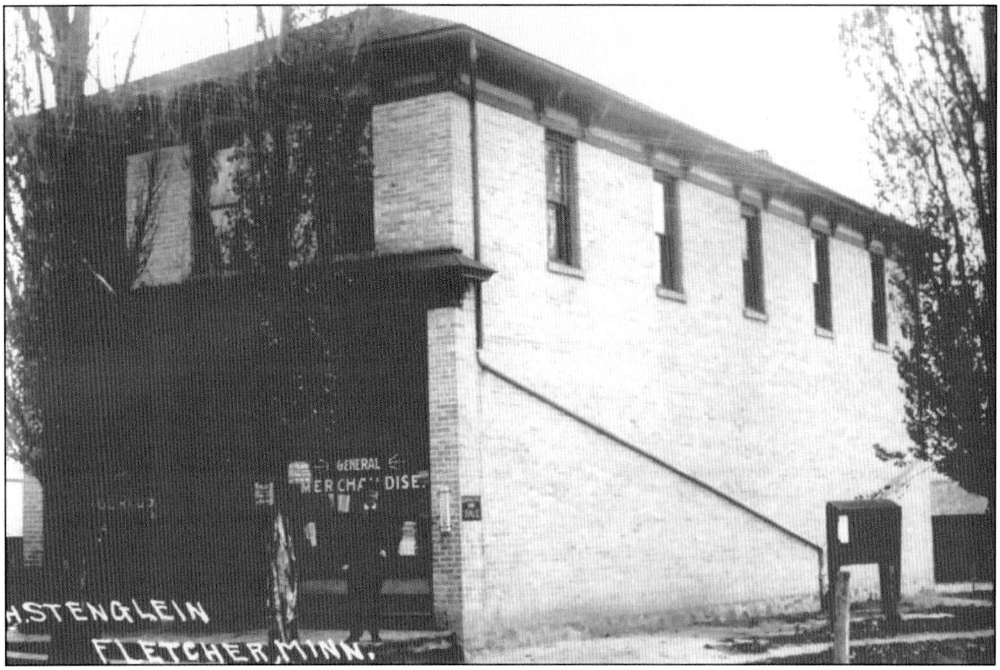

Historic research of the area reveals that Frank Stenglein and Magnuys Nelles opened the two-story brick veneer Fletcher store at the southwestern corner of Territorial Road and Corcoran-Dayton Road in 1900. This building served as an all-purpose store for the area, carrying staples, dry goods, hardware, and other items. The Stenglein house, which was located in the back of the store, served as a tavern in the early part of the century, and by the 1930s, a gas pump was added outside. Frank and Lenore Stenglein also built a residence just south of the store to live in during the hot summer months. (Courtesy of Andrew Stueve.)

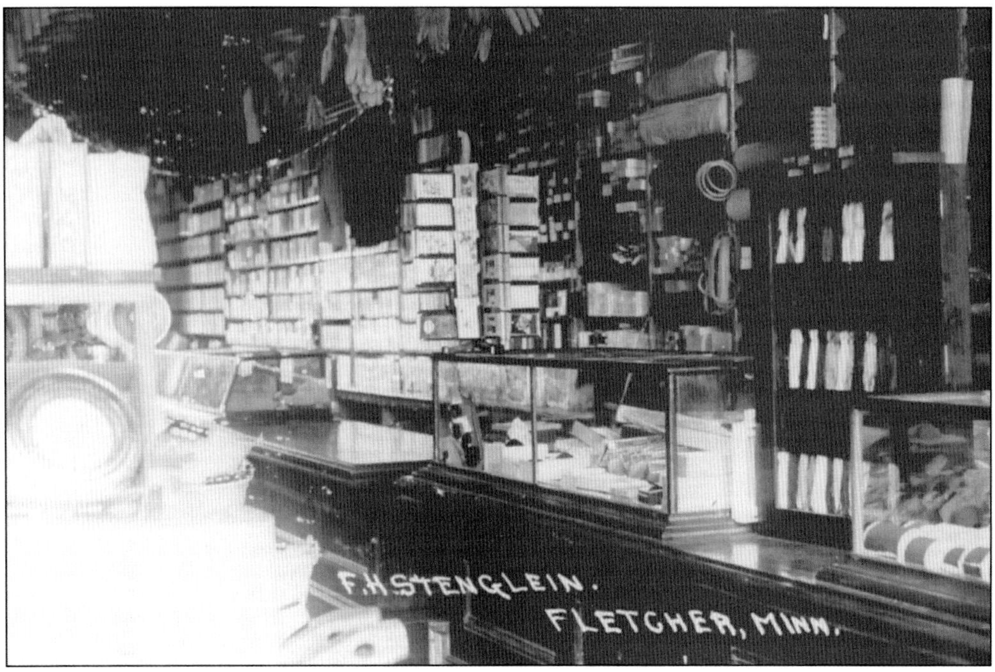

Six

A Few Good Men

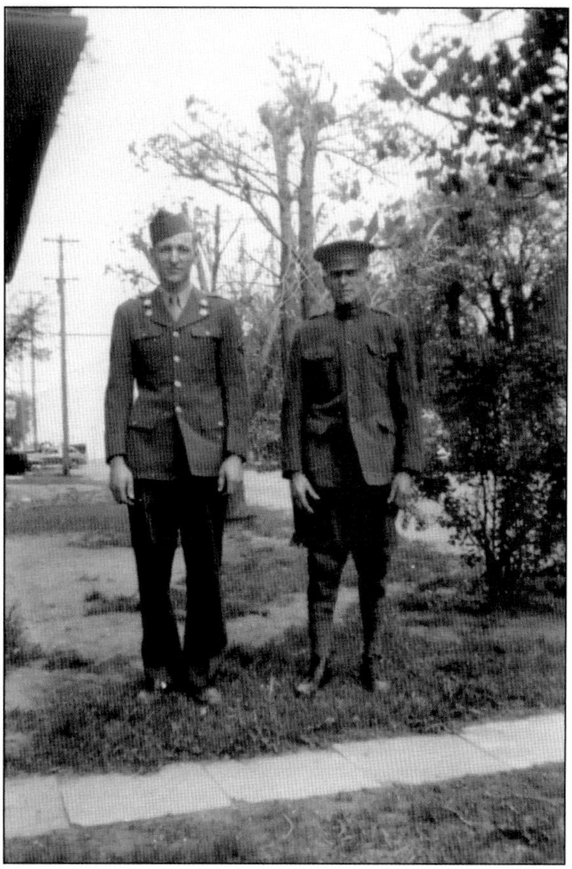

Several residents of Rogers, Hassan Township, and Fletcher served the nation proudly. Lenny Schlegel was in World War II and his father, Arthur Schlegel, served in World War I. They are pictured here in their uniforms. Lenny was stationed in Missouri, Louisiana, and New Jersey; he did not travel overseas during the war. Lenny explained that he was a cook, and they only could heat the food using steam from hot water. He often made pudding for breakfast. However, one morning he added too much water, and there was no corn starch to stiffen the pudding, so he mixed in a case of Kix cereal to thicken the mixture. The boys really liked it; they wanted to know when they were going to have it again. Eugene Ahlstrom also served the country. He was a pilot in the U.S. Marine Corps; his unit was presented with a citation by Pres. John F. Kennedy. (Courtesy of Lenny and Lila Schlegel.)

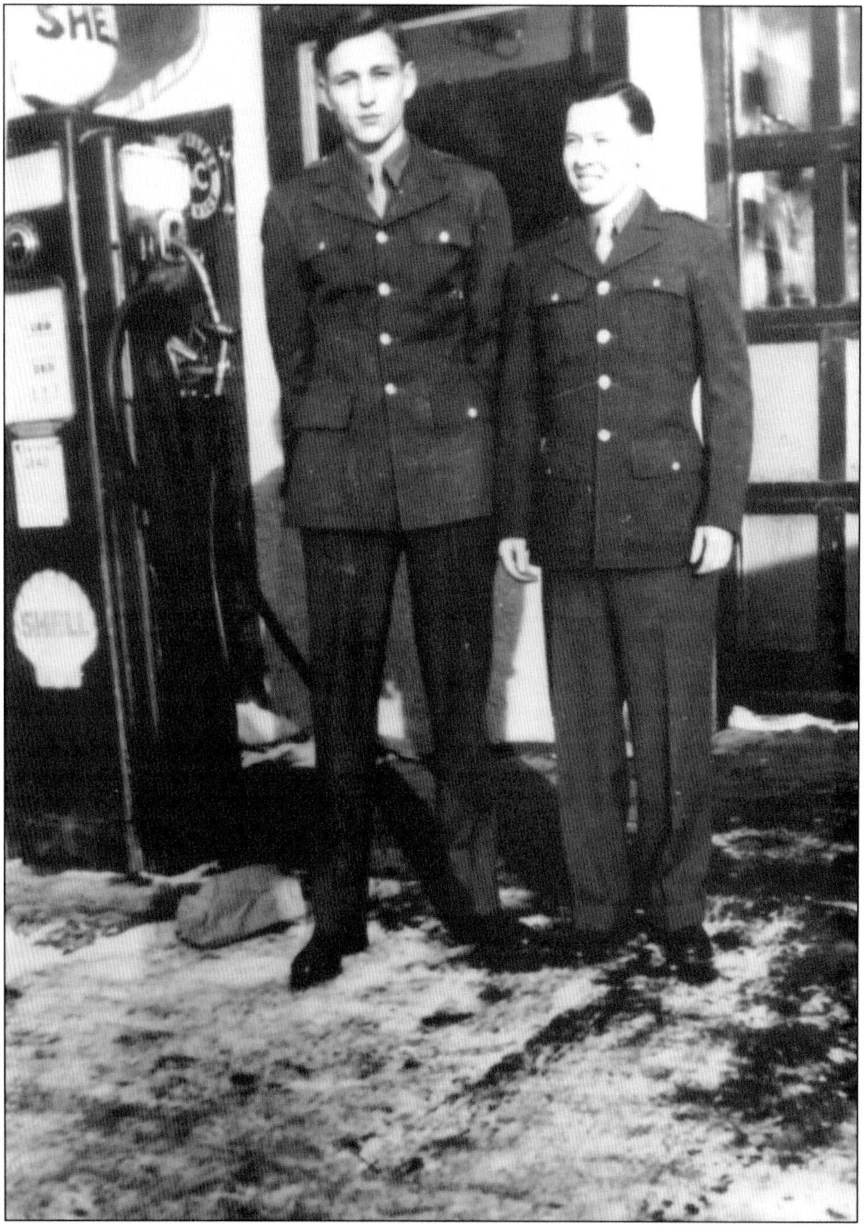

Lenny Schlegel and Leo Scharber are ready to leave for World War II in this picture. It was taken in front of a gas station on Main Street. Scharber remembered driving a lot of miles, in Schlegel's first car, going back and forth to Fort Snelling before they left. Jim Rogers's uncle Alvin Rogers sent a letter on Saturday before the bombing of Pearl Harbor, telling about the beautiful place he was stationed, the island of Hawaii. On Sunday morning, the Japanese bombed the island. They came in from the north and bombed the ships in the harbor. Years later, Alvin submitted a story to *Reader's Digest* about how he shot down the first plane of World War II. He was between two hangers and jumped in the gunner's turret of a C-plane. His major said, "You got that one!" and Alvin shot it down. *Reader's Digest* did not accept his story stating, "The first plane was shot down by a Japanese Major." Rogers had several uncles serve in World War II. (Courtesy of Lenny and Lila Schlegel.)

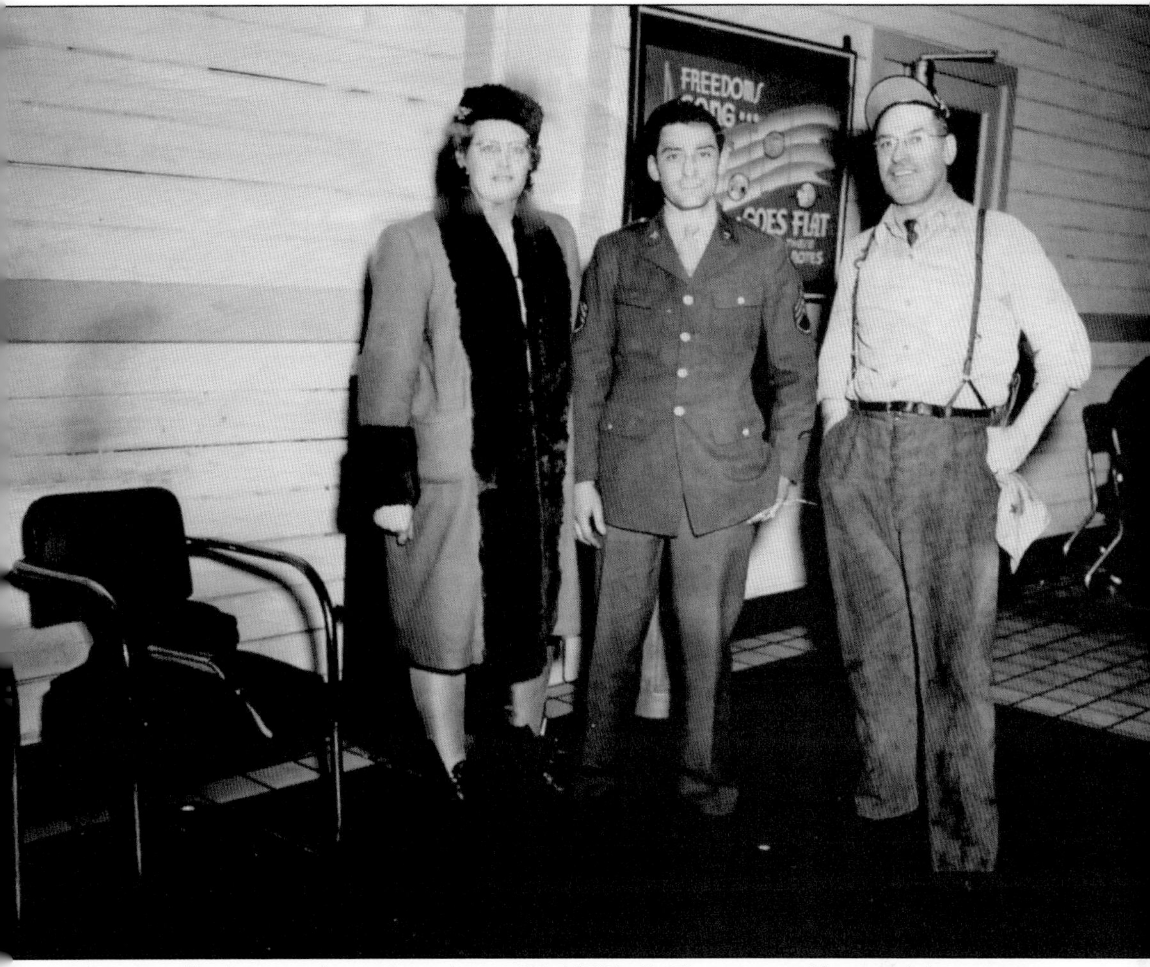

Melvin Rouillard was in the air force during World War II. He is pictured here with his parents, Ethel and Henry Rouillard, while home on furlough. According to Melvin, three men from Rogers, Hassan Township, and Fletcher were in the air force during the war. Melvin was trained as a B29 bomber. Jerome Gmach launched B17 and B29 bombs during the war. Jerome served for 38 months, until 1946. He moved around quite a bit and was on the ship headed overseas when the war ended. Both men thoughtfully remembered, "There were good times and bad times. It was rough, but overall we had good times." Ferdella (Rouillard) Gmach remembered "the boys coming and going." Ferdella distinctly remembers hearing Donald Dahlheimer say, "If you hear I am missing, I am gone." Pretty soon word was delivered that he was missing and everyone knew he was gone; Dahlheimer had been on a submarine. (Courtesy of Melvin Rouillard.)

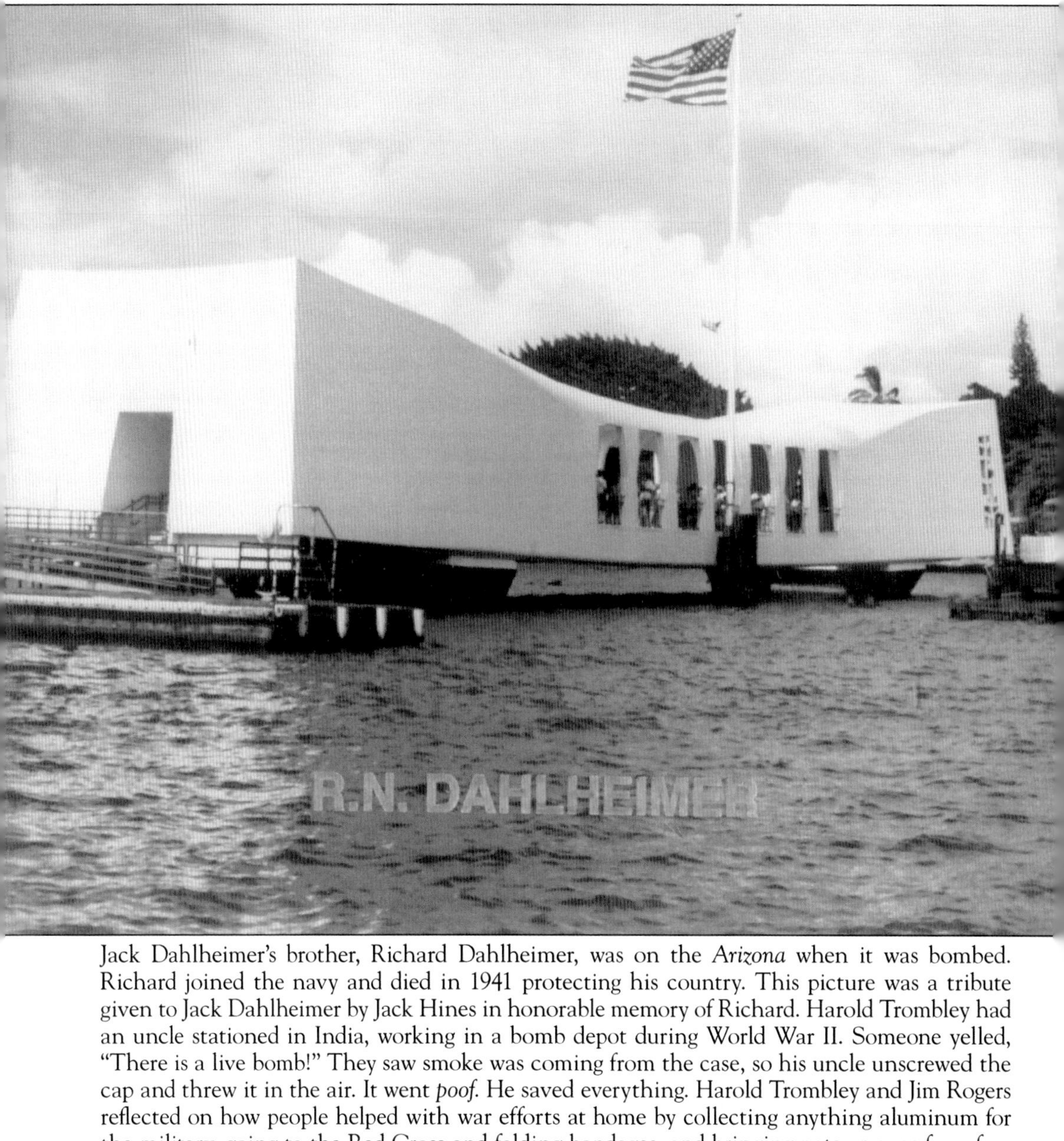

Jack Dahlheimer's brother, Richard Dahlheimer, was on the *Arizona* when it was bombed. Richard joined the navy and died in 1941 protecting his country. This picture was a tribute given to Jack Dahlheimer by Jack Hines in honorable memory of Richard. Harold Trombley had an uncle stationed in India, working in a bomb depot during World War II. Someone yelled, "There is a live bomb!" They saw smoke was coming from the case, so his uncle unscrewed the cap and threw it in the air. It went *poof*. He saved everything. Harold Trombley and Jim Rogers reflected on how people helped with war efforts at home by collecting anything aluminum for the military, going to the Red Cross and folding bandages, and bringing pots or pans for a free movie on Saturday. Harold remembers rations, such as limited gasoline, tire and butter purchases were minimized, sugar required a coupon, and other restrictions. Harold knew the war was over when a high school girl gave him a big hug and said, "The war is over Harold!" He remembers feeling relieved. (Courtesy of Jack and Peggy Dahlheimer.)

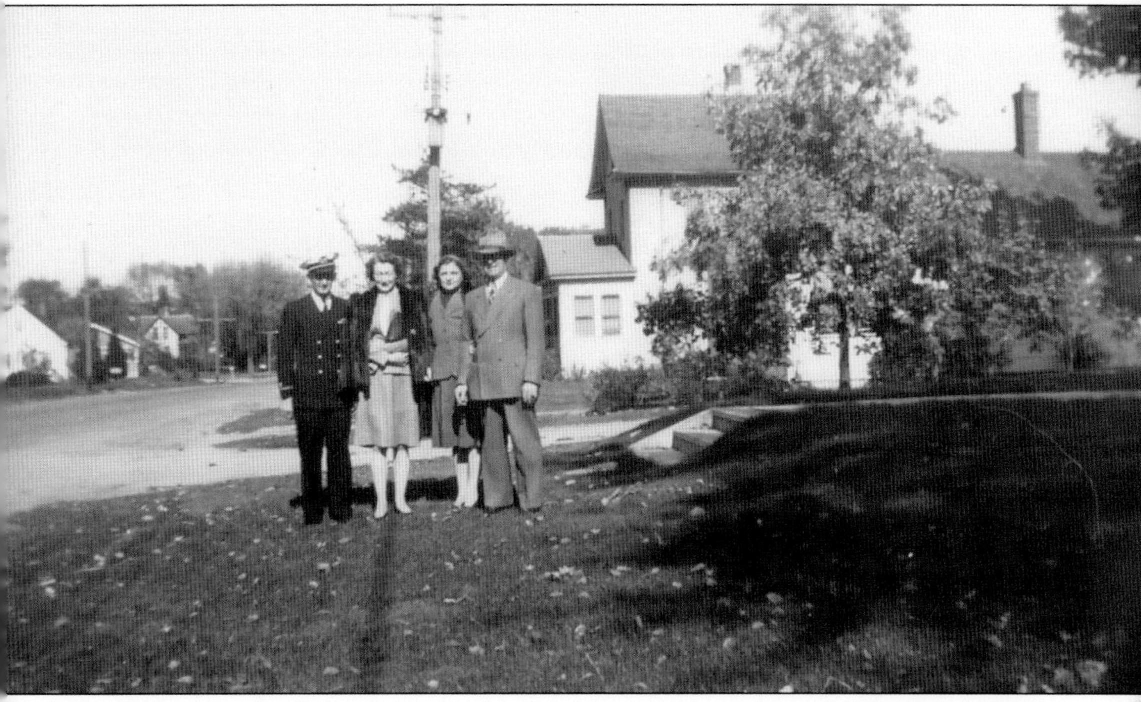

Here Gordon Rouillard poses with his family as he prepares to leave for the Korean War. Rouillard shared that Howard Dahlheimer told him they could join the reserves and not go to war. They met with a recruiter who said it was the "greatest deal in the world." Dahlheimer and Rouillard enlisted on December 12, 1950, and their unit got called to active duty on December 21, 1950; they were on a train to San Diego. Rouillard was assigned to a seagoing marine and played baseball for the U.S. Marine Corp. He remembered a game in Seattle. They switched trains in Oakland, California. After asking the porter what time "this" train leaves, they went to a bar, watchful to return on time. When they returned, they learned "this" train was not headed to Seattle; their train had left three hours earlier. They were AWOL and thrown in the brig. Stanley Scharber went to see Rouillard's game and heard about his situation. The admiral he was flying around made some calls, and Rouillard was released. (Courtesy of Gordon Rouillard.)

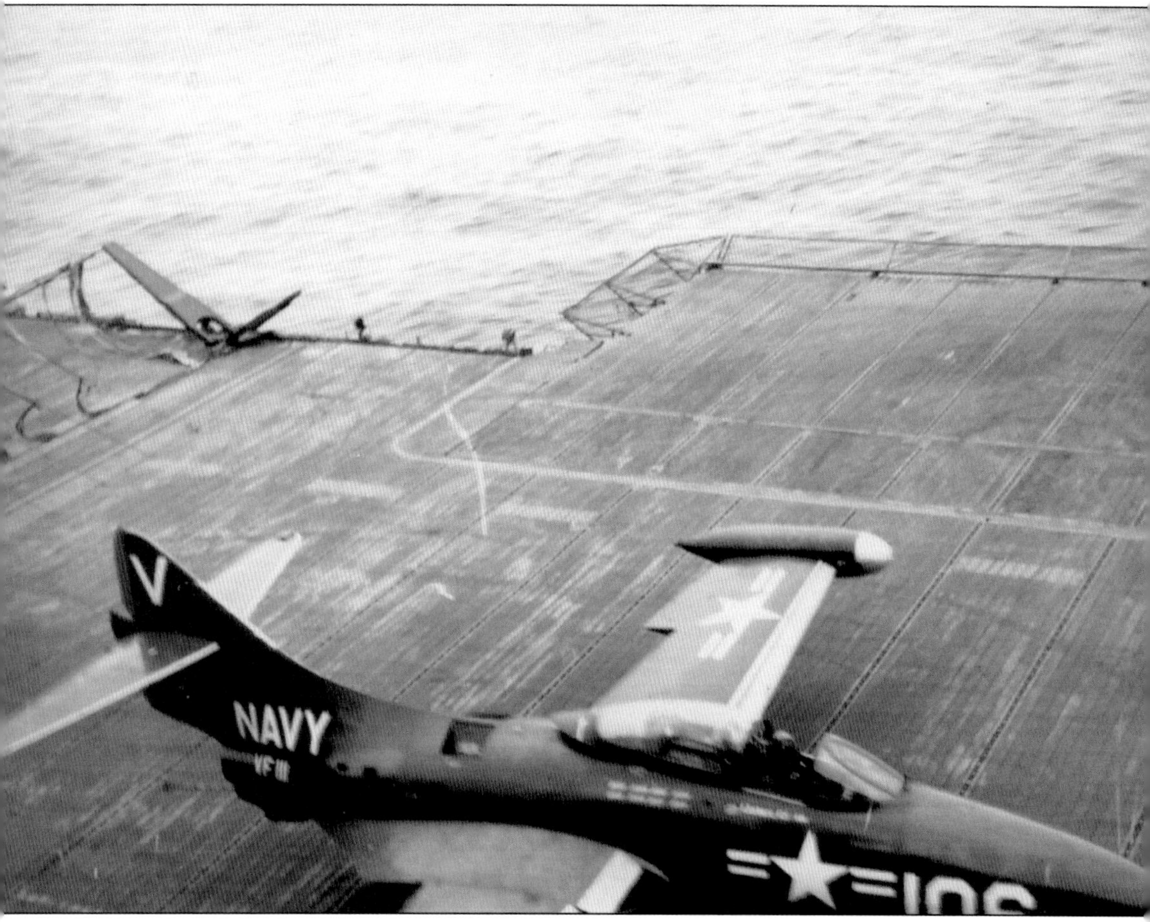

Gordon Rouillard was stationed in Hawaii, while Howard Dahlheimer served at Camp Pendleton, California. According to Rouillard, that was "where Howard played with big guns and played poker." Dahlheimer never left California, but Rouillard went to Korea. Rouillard claims he won the war for the United States because he "scared the death out of them." In 1950, another local, Florian Heinen, was assigned to the survey section of the army in Korea. His unit traveled in two Jeeps to survey an area. Heinen remembered a certain survey. It was close to dark, and the team wondered if they should go back to camp. They decided to return, which was good because the enemy overran the area that night. Two days later, navy planes bombed the area; three of the five guns were lost in the bombing. While Heinen was at war, he got a "Dear John" letter, which was a common occurrence for military men. (Courtesy of Gordon Rouillard.)

Seven

THE GOOD OLE DAYS

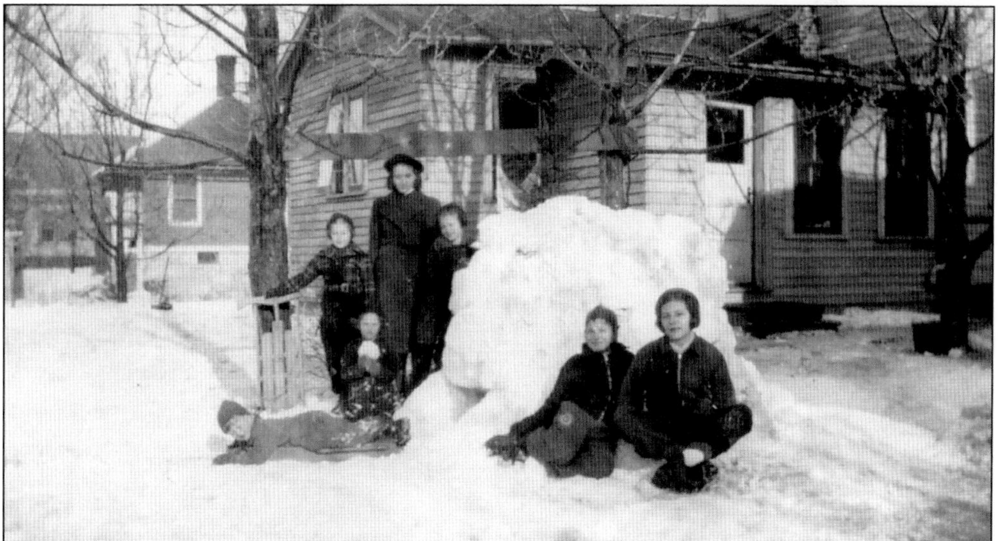

The Schlegel kids loved to play on their farm; they would start at the top of the hill and slide all the way down. The hill was the road, but there were so few cars there was never a concern about getting hit. Life was a slower, simpler time. In the words of Melvin Rouillard, it was "the good ole days." Lenny and Lila Schlegel's fondest memory was that they knew all their neighbors. When they first moved into their home, everyone had children, then everyone grew older, and now young people are moving in again. Lenny kept the vacant lot across the street mowed, and all the children played ball; no one had to wonder where their children were because they knew. Chuck and Jeff Christian shared, when a neighbor called and needed help you went. If someone asked for help, they needed it, and neighbors were there to help each other. (Courtesy of Lenny and Lila Schlegel.)

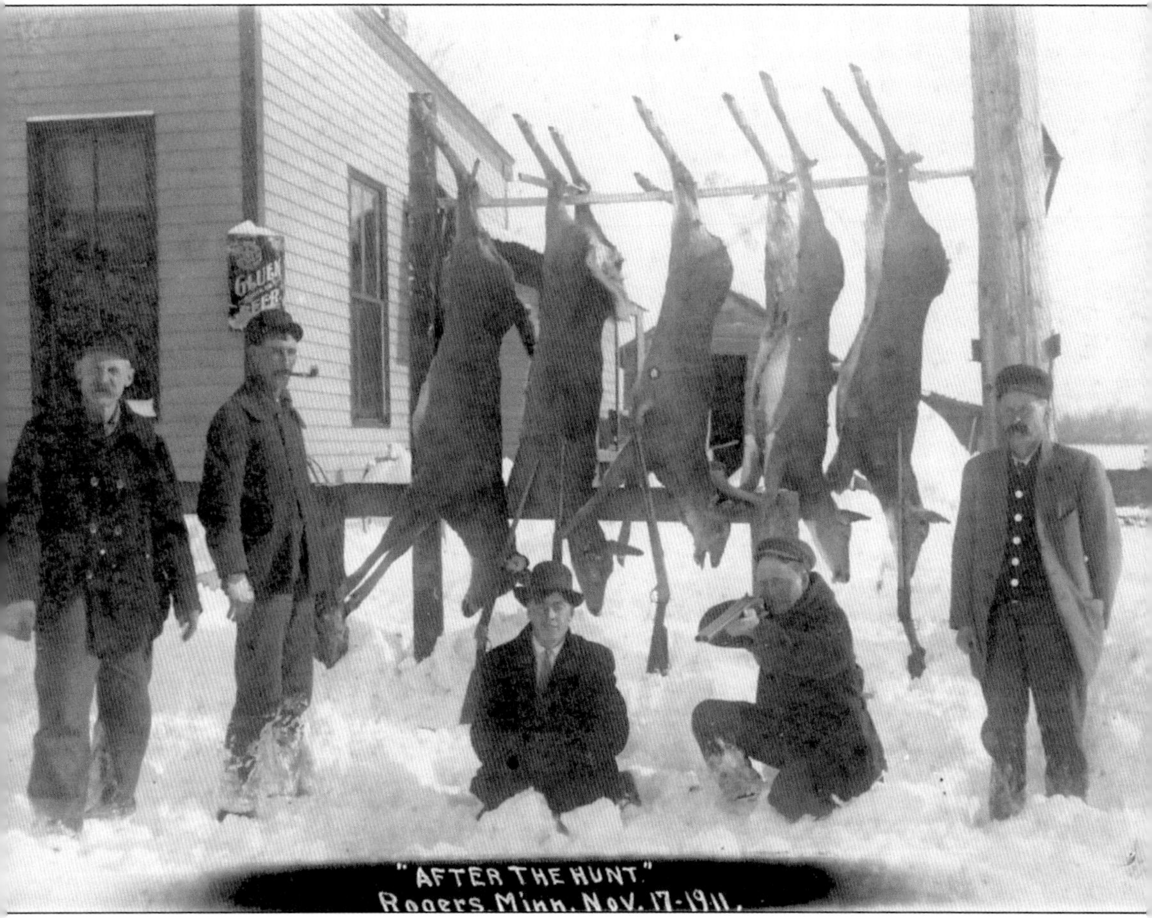

This picture, titled "After the Hunt," was taken on November 17, 1911. The mighty hunters posing from left to right are Jess Babler, John Hines, John Scharber, Rudolph Babler, and Chris Babler. Hunting was not only a sport, it was also a source of food for the family. During a conversation with Grady Kinghorn, he shared that Andrew Kinghorn came to Hassan Township from Scotland in 1858. He cleared his land with a horse, ax, and shovel. Andrew worked hard and was rewarded with a healthy farm. In the 1920s, when times were tough, William Kinghorn, Grady's great-grandfather, would tie a cow to a post so a farmer in need could take the cow home for his family. This neighborly support attracted people to the community. A fond memory for Jack Hines was when people would take a hot dish or pan of bars to a family with an illness or death. Those forms of kindness are still shown throughout the community. (Courtesy of Jack and Carol Hines.)

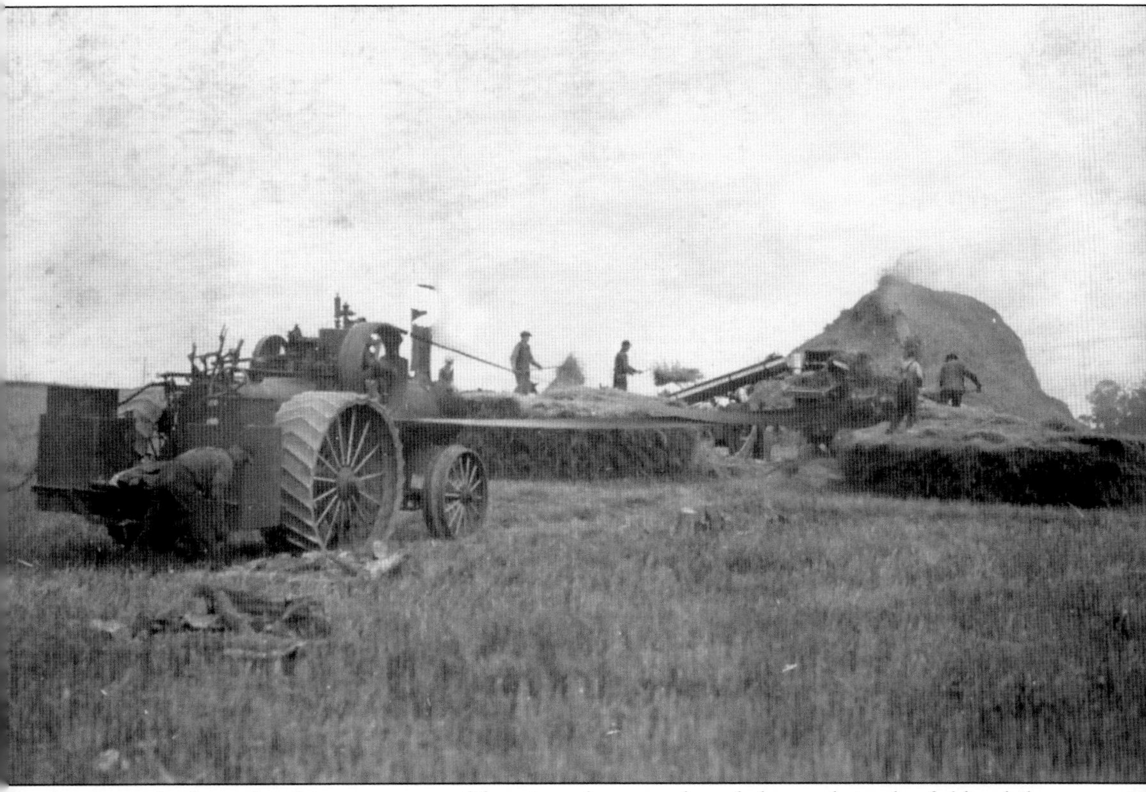

In the early days, threshing was part of farming; the men shared the work in the fields while the women worked side-by-side in the kitchen preparing gigantic feasts. This picture was taken in 1924 during threshing on the Louis Zachman farm. After time, processes improved, and threshing machines became outdated. In 1971, Adrian Milless had to move his old threshing machine because the freeway would be constructed through the Milless farm. His friends Walter Dehn and John Altenweg helped pull the 44-year-old machine from its 22-year-old resting place to restore it. Word got around, and in the fall of 1971, about 80 people attended the first threshing machine demonstration. Dehn, Altenweg, and Milless promptly began planning the 1972 threshing show, which was held where Burger King is now. Later shows were held on land behind the St. Martin's Cemetery. Over time, the show attracted thousands to the community. The Rogers Threshing Show was discontinued when the annual one-day FunFest was extended to a three-day event and renamed Rockin' Rogers Days. (Courtesy of Mary Lou and Ray Dahlheimer.)

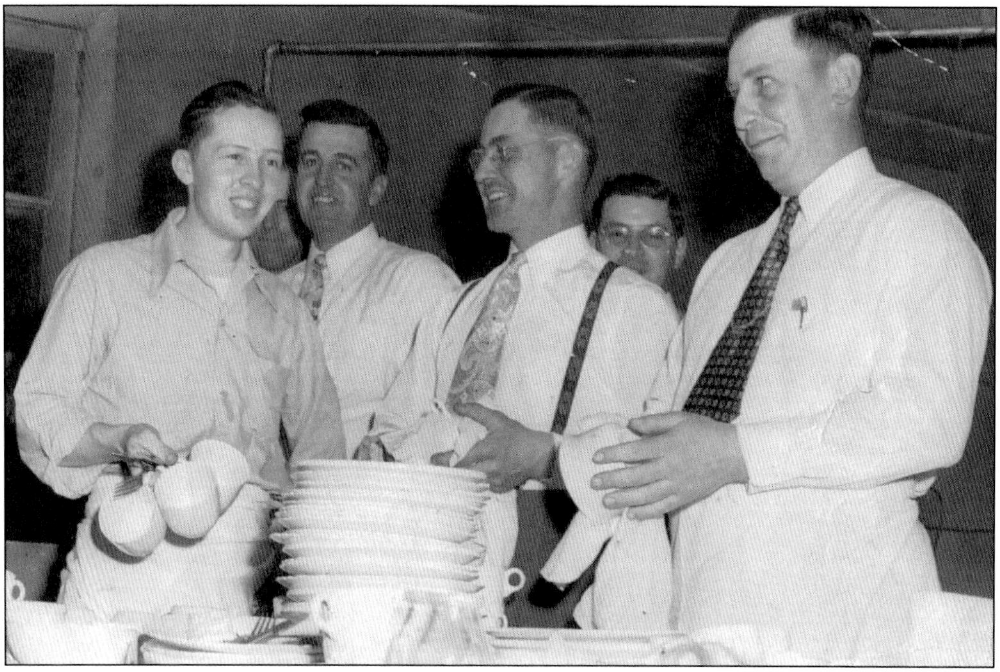

St. Martin's Church — Rogers, Minn. 55374
SUMMER FESTIVAL
CHICKEN DINNER 11 A.M. TO 4 P.M.
SUNDAY, JULY 28, 1968

ADULTS $1.50 CHILDREN UNDER 12, 75c
TICKET 25c—5 FOR $1.00 — WINNER NEED NOT BE PRESENT

C A S H — TOTAL PRIZES APPROXIMATELY $800.00

$100.00—Heinen Mercantile, Rogers
50.00—Rouillard Beverage, Rogers, Minn.
50.00—Dayton Trailer Park, Ben Dehn
25.00—Rogers State Insurance Agency
James W. Peterson, Oliver L. Kapsner, Agents
25.00—State Bank of Rogers
25.00—Al Kemmetmueller - Water Care Service, Osseo
25.00—Rogers Lumber Company
25.00—Richard F. Zahler Building Contractor, Rogers
20.00—Doug Scharber Implement, Rogers
20.00—Scharber Oil Company, Rogers
20.00—Rogers Motor & Implement
20.00—Pat's Auto Sales, 442 N. Main, Anoka
20.00—Zackman Plumbing & Heating Co., Rogers
15.00—Rogers Grain and Feed
10.00—Erwin Greeninger—Portable Mill
10.00—Medina Ballroom, Hamel
10.00—Rogers Ballroom
10.00—Al Hagel Auto Salvage, Rogers
10.00—Menzel's Realty & Insurance, Osseo
10.00—Berning's Mill
10.00—Lowell Zachman, Excavating, St. Michael
10.00—St. Michael Veterinary Clinic
10.00—Henry Van Lith—Milk Hauler
10.00—Burrill Contour Tops, Rogers
10.00—Griffith Oil Co., Rogers
10.00—Griffith Oil Co., Rogers
10.00—Weber Quality Sod, J. A. Weber, Prop.
10.00—Threatt's Barbecue & Cafe, Rogers
10.00—Ahlstrom Hardware, Rogers
10.00—Merle Dahlheimer, Glueks & Schlitz Beer at St. Michael
10.00—Lefty Schaber, Agent, State Farm Insurance
10.00—Lindenfelser Garbage Service, Albertville
10.00—Beck's Floor Covering Service
10.00—Donahue Cabinet, Elk River
5.00—Elmer (Hank) Schaber—Trucking, Hamel
5.00—Campbell Commission, South St. Paul
5.00—Bennett Commission, South St. Paul
5.00—McAlpine Bros. Well Co., Rogers
5.00—Crow River Farm Equip., Ralph Lahn & Sons
5.00—Crow River News
5.00—Fricke's Sod, Fletcher
5.00—Aime Morin Barber Shop, Rogers
5.00—Fletcher Store, Vick Dick, Prop.
5.00—Osseo Paint and Wallpaper Supply
5.00—Heinen's Champion Auto Store, Osseo
5.00—Millside Tavern, St. Michael
5.00—Chuck's Bar, Dayton
5.00—Al Langers Bar, Dayton
$10 in Trade—Milless Grocery & Lockers, Rogers
$10 In Trade—Rogers Grocery
$10 In Trade—Upton's Superette, Dayton Trailer Park
$5.00 in Trade—Allan Nott Rawleigh Products
Redwood Picnic Table—Independent Lumber Co., St. Michael.
2 Cases of Beer—Rogers Liquor Store
5 Pizza— Becher's 101 Club
15 Gallon Gas—Dayton Park North Star Station
2½ Gallons of Ice Cream—Anoka Dairy

$25 CASH TO PERSON SELLING MOST BOOKS
Given by Evans-Nordby Funeral Home—Osseo
DRAWING TO BE HELD AT 9:30 P.M

Pictured from left to right, Leo Scharber, Walter Dehn, Chuck Christian, Doug Scharber (behind Chuck), and Art Zachman are shown here washing dishes after a Men's Club breakfast. There were many church events that brought parishioners together. Another was the Annual Summer Festival and Chicken Dinner. Peggy Dahlheimer shared that every family was asked to bring three fried chickens and three pies to the festival, but in the later years, the chicken had to be made at the church because some people did not know how to cook chicken properly. Jack Dahlheimer remembered his mom as one of the pillars of the church; Alice Dahlheimer helped run the festival and was the "chief cook." Jack still envisions her wearing her pretty lace dress. This example of prize offerings is from 1968. (Above, courtesy of Norb Zahler; below, courtesy of Rogers Library.)

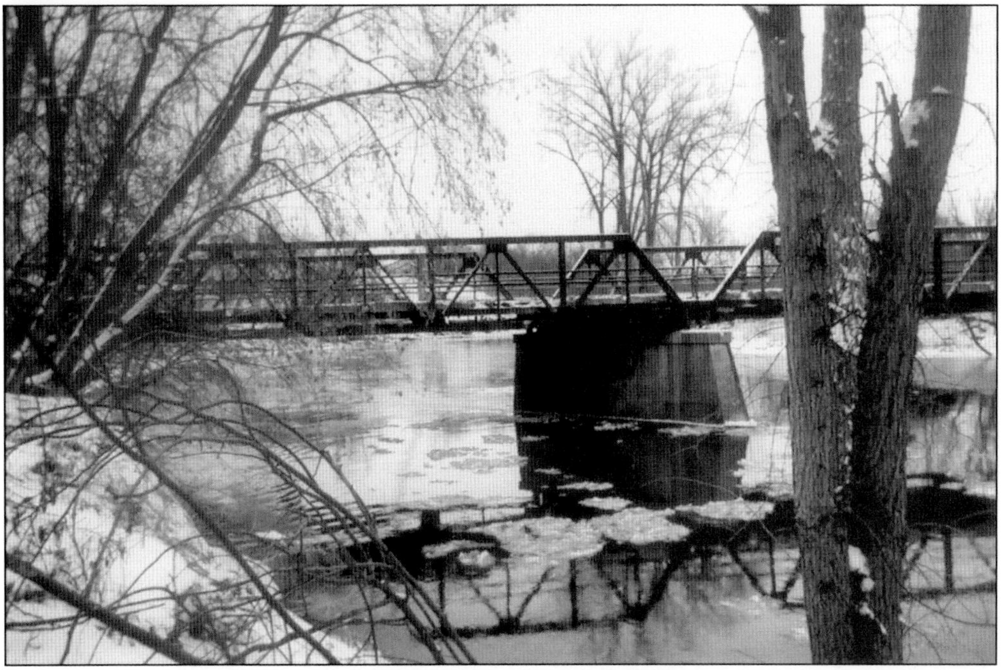

A highlight in many families' lives was going to Berning's Mill to watch feed being ground. It took about an hour to travel from the Fletcher-Rogers area to Berning's Mill by horse and buggy. This attraction, located on the far western edge of Hassan Township, was situated on the Crow River. The original bridge was built in 1885; however, after repairing the structure, it was replaced in the early 1930s with a three-span, rigid-connected Warren pony truss bridge in a concrete substructure, one of the few still remaining in Minnesota. The bridge has historical significance to the area, but due to heavy traffic on Territorial Road, is slated to be torn down and replaced with a new bridge. (Above, courtesy of John Hagel; below, courtesy of Norb Zahler.)

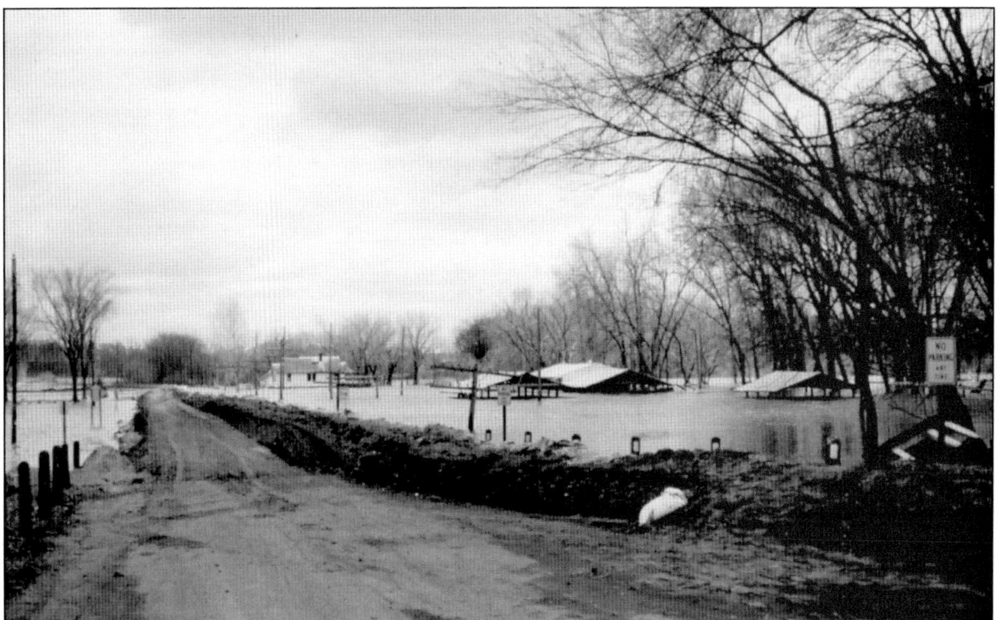

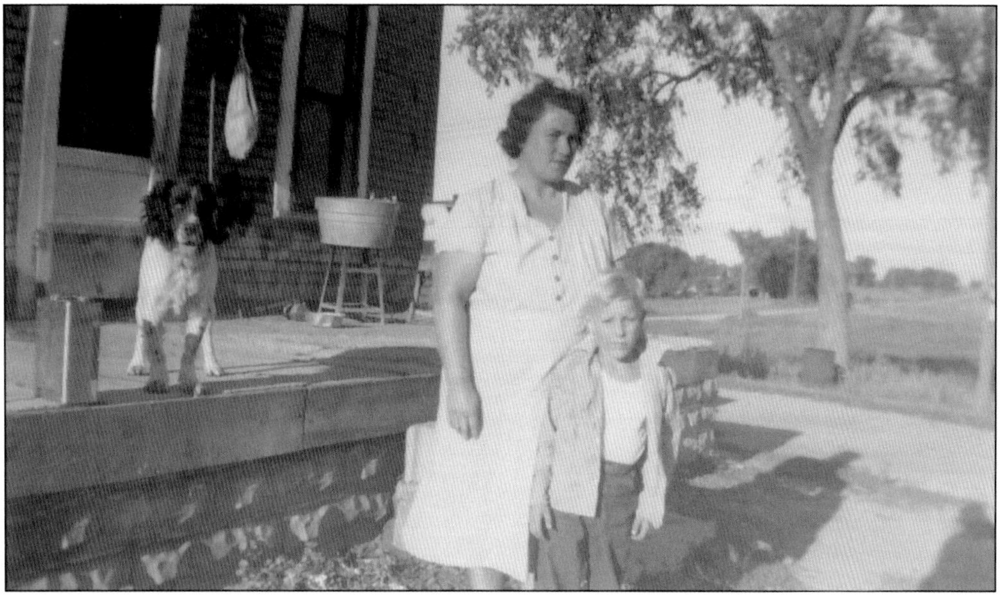

Jack Hines and his mom, Lillie, are seen here with their dog Suds at their home, which used to be located on the land where Walgreens now stands. This picture was taken in 1950. Notice the wash bucket on the porch. Every home had a wash bucket, and they served many purposes, as Howard Dahlheimer is demonstrating in the next picture. This picture was taken almost 20 years earlier, in 1931. (Above, courtesy of Jack and Carol Hines; below, courtesy of and Jane [Dahlheimer] Heinrich.)

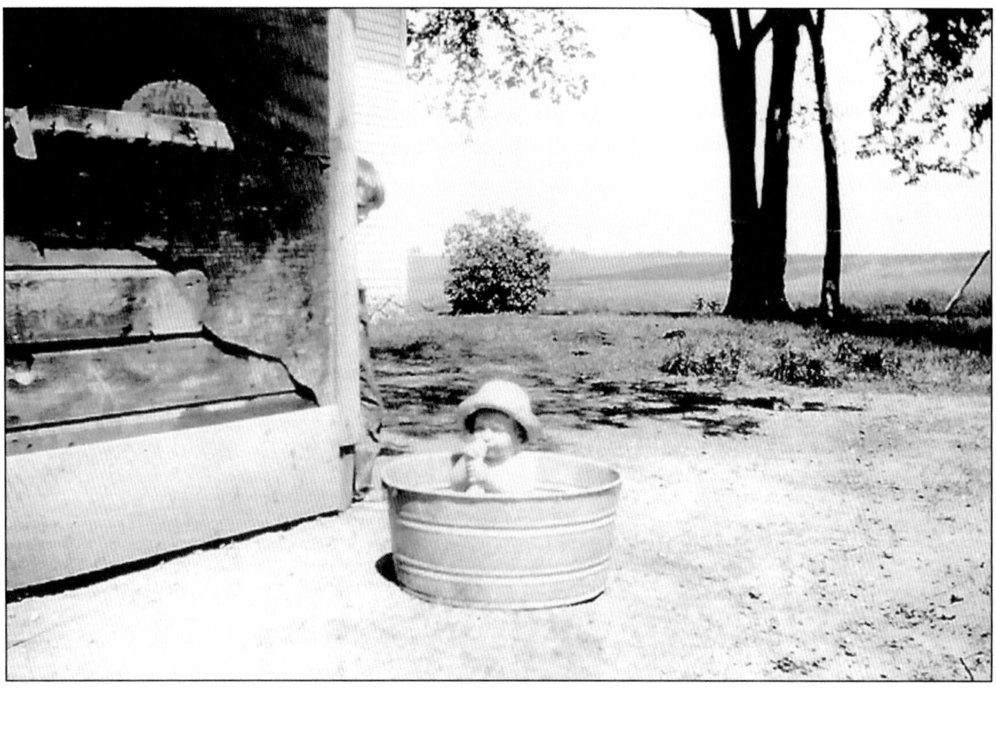

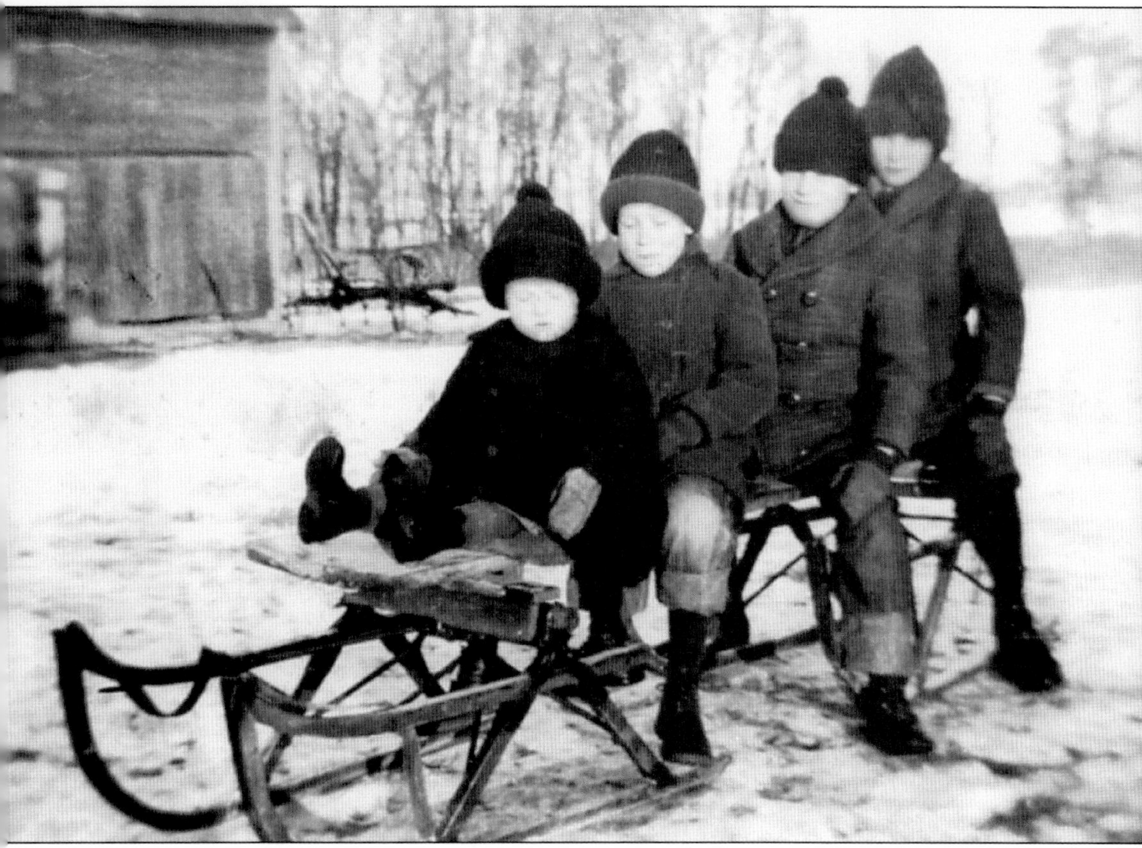

Carmen (Rouillard) Hawkins shared that a friend who worked at the grocery store would bring cherries and her mom would make pie while the kids went sledding or ice-skating. Everyone remembers sledding on the big hill behind Rich Weber's home. Gordon Rouillard reminisced about the trails for toboggans and sleds. Rouillard remembers a particular time sledding: he was running with his sled, to get a good head start, and he dropped onto the sled and the runner cut his thumb. Rouillard told Abby Adyt and Bobby Holland, but they told him to go home; they were going to stay and have fun. Rouillard started to walk home and got dizzy. Weber's sister saw him from their house and took him home so they could stitch his thumb up. Later the boys teased Rouillard, "It was not hard to find Rogers. We just followed the blood trail." Marcellus, Gerold, Leo, and Jerome Gmach are bundled up for this picture taken on February 6, 1925. (Courtesy of Jerome and Ferdella Gmach.)

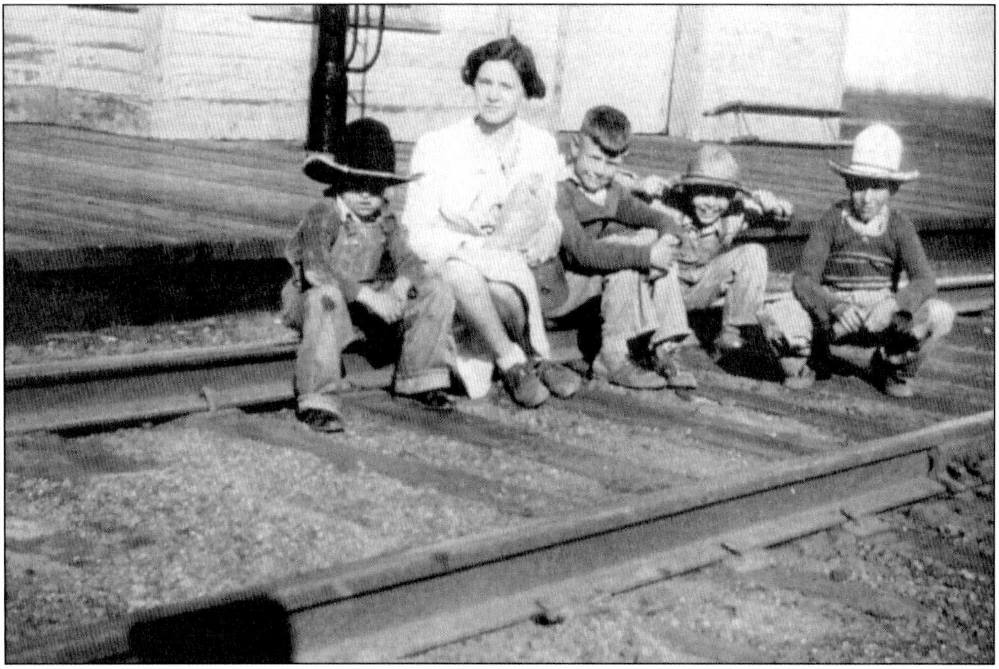

Sitting on the railroad tracks at the end of Main Street are (from left to right) Gordon Rouillard, Audrey Greeninger, Rayburn Couett, Leo Scharber, and Abby Aydt. Greeninger was watching Rouillard for the day, and his friends decided to join them for a picnic. Everyone enjoyed going to the railroad tracks and watching the passenger cars roll into town. (Courtesy of Leo Scharber.)

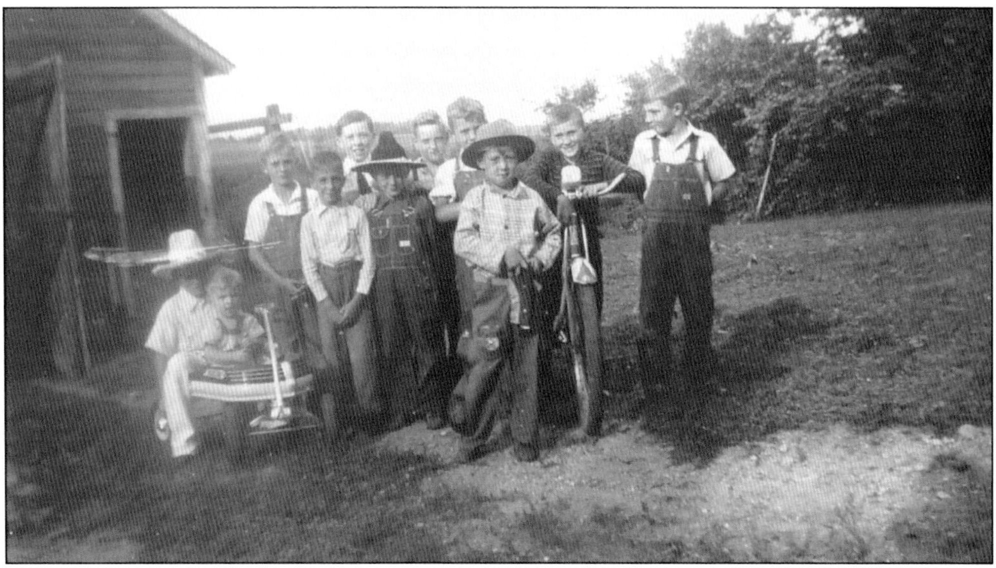

Gordon Rouillard had a big birthday party to celebrate turning eight. He remembers everyone had a lot of fun. Rouillard shared that each year he visited his godmother, aunt Hazel Scharber, at the Red and White grocery store. She would give him a birthday card that was signed "Happy Birthday, Hazel your Godmother," but when he looked inside, it was empty; then she would take it back. As Rouillard got older, he realized she gave all her godchildren the same card every year. (Courtesy of Gordon Rouillard.)

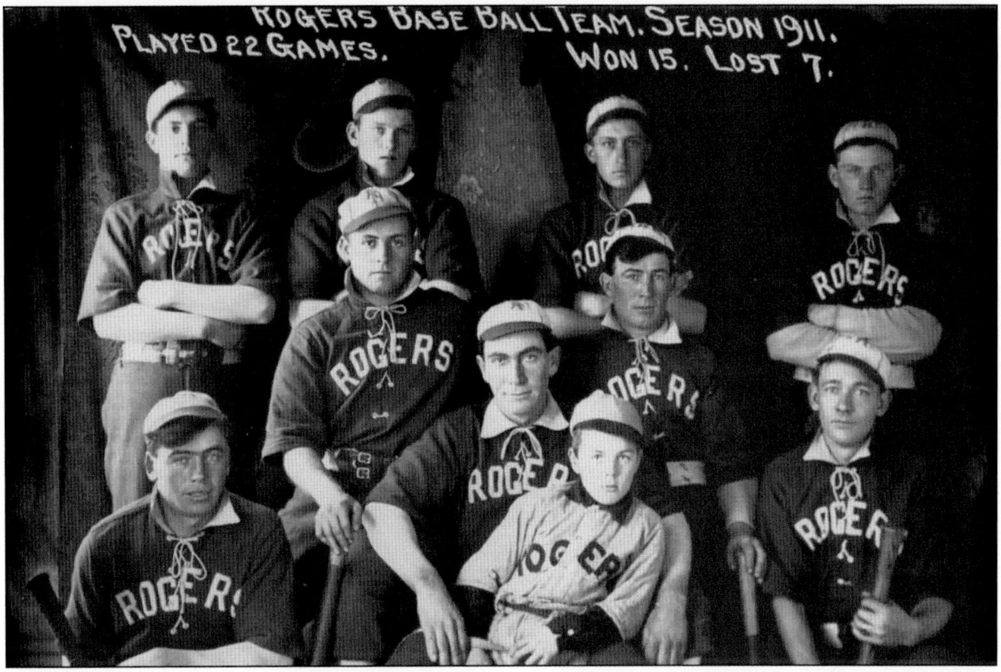

Pictured is the team of 1911. Melvin Rouillard shared that his father, Henry, played on this team. Rogers was known for its excellent ballplayers. The 1959 Rogers peewee team shown below was coached by Bob Milless (left) and Melvin Rouillard. The roster included Michael Ahlstrom, Jerry Sipe, Jerome Fehn, Lee Peterson, Gary Koneig, Kenneth Milless, Gerald Mitling, Quentin Weber, Arnold Daluge, Nicky Weber, Steven Gmach, Steve Dehn, Jerome Weber, Joseph Nelles, Kenneth Scherber, Bob Raudenbush, Tom Scharber, and Mike Rouillard. The 1959 baseball team roster included Earl Kottke, Lawrence Lynch, Donald Milless, Gerry Milless, Eddie Zirngable, Lefty Schaber, Dick Johnson, Ron Kish, Walt Lechner, Arnold LaVasseur, Gordon Rouillard, Eddie Ghostly, Jim Coughlin, Carl Leadens, Gordon LeFebvre, Dwight Skinner, and Ron Fricke. (Above, courtesy of Noreen Durant; below, courtesy of Melvin Rouillard.)

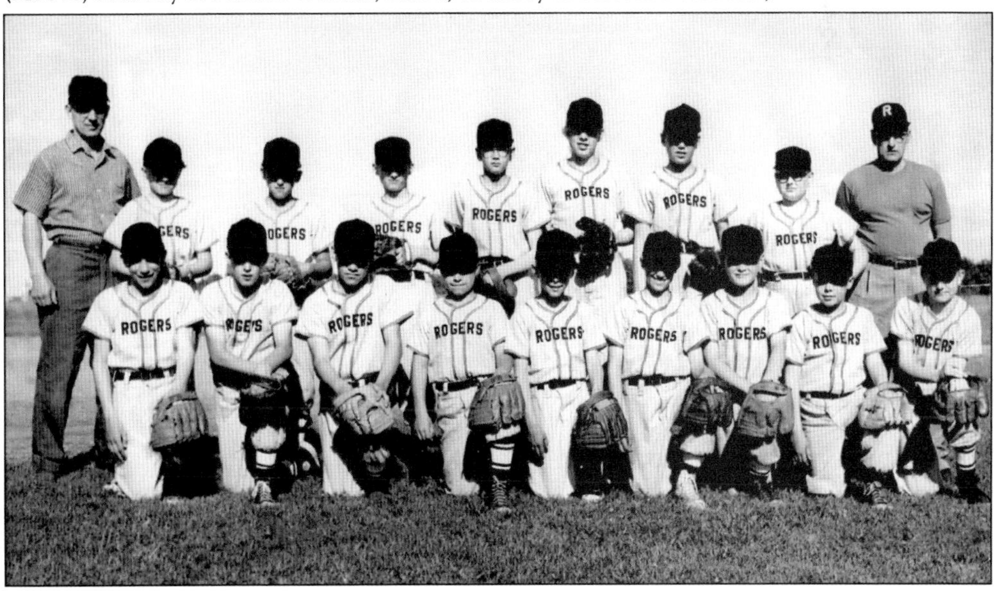

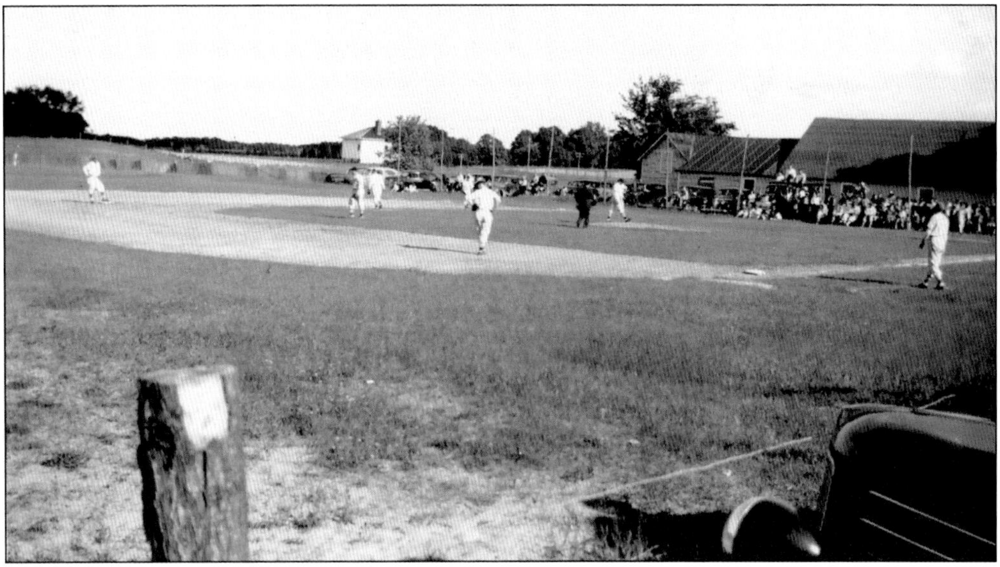

Every Sunday afternoon, the Rogers Red Devils, as Gordon Rouillard proudly noted the team was named, played ball. The team traveled to neighboring communities such as St. Michael, Dayton, and Hamel. Melvin Rouillard shared that no one wanted to miss a game, so several people packed into an automobile and more climbed into the trunk; a baseball bat was used to hold the trunk open for air. People throughout the community agreed that Rogers had really good baseball teams. Norb Zahler reminisced about sitting outside at the baseball games when the sun was blinding or the wind was blowing or rain was pouring, but nobody cared. Lenny Schlegel shared this 1947 picture of the Rogers team in action and another of the spectators. (Courtesy of Lenny and Lila Schlegel.)

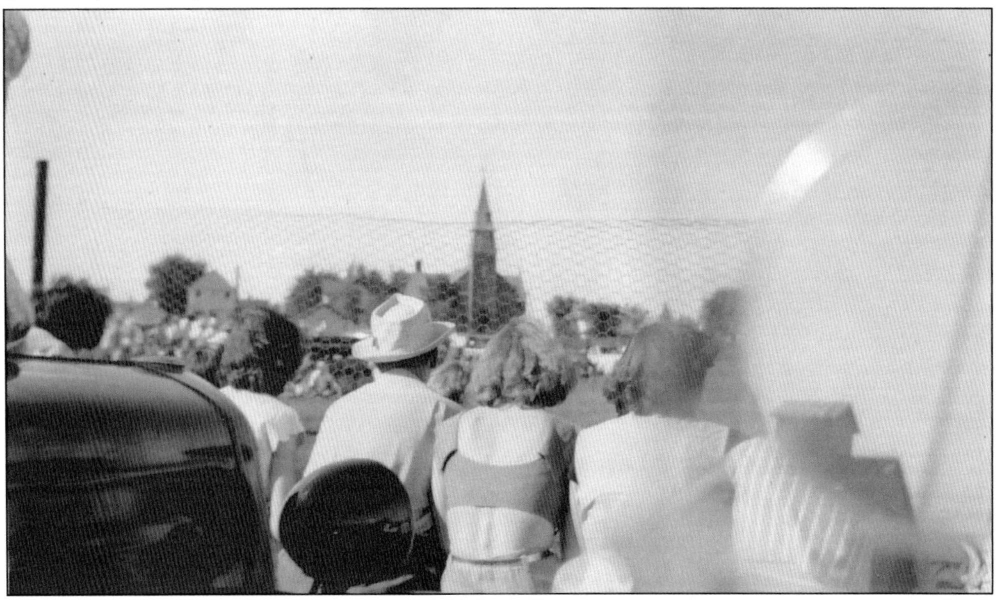

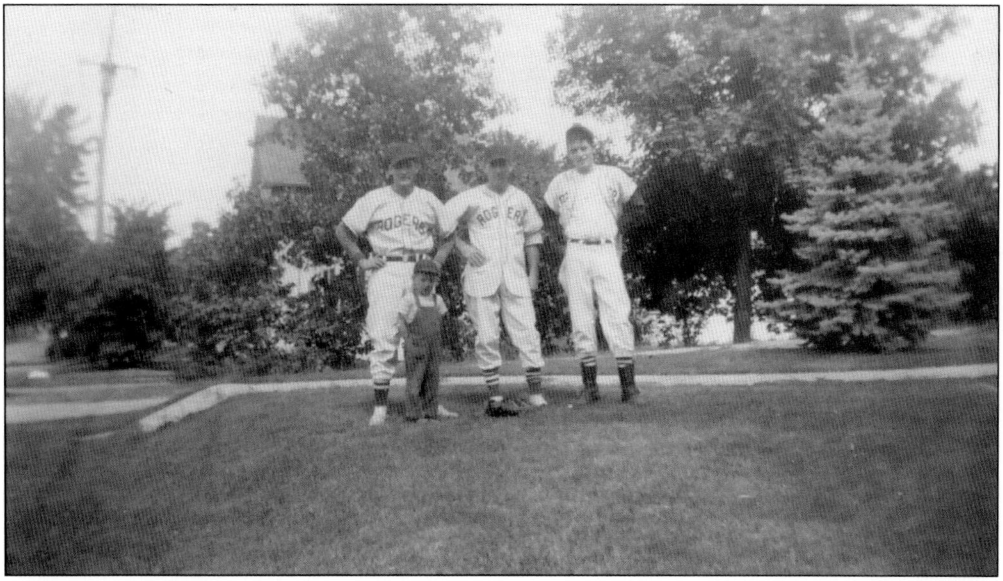

Many of the ballplayers from the glory days still reside in the area. Pictured from left to right are Melvin Rouillard with his son Mike, Donald "Dude" Milless, and Gordon Rouillard. The other picture includes, from left to right, Melvin, Dude, Gordon, Lou Greeninger, and Mike in front. Norb Zahler shared that he thought those pictured, along with Bob Milless and Lefty Schaber, were really good players. The baseball field was located where the Rogers Community Center and Fire Hall currently resides. Because children began playing baseball together in grade school, they had the opportunity to learn to work well together. In the 1930s and 1940s, people remembered running from home to home gathering children and starting a game in a pasture or field. Life was not as structured as it is today, and children seemed to have more fun and be able to entertain themselves better. (Courtesy of Gordon Rouillard.)

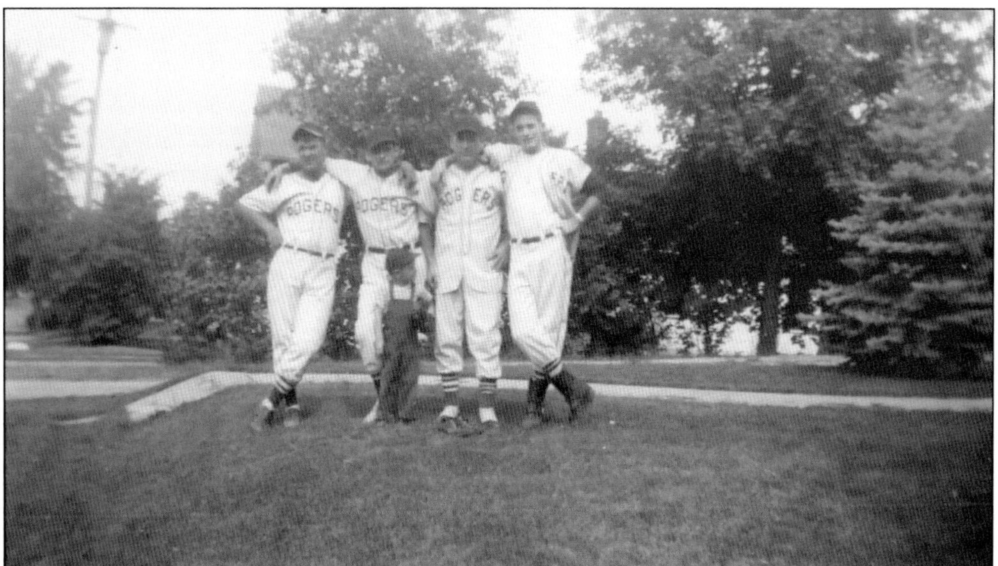

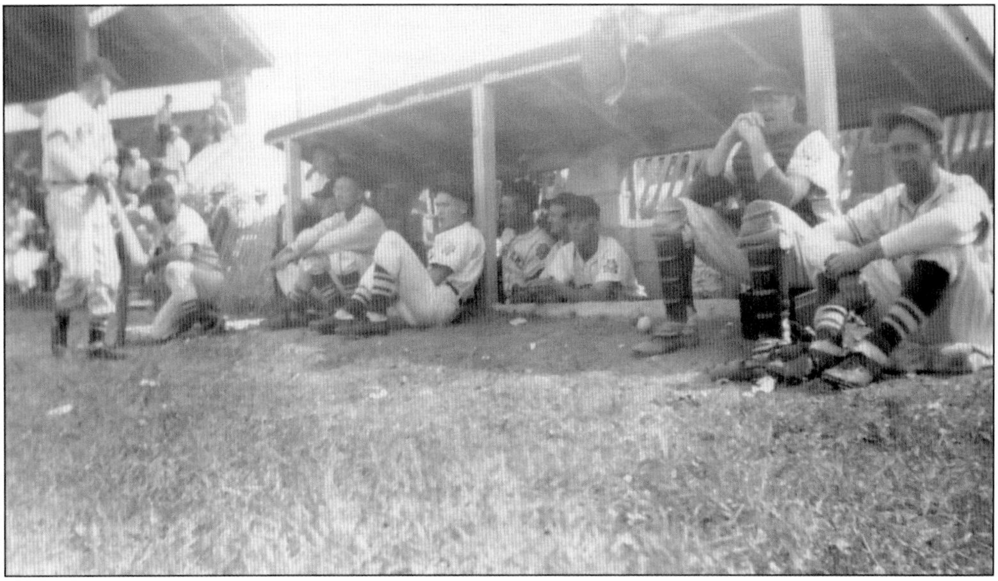

Baseball was the biggest summer event to hit Rogers back when stores were closed on Sunday. There was a town baseball team for 40 or 50 years. The team played neighboring communities, and if they were lucky, they could go to the playoffs, as shown in these pictures. The Rogers Red Devils actually won a few titles. The Sportsmen's Club was formed to provide funding for the baseball team. Leo Scharber shared that his cousin Vern Gagne was recently inducted into the Wrestling Hall of Fame. Gagne grew up in the area and spent summers with Scharber. Another community member known for sports was Dave Christian. Christian shared that he played baseball and was a boxer. He earned the Light Weight Golden Glove title in 1962. (Courtesy of Gordon Rouillard.)

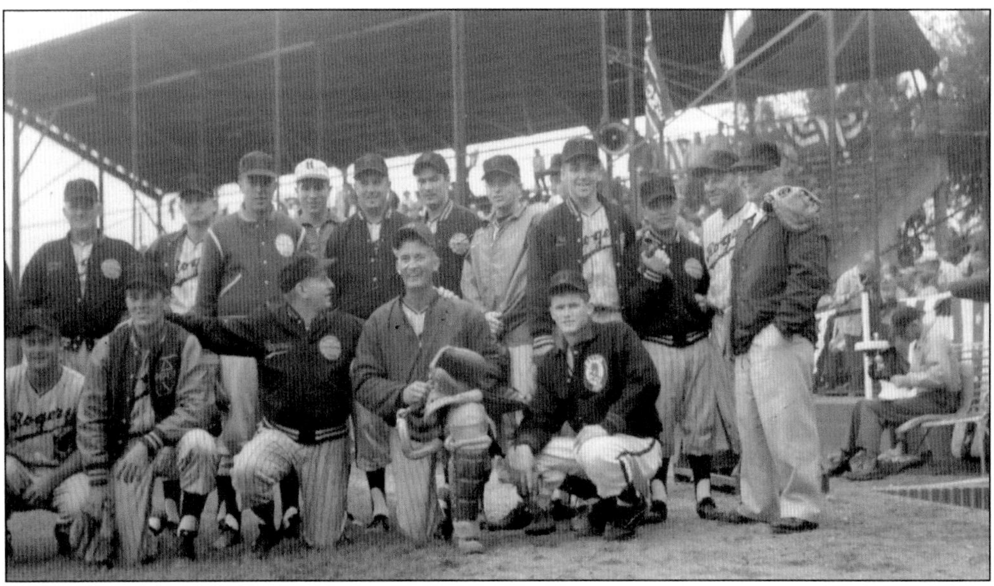

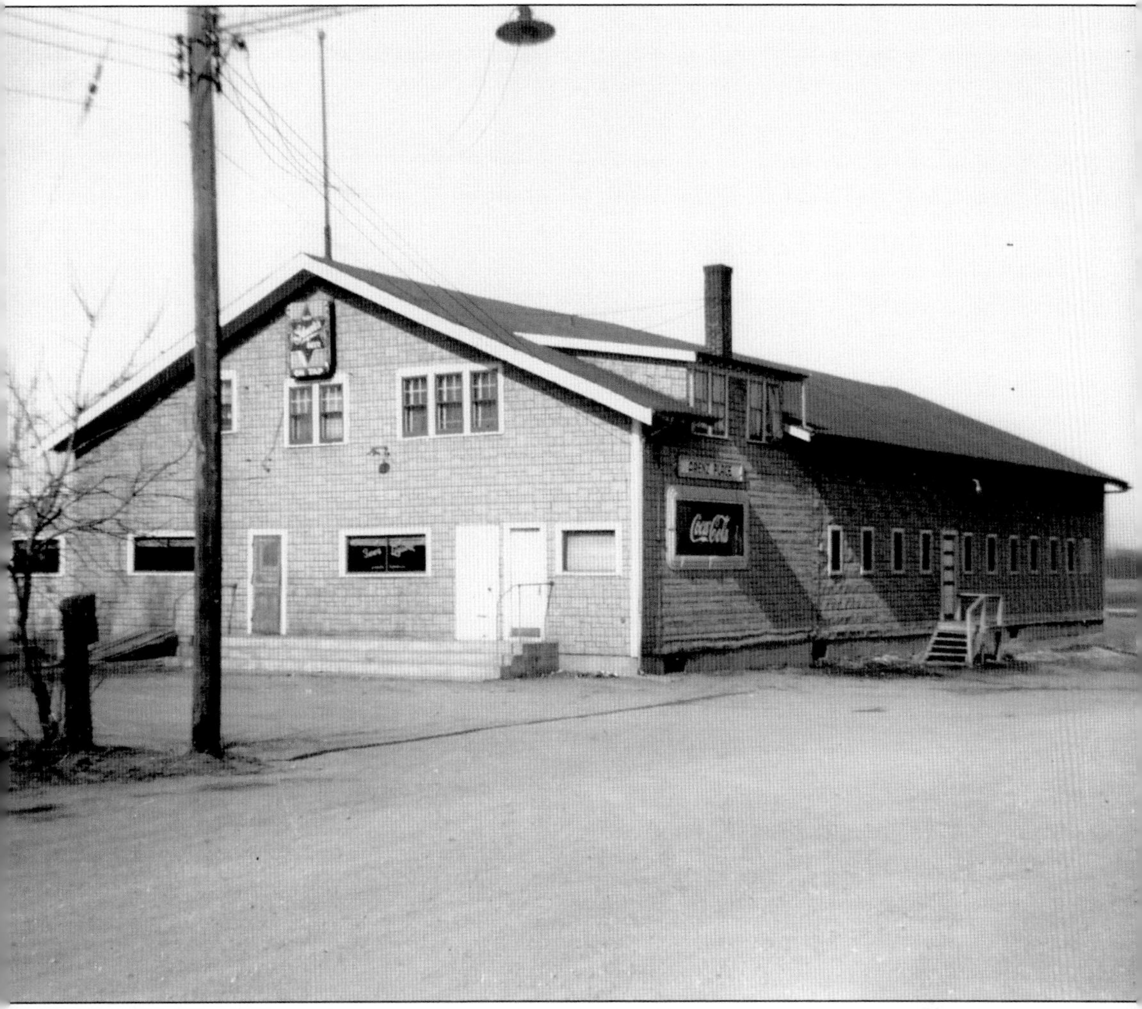

Lucy Harves and Frank Stenglein built the dance hall in Rogers. It was later owned by Andy Wishy, Louie Arenz, and the Weber family. The dance hall may have had other owners as well. Jack and Peggy Dahlheimer met at the dance hall during a wedding dance. Jack had planned to travel the United States; instead he married Peggy. Bob and Alice Milless and Jerome and Ferdella Gmach had their wedding dances there too. Bob Milless came from a family of 13 children. Since his aunt Lucy owned the building, he got to roller-skate for free. The roller skates were not fancy, they strapped to the bottom of street shoes. Everyone enjoyed watching when the couple with white shoe skates came from Minneapolis. Eugene Ahlstrom enjoyed roller-skating as a child and just three years ago went skating in Monticello, Minnesota. At the time, he was 84 years young. The dance hall was located where the Word of Peace Church is now. (Courtesy of Chuck Christian.)

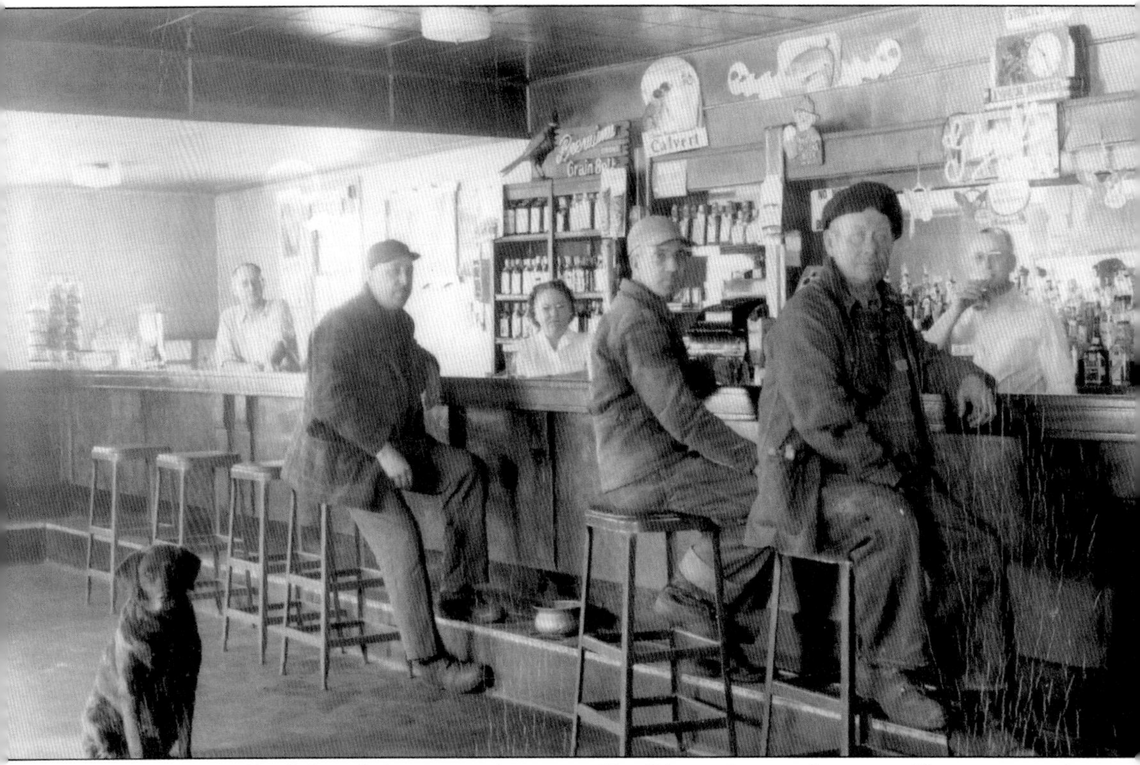

Gordon Rouillard shared that Louie Arenz would tell him when undercover officers were at the dance hall. Since Rouillard's dad was the beer distributor in town, he had a key to the warehouse and would stash a few in his car. When they got thirsty, Rouillard and Rich Weber would go to the car to quench their thirst. Denny Stieg remembered hearing a rumor one night: Alfred Hagel was going to roll his car down Main Street. Everyone left the dance and hurried out to Main Street. All of a sudden, there was a car roaring down the street, then he cranked the steering wheel hard to the left and the car flipped on its side and rolled over and over, down the street in front of Farrian's Malt Shop. Another form of excitement was the free movies shown on the side of the building each Friday night; this event was sponsored by the local businesses. The dance hall burned down in 1978. "It was the end of an era," said Judy Volkers. (Courtesy of Priscilla Arenz.)

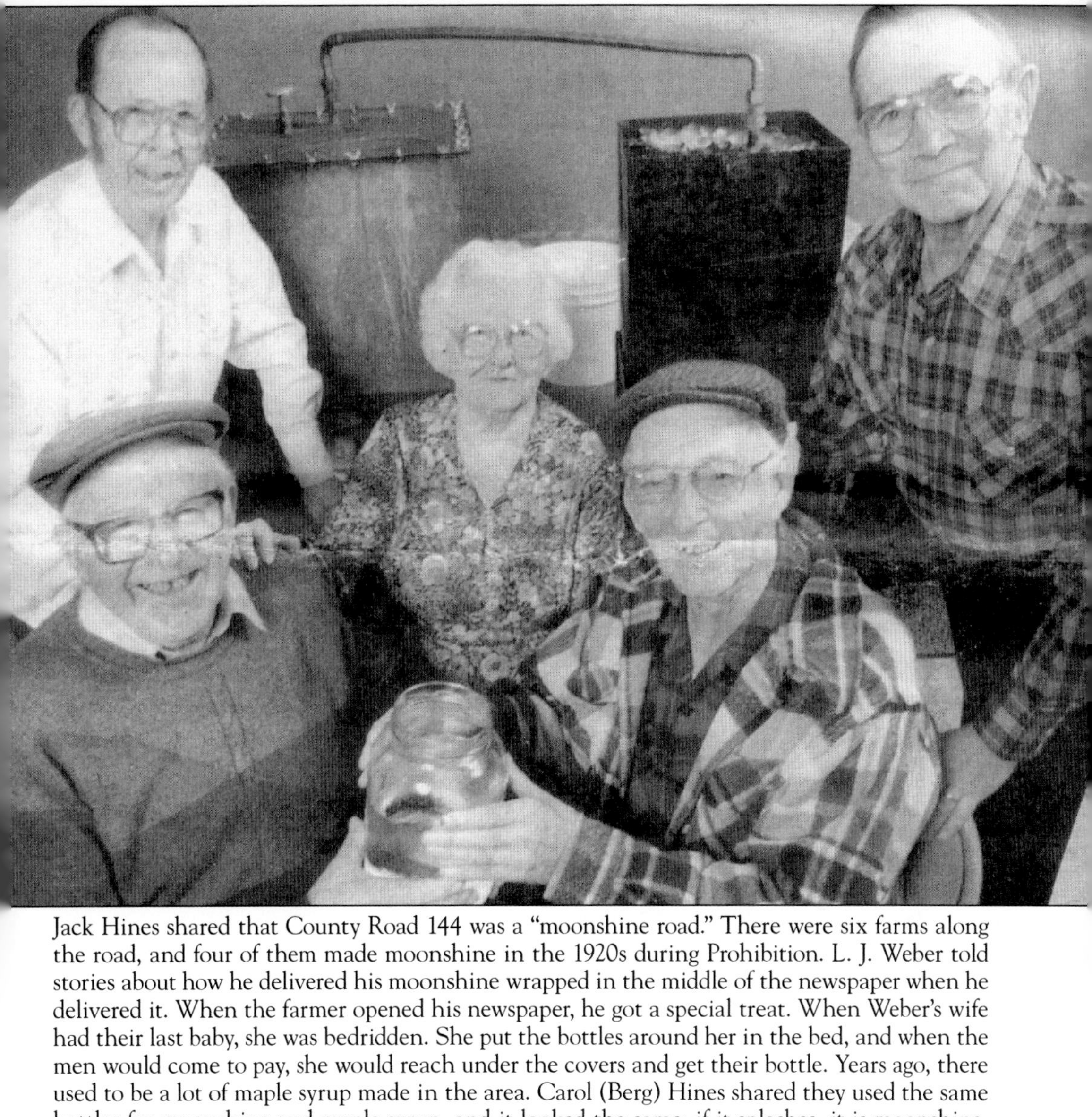

Jack Hines shared that County Road 144 was a "moonshine road." There were six farms along the road, and four of them made moonshine in the 1920s during Prohibition. L. J. Weber told stories about how he delivered his moonshine wrapped in the middle of the newspaper when he delivered it. When the farmer opened his newspaper, he got a special treat. When Weber's wife had their last baby, she was bedridden. She put the bottles around her in the bed, and when the men would come to pay, she would reach under the covers and get their bottle. Years ago, there used to be a lot of maple syrup made in the area. Carol (Berg) Hines shared they used the same bottles for moonshine and maple syrup, and it looked the same; if it splashes, it is moonshine. Hines's grandparents farmed on the old Dehn land and ran moonshine. Pictured at a moonshine reunion party thrown by Jack and Carol Hines are, from left to right, (first row) Douglas McLean and Adlore Leger; (second row) Leo Scharber, Annie Weber, and Wallace Hagel. (Courtesy of Leo Scharber.)

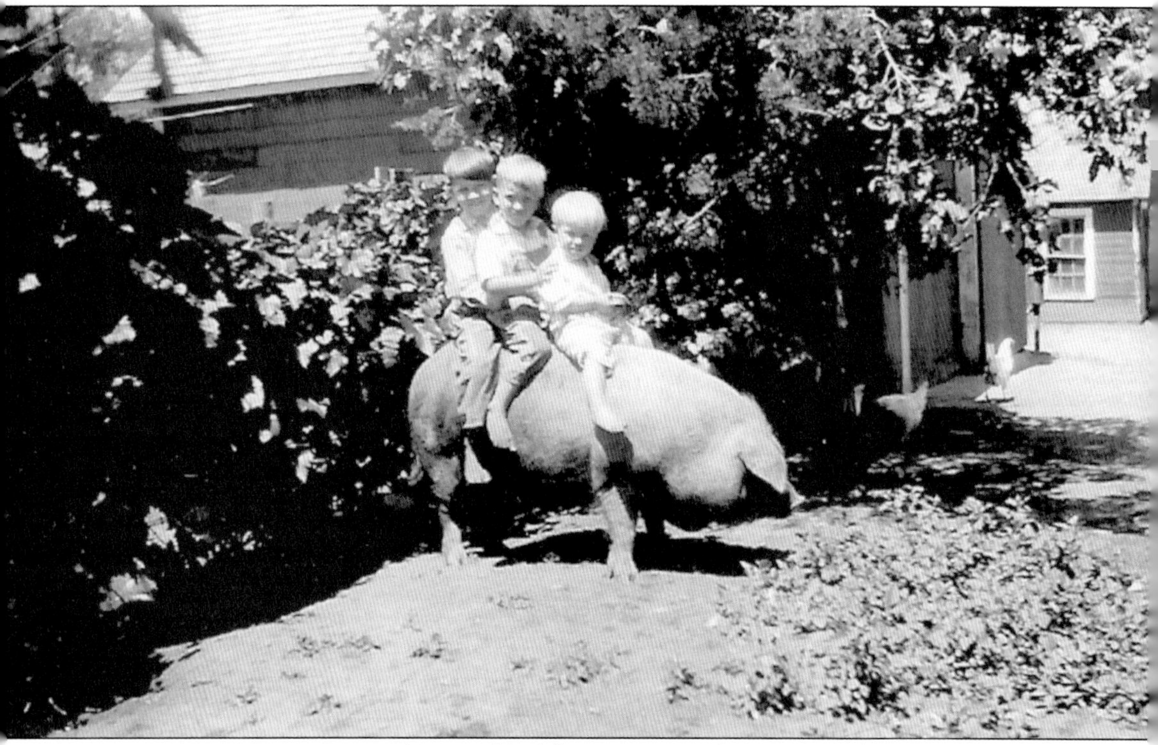

In 1932, George, Harvey, and Howard Dahlheimer were riding a pig on the Werner Dahlheimer farm. Children entertained themselves by playing with each other and having fun outside. There was no television or technology, and organized sports meant running down the street yelling, "Meet me at the ball field!" Life was simpler, but according to each person interviewed, it was also more fun. Howard Dahlheimer shared a story about how they had one pair of skis to share. They would stand on the skis and hang onto the horse's tail and get him galloping down the street. Jack Dahlheimer explained how to play the game "hunt the greyhound." One person is the "greyhound." He or she takes off running in the dark while everyone else counts to 50, then the group of three or four starts yelling, "Hunt the greyhound," and the person hiding responds and then moves; this goes on until the "greyhound" is caught. Mary Lou (Zachman) Dahlheimer enjoyed playing kick the can, and her husband, Ray, remembered how fun dodgeball was back then. (Courtesy of Jane [Dahlheimer] Heinrich.)

Eight

THEY CALL IT PROGRESS

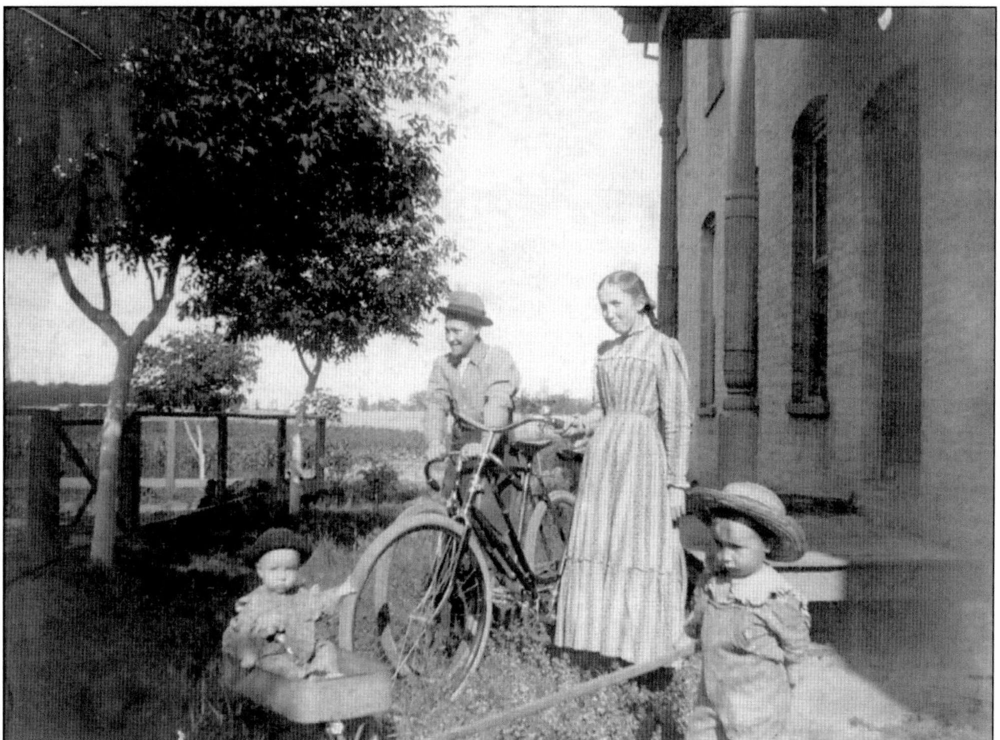

Life in this quiet farming community was not always as peaceful as this picture makes it appear. In August 1862, news of a recent massacre spread through the area like wildfire and terrified the settlers of Hassan. Many of them fled to Minneapolis, and others went to Fort Snelling for safety. Although there is no proof of any massacre in Hassan Township, Evelyn Henry, Lloyd Henry's wife, shared a story her mother-in-law told her. She remembered when Native Americans lived in the territory. One day, she was baking bread when the women and children were all taken to the river and sent to Dayton because there was fear the Native Americans would attack; the bread was done when they returned home. (Courtesy of Leo Scharber.)

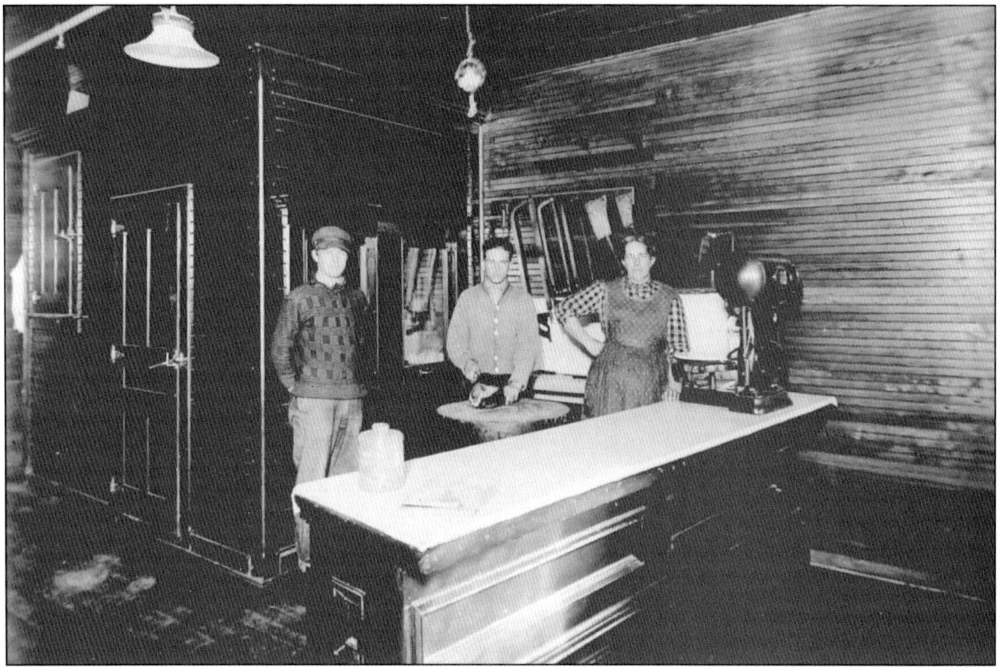

These pictures were taken inside the original J. N. Heinen General Merchandise and Hardware store, which opened about 1899 on Main Street, blocking the current Church Avenue. Joe, Rudy, and Katherine (Katie) Heinen are pictured in these images. Florian and Merle's father, Rudy, was active in the company, along with his brothers John, Martin, Otto, and Hubert. Dale Durant (Rudy's son-in-law) began working at the store in the early 1950s. The company operated a service shop next to the store where Danny Durant worked on equipment. The Heinens and Durants greatly appreciated the support through over 100 years; however, due to development of the area, farmers sold their land because the price of their land became more valuable than farming and Heinens closed. (Courtesy of Danny, Janet, and Noreen Durant.)

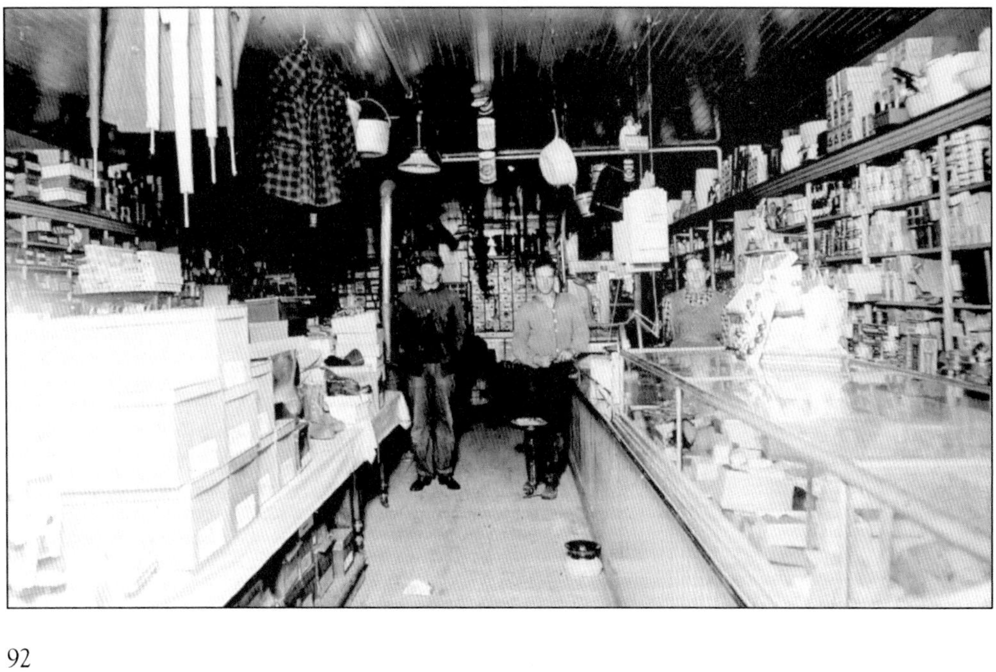

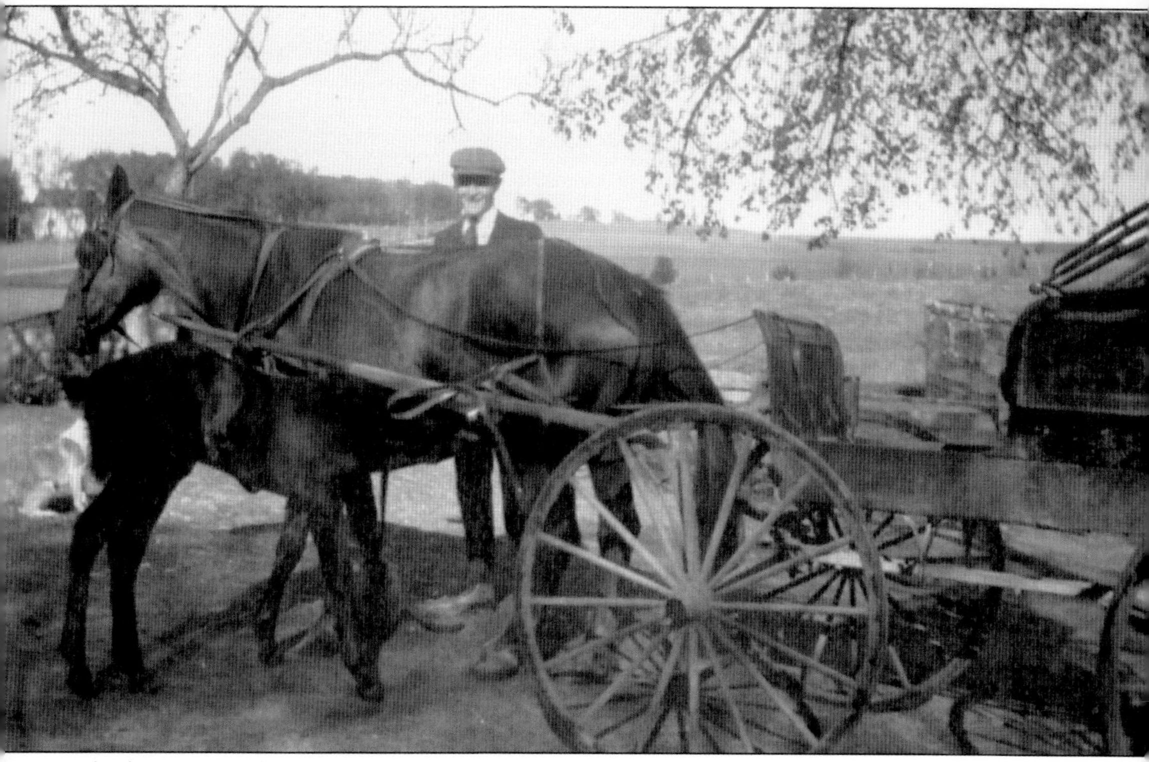

At the beginning of the 20th century, it was common to see locals travel by horse and buggy. Norb Zahler shared that his father, Victor Zahler, liked to travel using a horse and cutter (a type of sleigh) during the winter when he was courting his future bride, Bernadette Dahlheimer. Victor would drive the cutter over to Bernadette's home, which was about five miles away. They would sit in the house and visit for hours. On the return journey, Victor would point the horses toward home, cover up with a blanket, and take a nap. When the sleigh crossed the railroad tracks, it woke him up; he knew he was a half block from home and it was time to sit up and steer the horses into the barn. Victor and Bernadette were married in 1926. (Courtesy of Gordon Rouillard.)

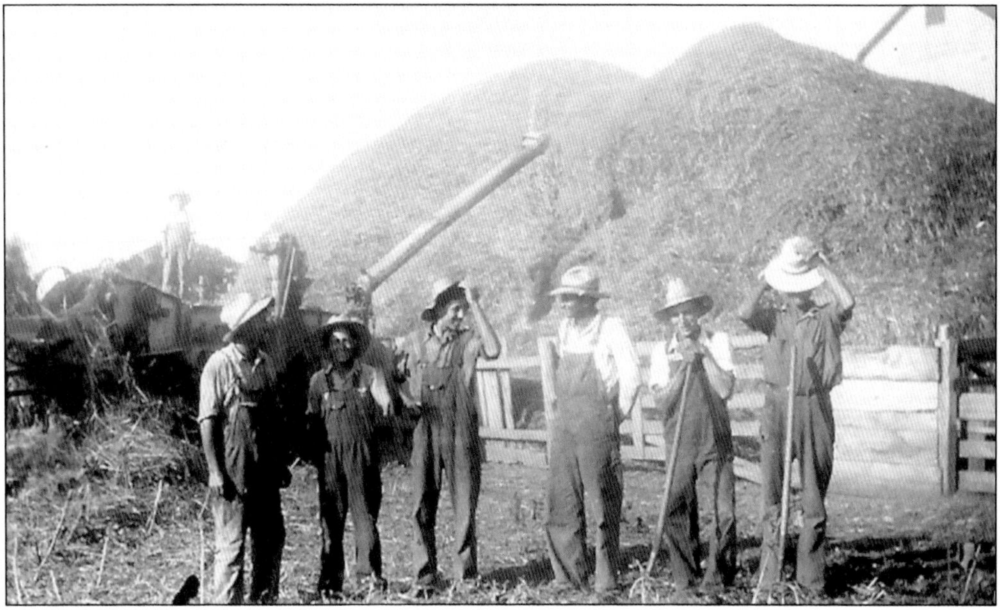

The first threshing machine was brought into the township by John Temple. It was powered by a two-horse treadmill. Farming was a way of life; equipment and buildings were important. Norb Zahler shared a story of a hobo who had been riding the rails and chose to sleep in Zahler's family's barn. It was during the winter, and when he awoke, he found his legs were frozen, so he lit the barn on fire and rolled out to get some attention. He was taken by horse and buggy to the train depot, where the agent put him on the train to get him some medical attention in the city; he died on the way there. The barn was lost as well. (Above, courtesy of Jane [Dahlheimer] Heinrich; below, courtesy of Jerome and Ferdella Gmach.)

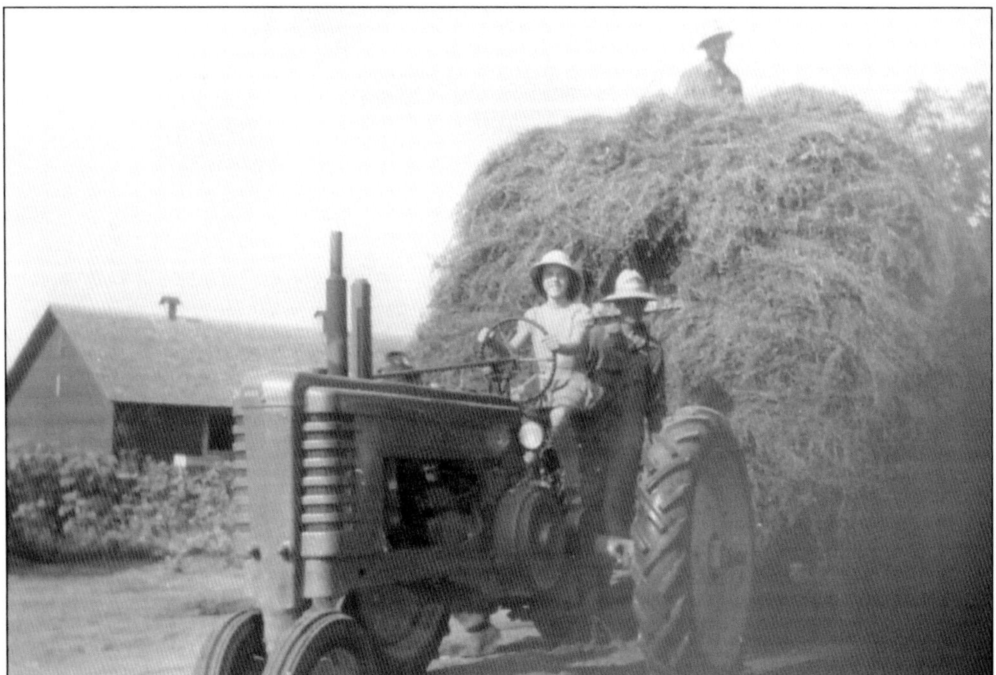

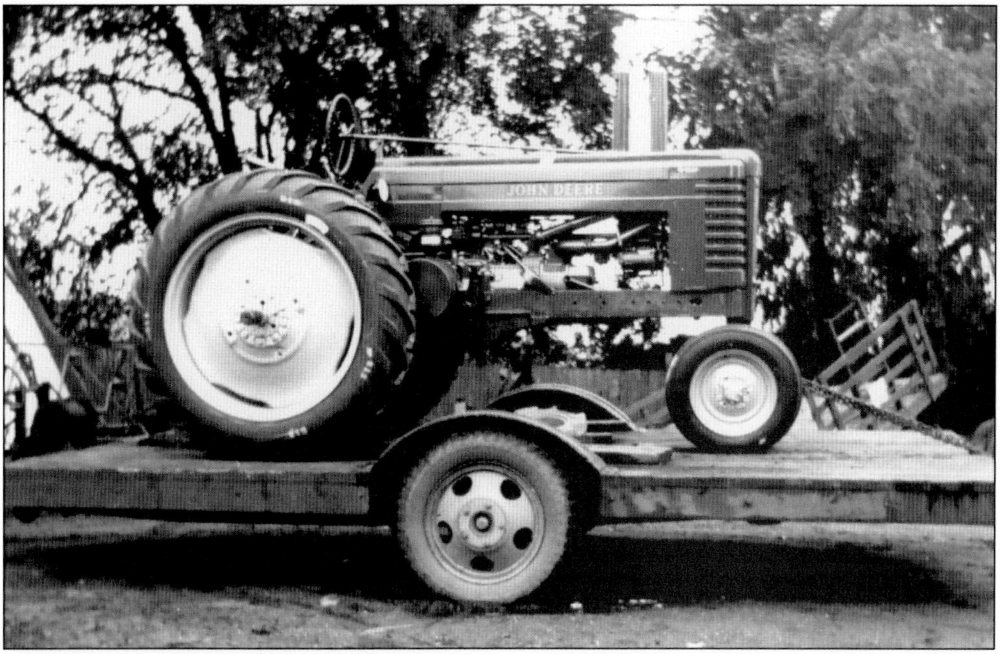

To support the rural community, the businesses provided choices. Scharber and Sons carried John Deere. Heinen offered FarmAll and International Harvester equipment and parts. Gerhart Scherber carried Minnesota machinery, which was made in Stillwater by the prisoners. Pictured here are a 1944 John Deere and Howard Dahlheimer on a 1946 FarmAll. (Above, courtesy of Melvin Rouillard; below, courtesy of Jane [Dahlheimer] Heinrich.)

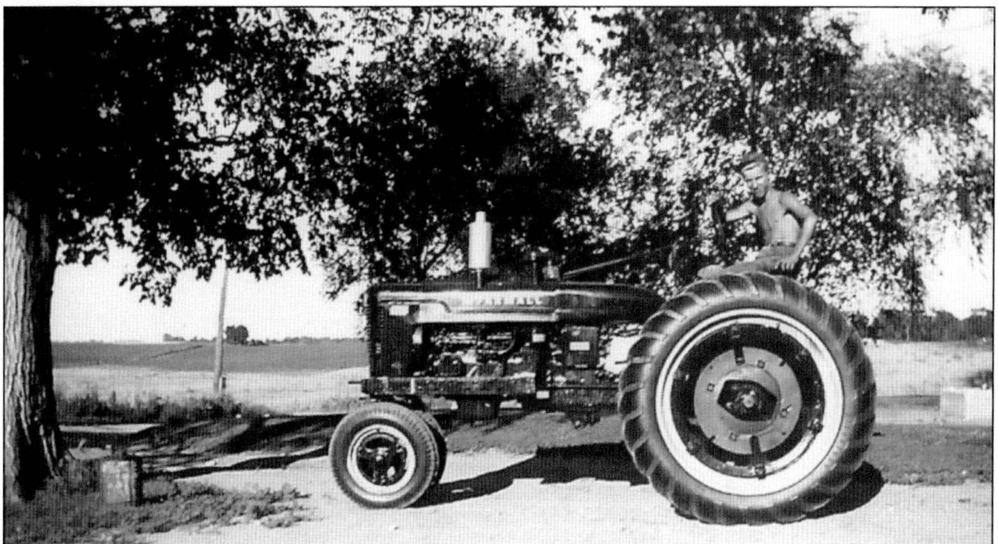

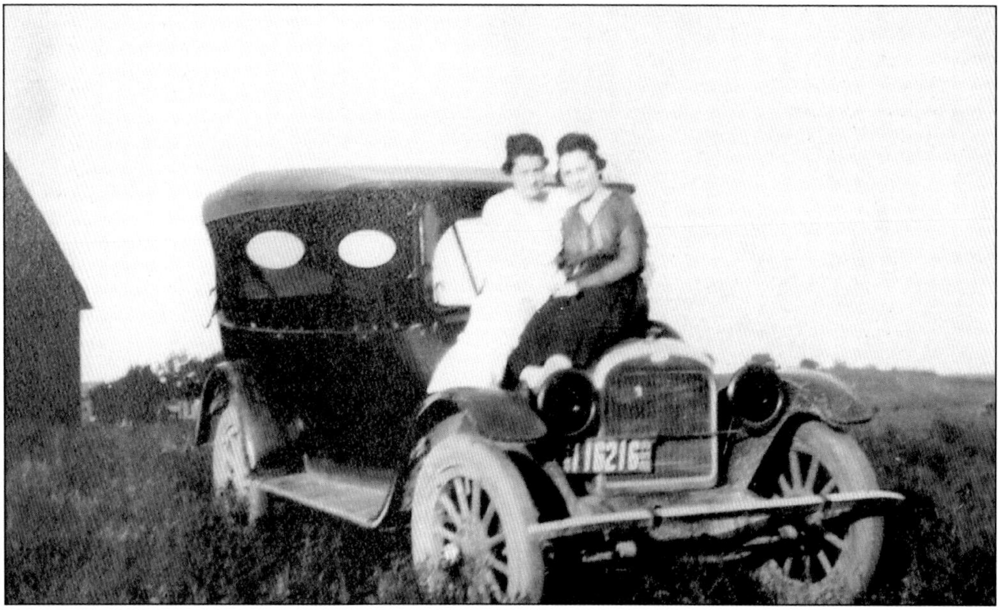

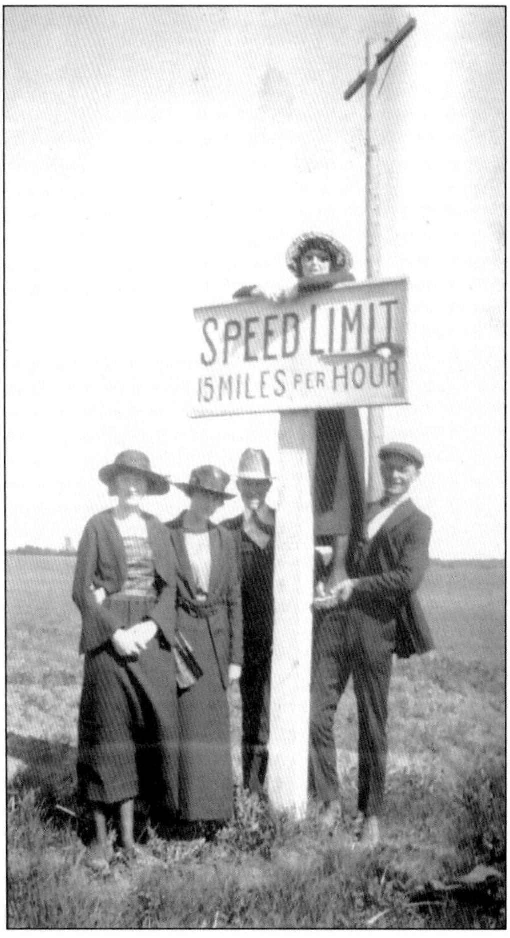

Territorial Road had been a primary thoroughfare between Minneapolis and Monticello since 1858; however, automobiles were relatively new to the scene. Looking at these pictures is cause to believe the phrase "Sunday drive" may have been derived from this era. These images were taken in 1919 as a group of friends enjoyed a Sunday afternoon tooling through Hassan Township. (Courtesy of Gordon Rouillard.)

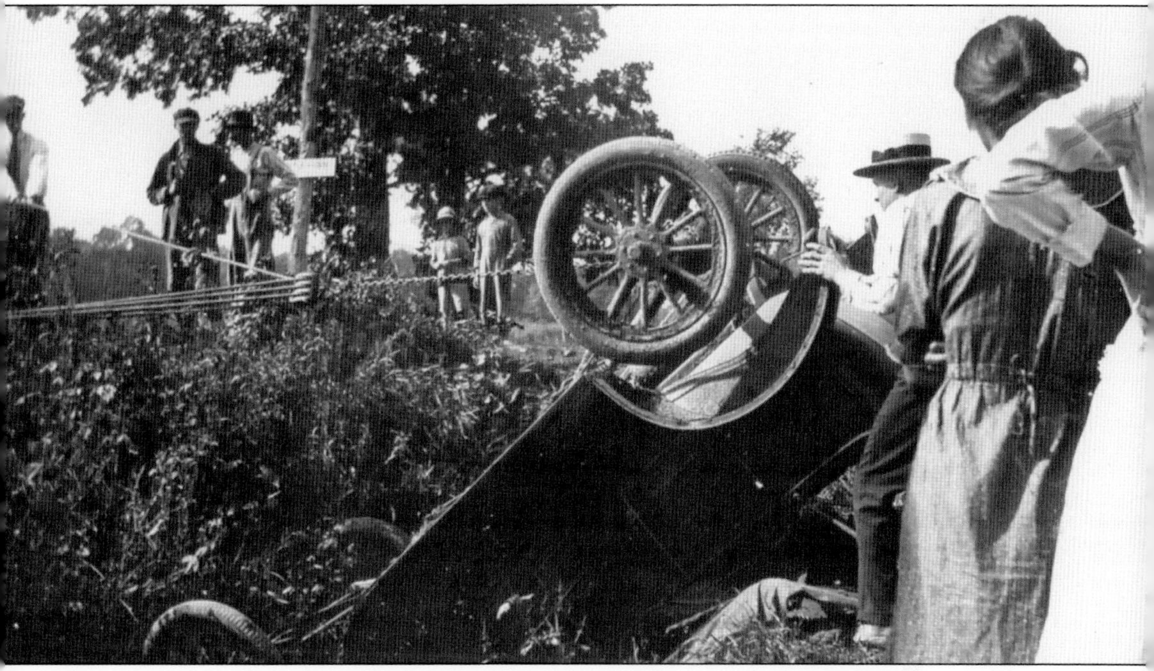

This unfortunate scene shows Gordon Rouillard's aunt Nell; she broke her back in this accident. There were a few tragic accidents in the early history of the community. Leo Scharber remembers going to Osseo for stamps and coming upon a 1937 Chevrolet against a tree. Mike Borck was hanging out the window with blood running from his mouth; he had been killed instantly. The driver, his hired man, had fallen asleep and hit a big tree; he did not get hurt. Doug Scharber shared when Eugene Ahlstrom's mom, Emma, had an accident. He and Otto Scharber were the first on the scene. They got her help, but she passed on a few days later. Gordon Rouillard told of the day when Leo Scharber, Bobby Holland, and he were shooting pool at Andy Wishy's. They heard about a big accident, so Leo drove them to check it out; that was how Bobby learned of his dad's death. Automobile accidents continue to plague the community. (Courtesy of Gordon Rouillard.)

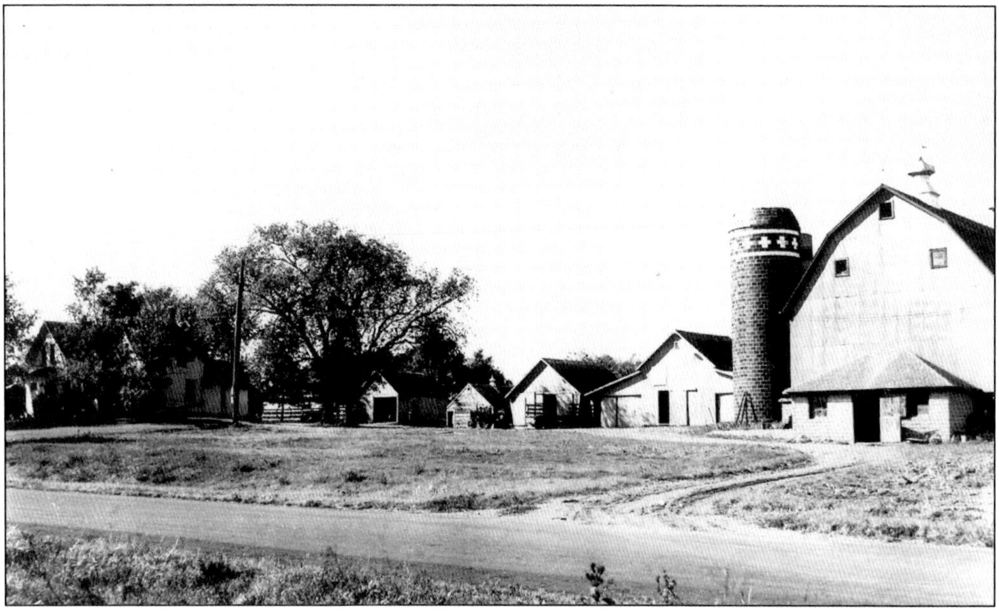

This picture of the Werner Dahlheimer farm was taken in 1946, and the other is of Werner in his buggy with his team of horses, the mode of transportation in 1917. The Werner Dahlheimer farm was a 160-acre farm many now know as the trade center housing Super Target, Kohl's, Culvers, several strip malls, and other fine shopping establishments. The land was originally acquired through homesteading. In 1928, when Werner's mother died, he bought out the family; he had been paying toward contract for deed and paid everyone off in 1928. According to Howard Dahlheimer, during the Depression, when the banks failed, Werner did not lose anything. They did not have any money, but did not owe anyone anything either. (Courtesy of Jane [Dahlheimer] Heinrich.)

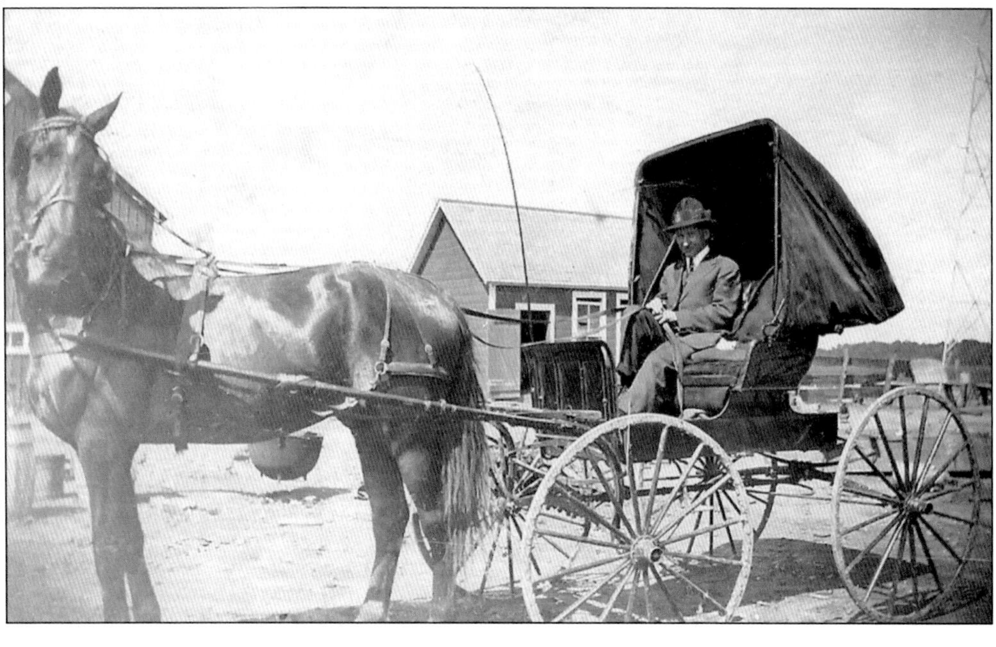

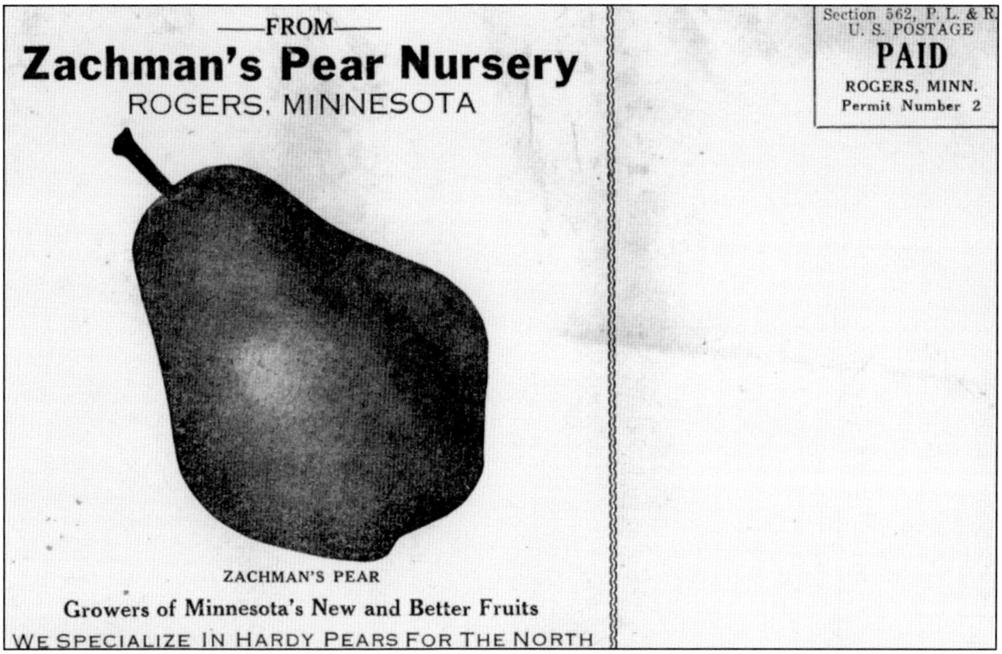

The Zachman's Pear Nursery was known for its hardy northern pear trees. Louis Zachman sold his fruit trees by the foot, measuring from the roots to the tip of the tree. A three-to-four-foot tree was 40¢, a four-to-five-foot tree was 50¢, a five-to-six-foot tree was 75¢, and a six-to-seven-foot tree was $1. Louis also offered quantity discounts. The Zachman's Pear Nursery was eventually sold, and the land was developed into housing; Arthur Street was named after Arthur Zachman, who is Mary Lou (Zachman) Dahlheimer's dad and Louis's son. (Courtesy of Mary Lou [Zachman] Dahlheimer.)

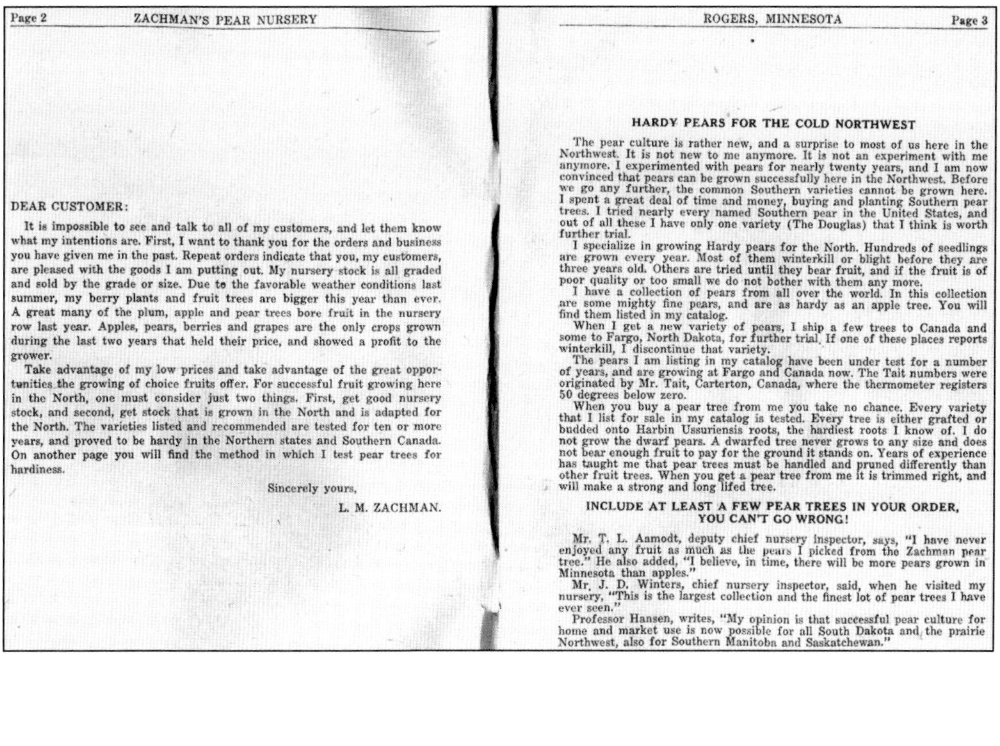

Page 2 ZACHMAN'S PEAR NURSERY

DEAR CUSTOMER:

It is impossible to see and talk to all of my customers, and let them know what my intentions are. First, I want to thank you for the orders and business you have given me in the past. Repeat orders indicate that you, my customers, are pleased with the goods I am putting out. My nursery stock is all graded and sold by the grade or size. Due to the favorable weather conditions last summer, my berry plants and fruit trees are bigger this year than ever. A great many of the plum, apple and pear trees bore fruit in the nursery row last year. Apples, pears, berries and grapes are the only crops grown during the last two years that held their price, and showed a profit to the grower.

Take advantage of my low prices and take advantage of the great opportunities the growing of choice fruits offer. For successful fruit growing here in the North, one must consider just two things. First, get good nursery stock, and second, get stock that is grown in the North and is adapted for the North. The varieties listed and recommended are tested for ten or more years, and proved to be hardy in the Northern states and Southern Canada. On another page you will find the method in which I test pear trees for hardiness.

Sincerely yours,

L. M. ZACHMAN.

ROGERS, MINNESOTA Page 3

HARDY PEARS FOR THE COLD NORTHWEST

The pear culture is rather new, and a surprise to most of us here in the Northwest. It is not new to me anymore. It is not an experiment with me anymore. I experimented with pears for nearly twenty years, and I am now convinced that pears can be grown successfully here in the Northwest. Before we go any further, the common Southern varieties cannot be grown here. I spent a great deal of time and money, buying and planting Southern pear trees. I tried nearly every named Southern pear in the United States, and out of all these I have only one variety (The Douglas) that I think is worth further trial.

I specialize in growing Hardy pears for the North. Hundreds of seedlings are grown every year. Most of them winterkill or blight before they are three years old. Others are tried until they bear fruit, and if the fruit is of poor quality or too small we do not bother with them any more.

I have a collection of pears from all over the world. In this collection are some mighty fine pears, and are as hardy as an apple tree. You will find them listed in my catalog.

When I get a new variety of pears, I ship a few trees to Canada and some to Fargo, North Dakota, for further trial. If one of these places reports winterkill, I discontinue that variety.

The pears I am listing in my catalog have been under test for a number of years, and are growing at Fargo and Canada now. The Tait numbers were originated by Mr. Tait, Carterton, Canada, where the thermometer registers 50 degrees below zero.

When you buy a pear tree from me you take no chance. Every variety that I list for sale in my catalog is tested. Every tree is either grafted or budded onto Harbin Ussuriensis roots, the hardiest roots I know of. I do not grow the dwarf pears. A dwarfed tree never grows to any size and does not bear enough fruit to pay for the ground it stands on. Years of experience has taught me that pear trees must be handled and pruned differently than other fruit trees. When you get a pear tree from me it is trimmed right, and will make a strong and long lifed tree.

INCLUDE AT LEAST A FEW PEAR TREES IN YOUR ORDER, YOU CAN'T GO WRONG!

Mr. T. L. Aamodt, deputy chief nursery inspector, says, "I have never enjoyed any fruit as much as the pears I picked from the Zachman pear tree." He also added, "I believe, in time, there will be more pears grown in Minnesota than apples."

Mr. J. D. Winters, chief nursery inspector, said, when he visited my nursery, "This is the largest collection and the finest lot of pear trees I have ever seen."

Professor Hansen, writes, "My opinion is that successful pear culture for home and market use is now possible for all South Dakota and the prairie Northwest, also for Southern Manitoba and Saskatchewan."

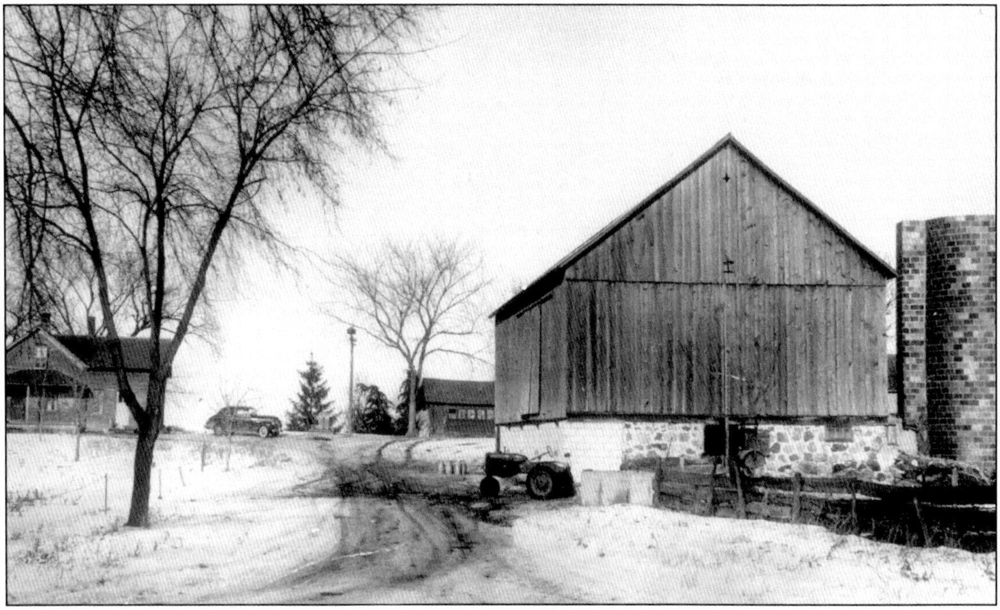

This was the home place of John M. Milless taken in about 1930. Bob Milless shared that the State of Minnesota contacted his family regarding plans to build a freeway through their land. The Millesses were offered $1 for about 65 acres of land. They were not happy with this offer and battled in court for a couple of years. Ultimately the state paid $20,000 for the entire piece of land that divided their property. In 1971, Texaco bought land for a gas station, which is now the Sinclair gas station. To offer perspective, the barn used to sit where the gas station is currently located, and the house would have been positioned within the cluster of trees on the current image. The freeway came through in about 1973. (Above, courtesy of Bob Milless; below, courtesy of Rob Bell.)

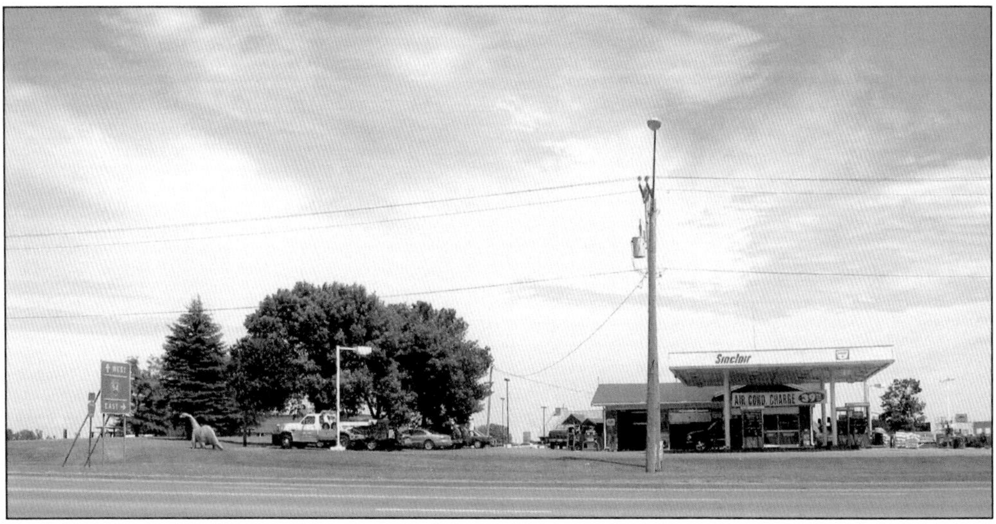

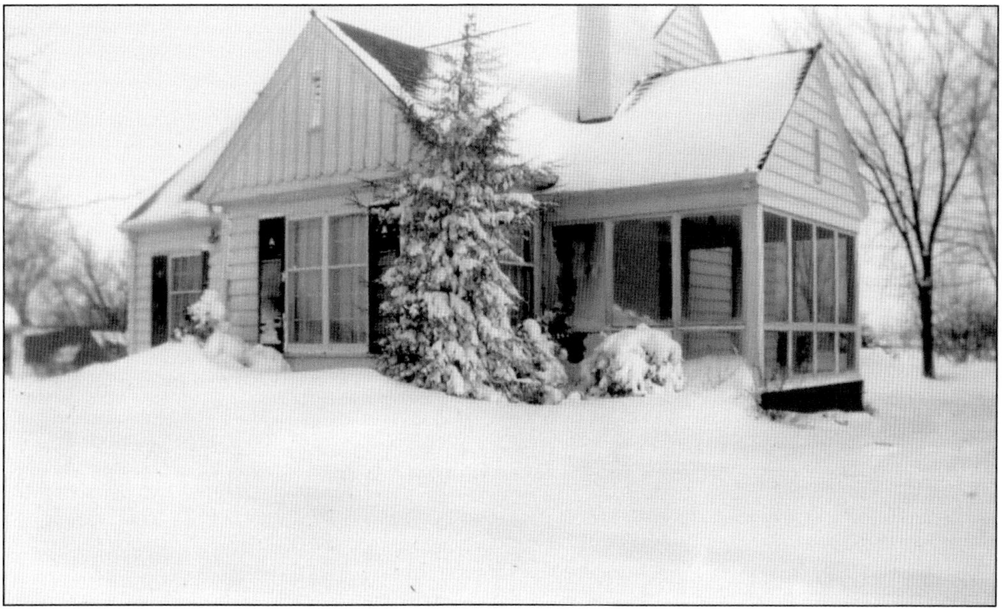

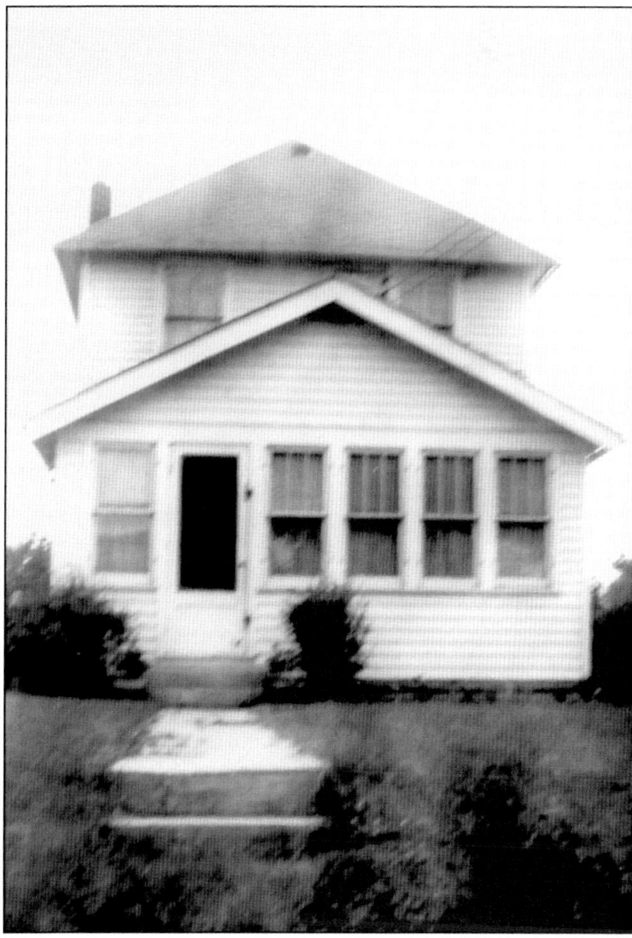

Both of these homes still exist on what was known as Church Street, but renamed Church Avenue in 2005. Gordon Rouillard shared that he was born on a Sunday in the first home. His mother was so embarrassed because everyone walked by on their way to church, and they knew what was happening. Rouillard also learned he was going to be named David; however, standing up to be baptized before them was Izzy Zahler, his wife, and their son, David "Buck" Zahler. Rouillard's mom said they needed to choose a different name, and Rouillard's dad did not want a junior. Rouillard never knew his name was not Gordon until he enlisted in the service; his real name is Joseph Gordon Rouillard. (Above, courtesy of Gordon Rouillard; below, courtesy of Danny and Janet Durant.)

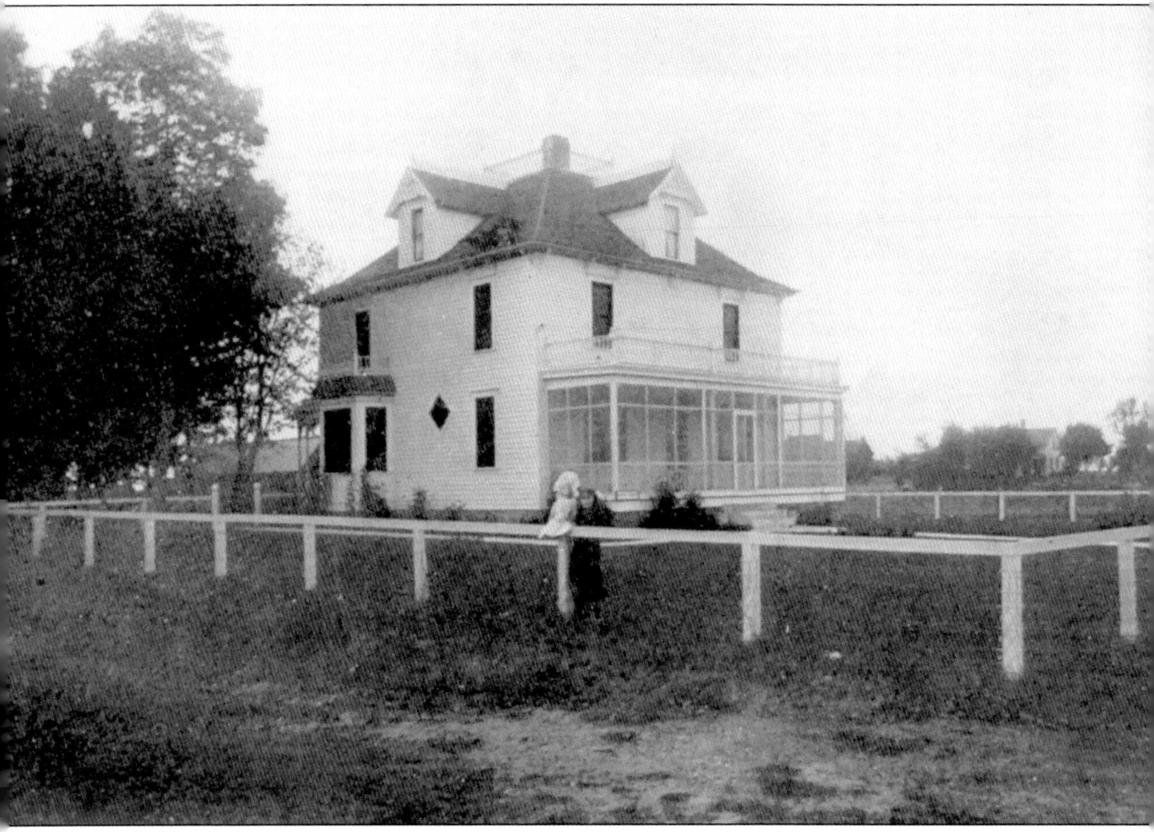

This home was the residence of prominent businessman Mike Borck. Donald "Dude" Milless and Rosemary (Rouillard) Milless currently reside in the home. According to Carmen (Rouillard) Hawkins, Rosemary's sister, the woodwork in this home is beautiful. (Courtesy of Jack and Carol Hines.)

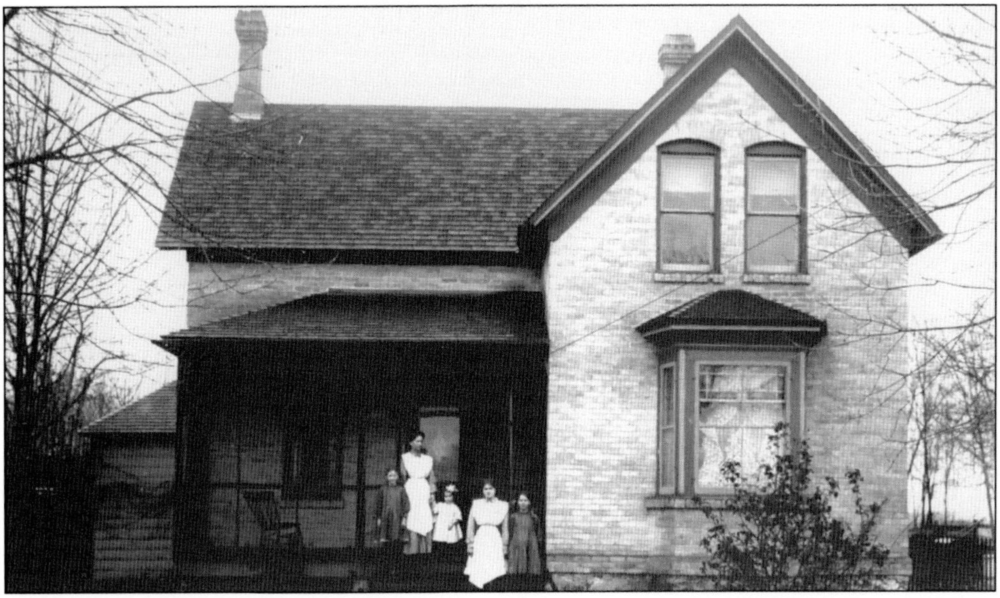

Originally the home of the John McNeil family, this beautiful brick-veneer home is now owned by Eugene Ahlstrom. Ahlstrom, grandson of Mike Borck, has lived in Rogers all his life. The original barn is still in the backyard, and he still has a large garden every summer. In the fall, Ahlstrom welcomes people to stop buy to purchase his apples, and if one is lucky, he will share stories about his childhood. Just down Main Street from Ahlstrom's home is the old Doug Scharber home. This home was located on the north side of the tracks, but due to business expansion, rather than destroy the home it was moved to a quieter side of town. It currently resides near the Rogers Elementary School. (Above, courtesy of Danny, Janet, and Noreen Durant; below, courtesy of Jack and Carol Hines.)

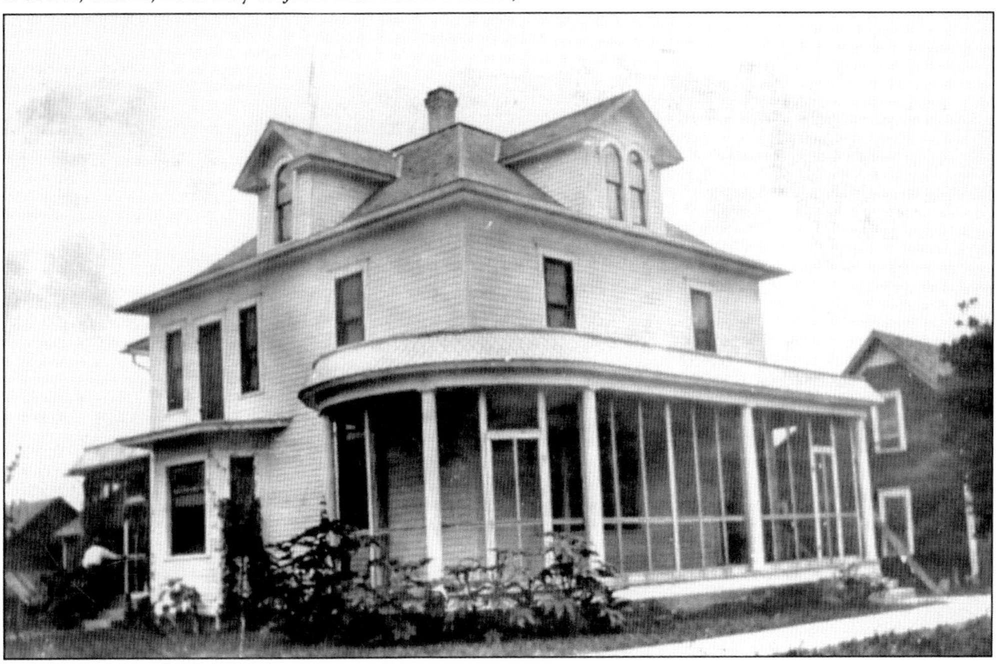

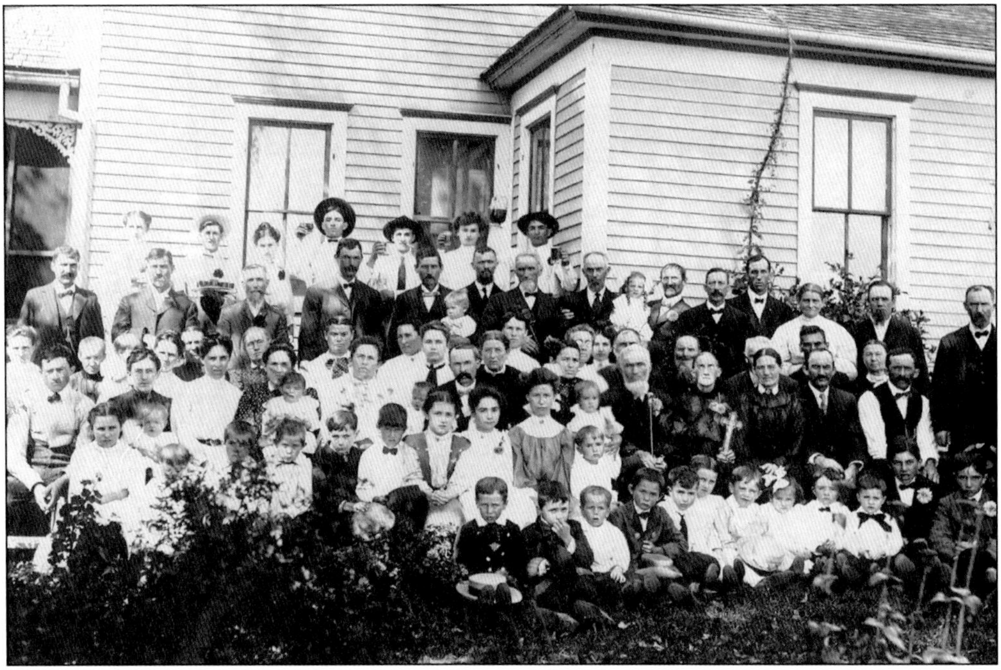

Both pictures are taken at the same farm place. The first was taken in 1904 during a golden wedding celebration for George and Mary Scharber. The second is of Willie Dahlheimer by the house, Ed and Phillip Dahlheimer in the buggy, John Dahlheimer and Mary (Scharber) Dahlheimer seated, and other family posing on the lawn. For a wedding gift, grandpa George Scharber gave John and Mary Dahlheimer 80 acres of farmland. They lived on the land until Willie and Alice Dahlheimer bought it from them. Jack and Peggy Dahlheimer farmed the land from 1951 until 1976, when they began selling the land to a developer. The T. A. Truck Stop is now located here. (Above, courtesy of Leo Scharber; below, courtesy of Jack and Peggy Dahlheimer.)

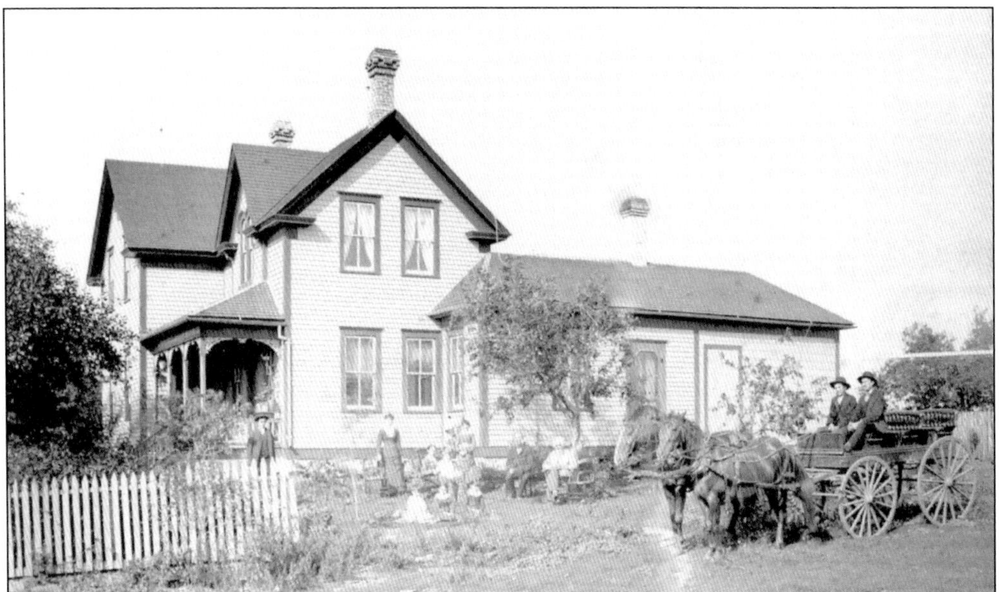

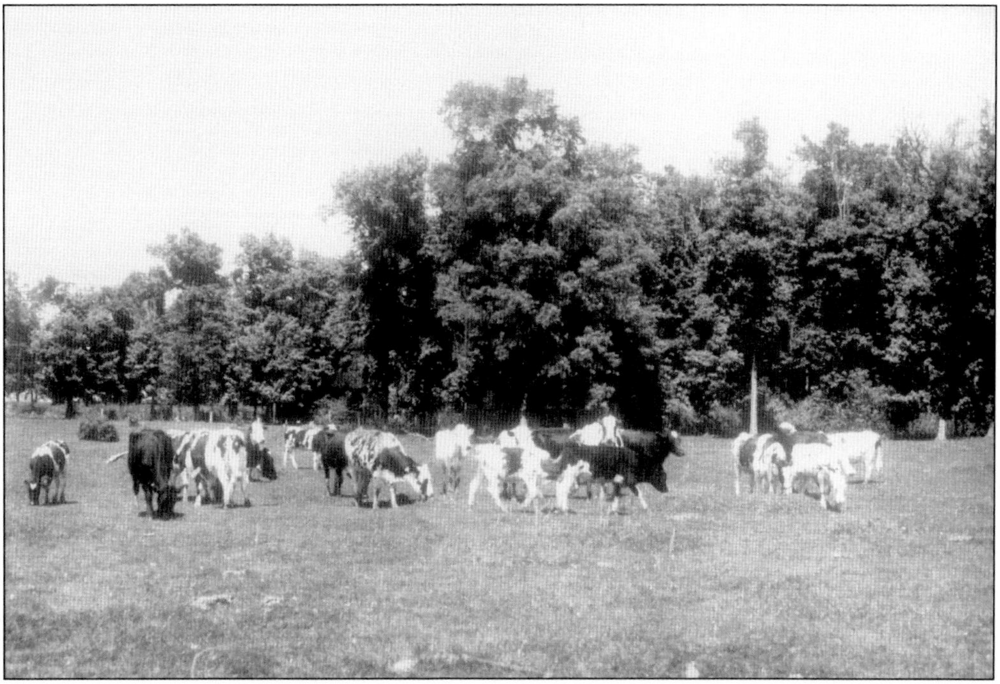

John M. Milless took this picture of his cows in the pasture not realizing in about 40 years the landscape would be changed forever. John passed away in 1964; his son, Bob Milless, shared that he believes his father would be utterly surprised at the development. Bob explained that a few of the trees are still standing behind Division Stamping, which is located on Commerce Boulevard. That was the first building constructed on that side of the freeway; however, at the time, it was a boating business. Bob shared that the businesses were there before the street was actually constructed. The city ran a storm sewer right through the woods; it was a disheartening day for Bob. The bottom photograph depicts the area today. (Above, courtesy of Bob Milless; below, courtesy of Rob Bell.)

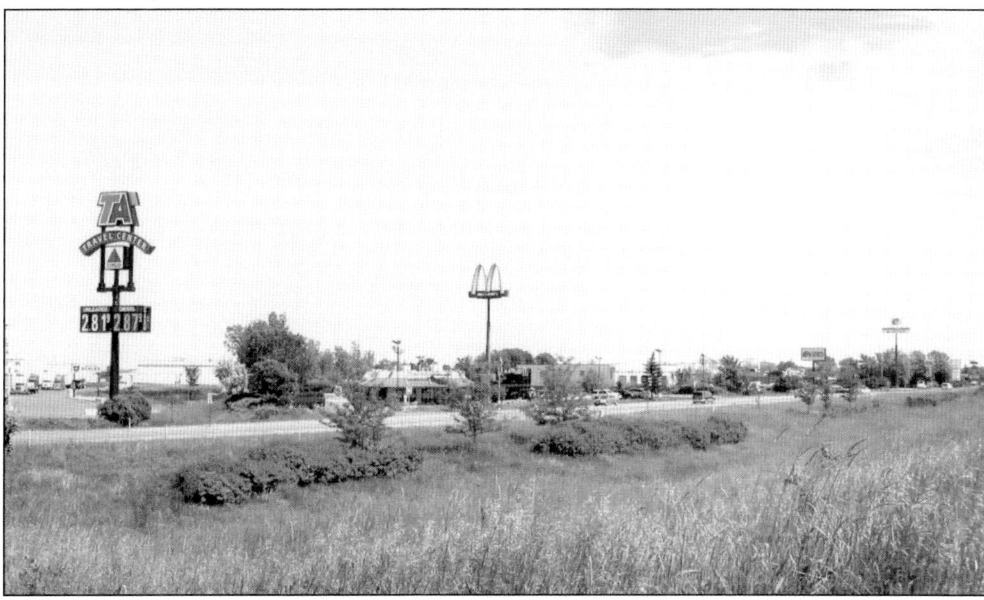

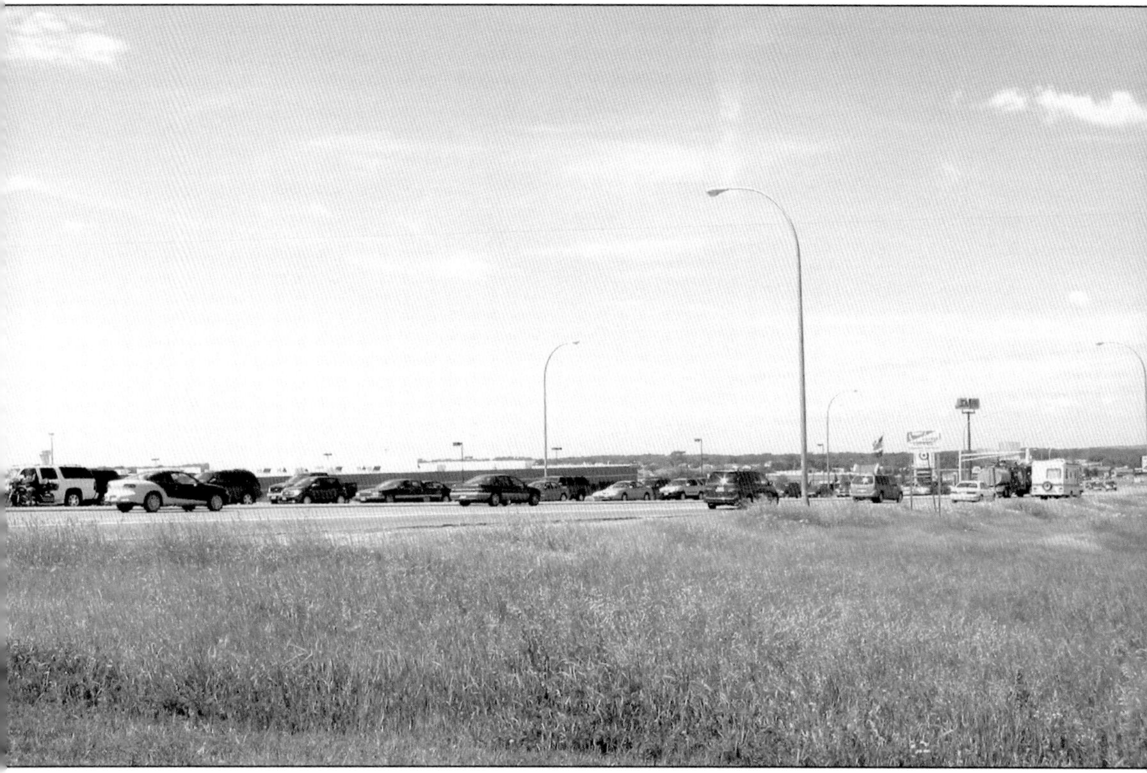

Growth in the area has caused increased traffic and crime. Dennis "Denny" Miltz moved to Rogers in 1970 and started working for the Rogers Police Department in September 1971. He taught the youth of the community to respect him and he would respect them. Miltz gave an example exchange: One young man drove down Main Street holding a beer can out the window and drinking it. He parked and walked up to Miltz saying smart words and drinking his beer. Miltz took his beer and poured it in his pants pocket, and then all of his friends laughed. The young man was always respectful after that moment. Miltz is very proud of the fact that he hired Terri Hanson, the police department's administrative assistant. He had several part-time officers on the force: Milt Miller, Tim Prill, Mike Miller, Joe Zerwas, and Keith Oldfather, to name a few. Ryan Franzen was the first full-time officer. The community began receiving 24-hour coverage in 2001 and began filing its own reports in 2005. The department continues to grow as community needs change. (Courtesy of Rob Bell.)

Nine

FAMILY TIES

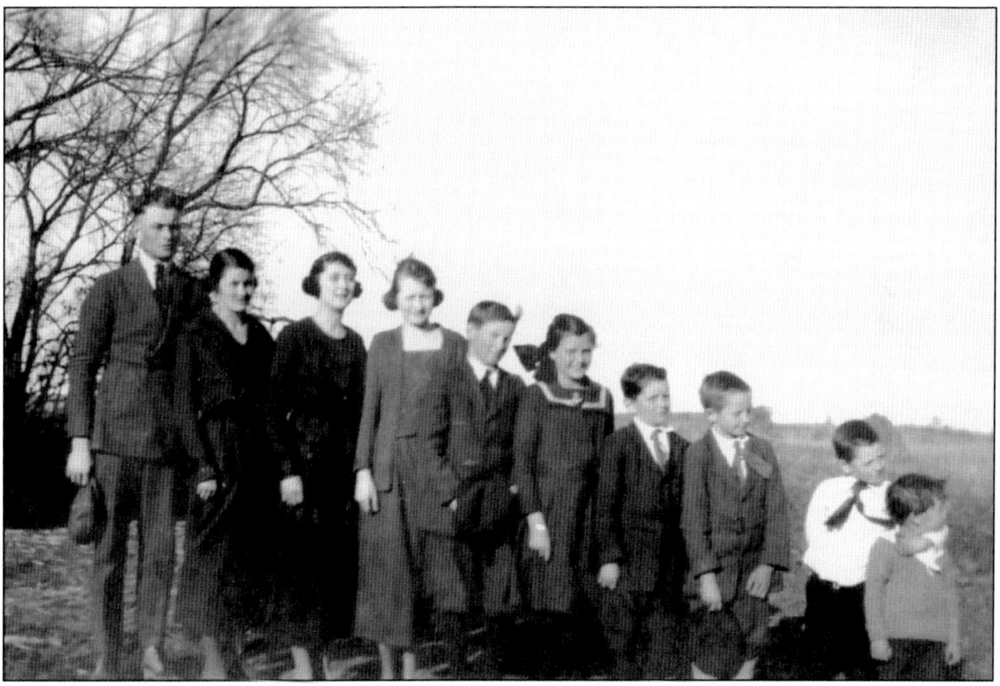

The Rogers family originally helped settle the area. Pictured here from left to right are Walter, Myrtle (Rouillard), Irene, Pearl (Rouillard), Earl, Nell, Robert, Gilbert, Roy, and Wilber Rogers. Alvin is not pictured; he was born in 1921. Jim Rogers likes to share this historical brainteaser: The Rogers came to the area in 1855. There were nine children that came from Ireland. William, born in 1866, was Thomas's youngest son of 11. Walter was William's oldest son. Jim is Walter's youngest son. (Courtesy of Gordon Rouillard.)

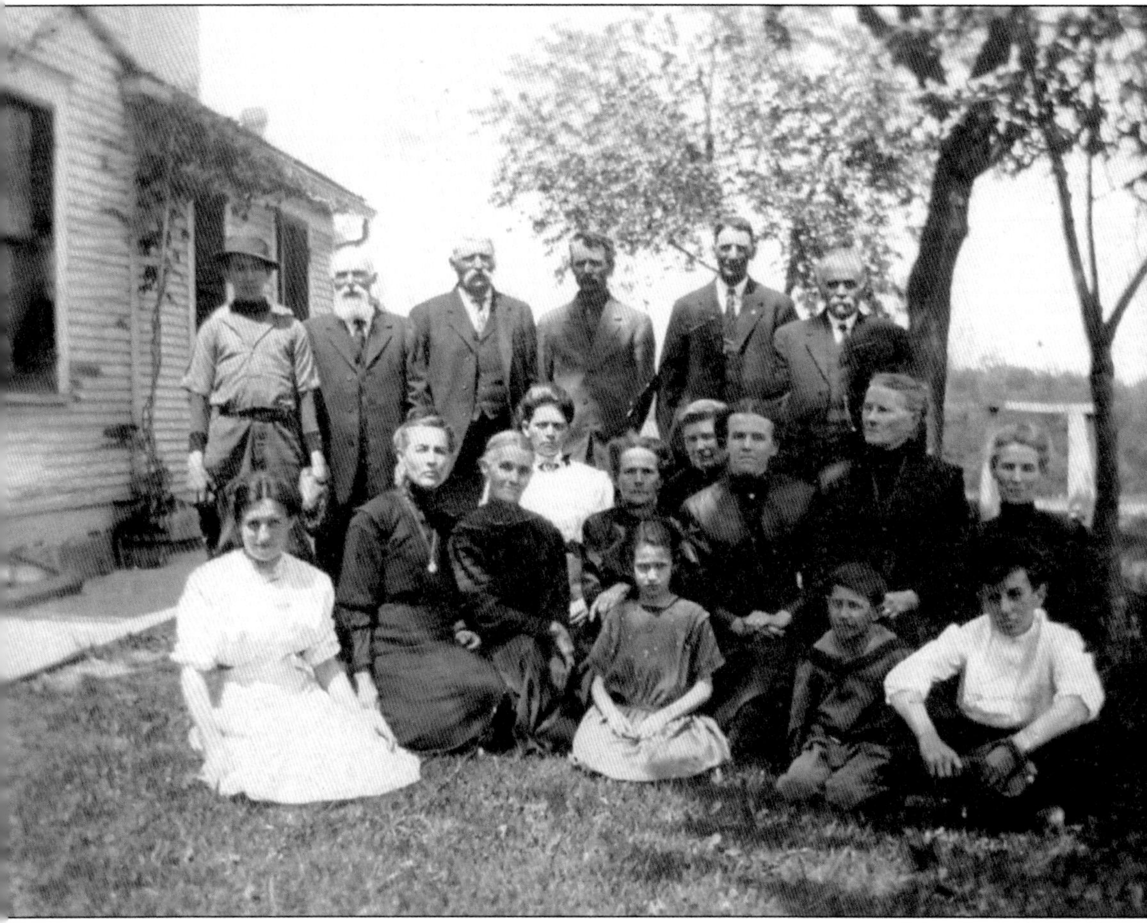

This Rouillard family reunion picture was taken in 1916 on the family farm. The Hassan Elementary School was built on this land. The Rouillard family women married into the Scharber, Gmach, Dahlheimer, and other families in the community. (Courtesy of Melvin Rouillard.)

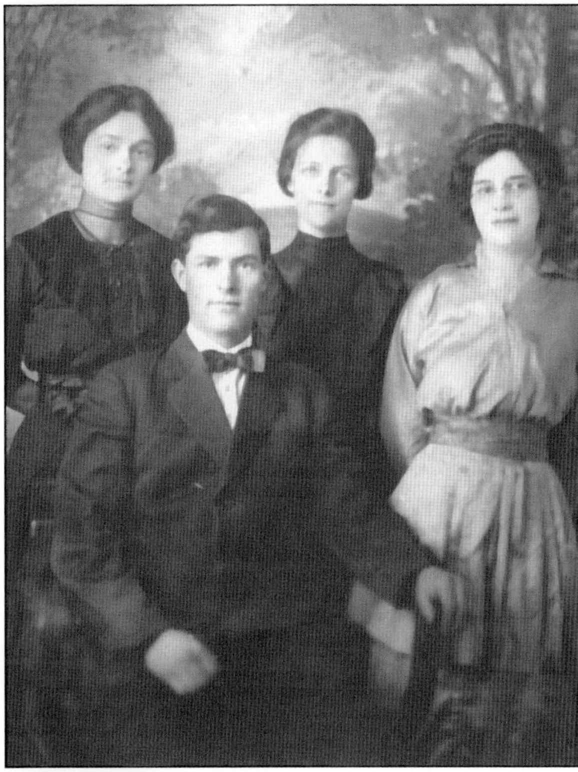

Pictured from left to right are Hazel, Henry, Dena, and Ida Rouillard. Hazel later married Otto Scharber. The other picture is of Ethel (Malone) Rouillard and Henry Rouillard, parents to Melvin, Rowland, and Merle Rouillard. (Courtesy of Melvin Rouillard.)

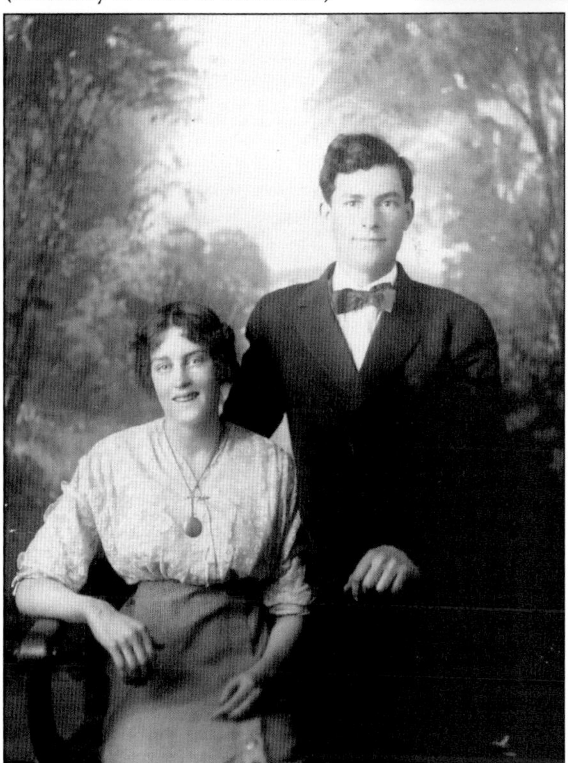

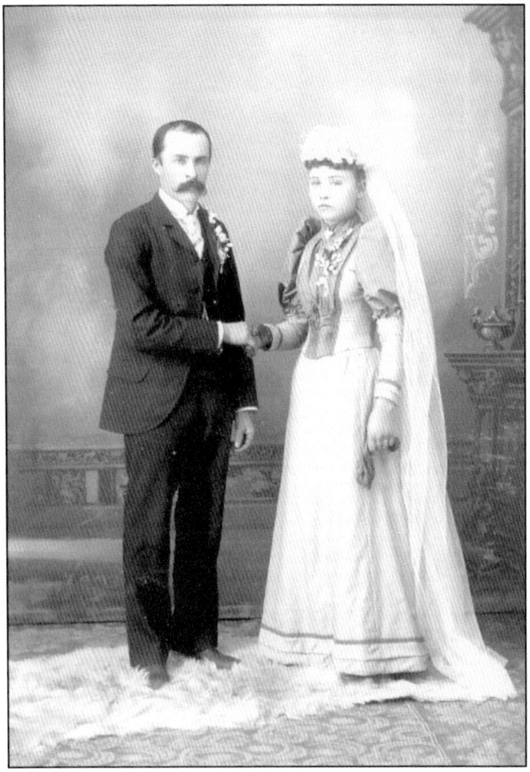

John Scherber was married to Rose Klersey, and they were the parents of Otto, Lawrence, Elmer, and Meletta. George Scherber married Lena Klersey. Their children were Matilda, Emil, Adeline, Grace, and Walter. John and George's father was George Scherber. (Courtesy of Norb Zahler.)

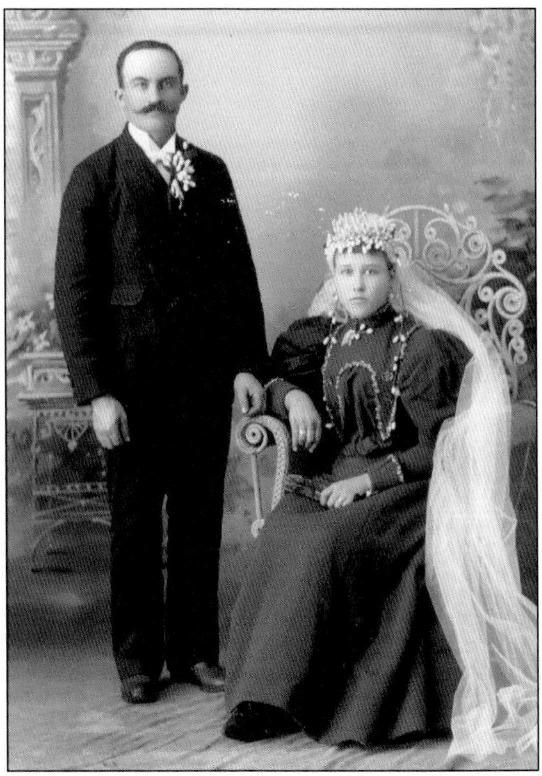

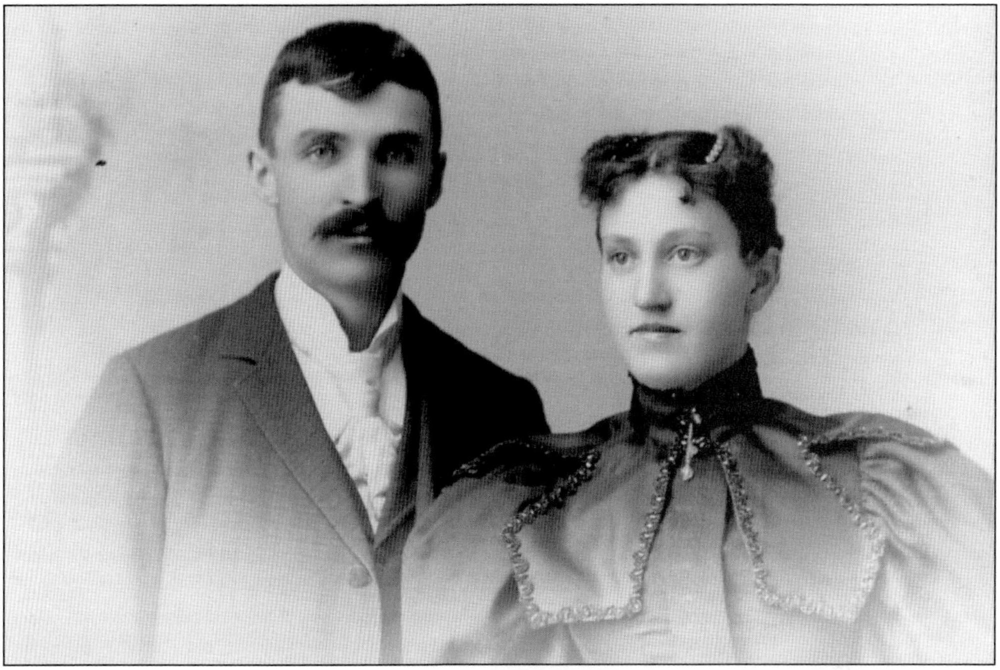

Henry Scherber, son of David Scherber, married Nellie Rech, and they were the parents of Colletta. Peter Scherber was also David's son and married Josephine Hoeben. They were the parents of Gertrude, Clara, Clarence, and Robert. (Courtesy of Norb Zahler.)

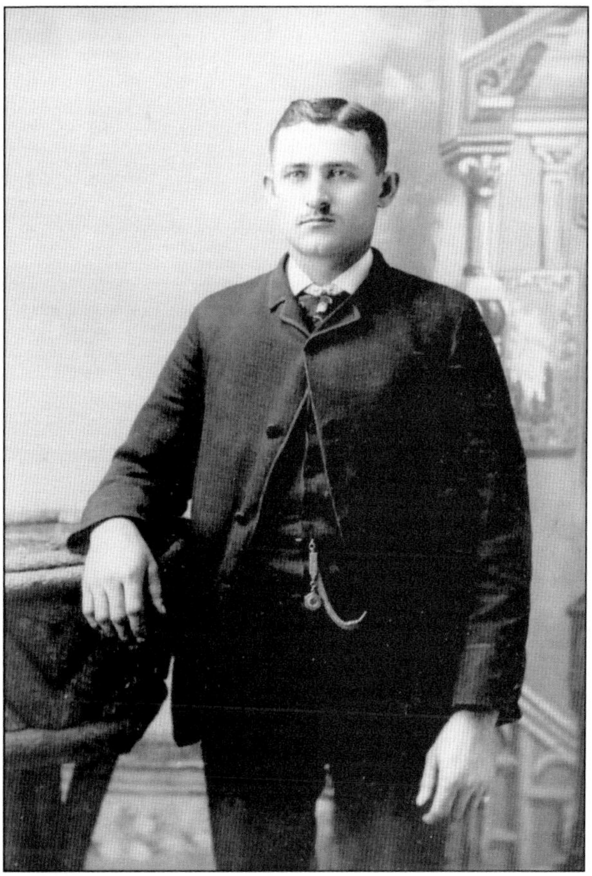

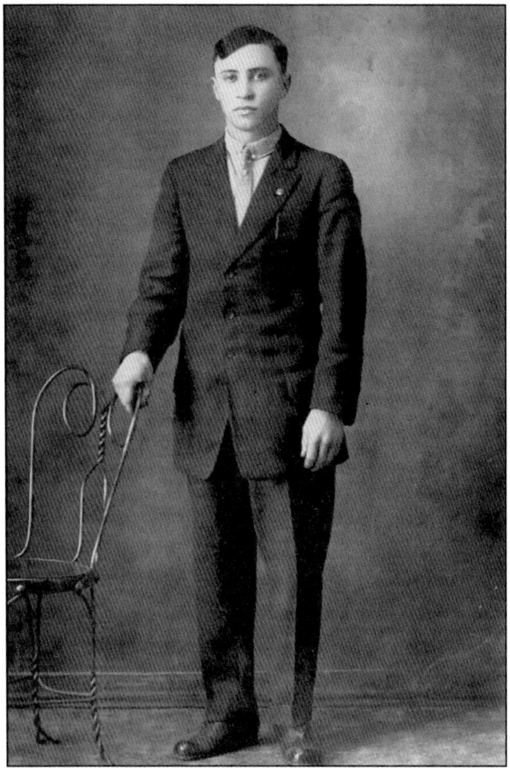

This portrait was taken of prominent businessman Otto Scharber, who later married Hazel Rouillard. Also photographed was Susan Scharber, daughter of George Scherber. She married Henry Miller, and they had one daughter, Lorena. Leo Scharber shared that although people may see the last names are spelled differently, the Scharbers and Scherbers are related. He explained that George Scherber had four sons who all had the same last name, but as their families grew, so did the number of homes with the same last name; this caused confusion for the postmaster. After a generation, the last names became Scharber, Scherber, or Scharver. A family member did research and learned that even brothers' last names were not spelled the same. (Courtesy of Norb Zahler.)

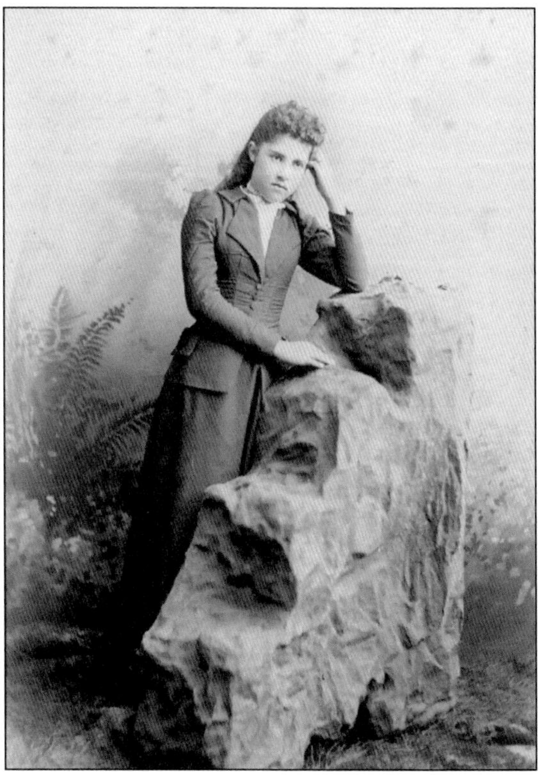

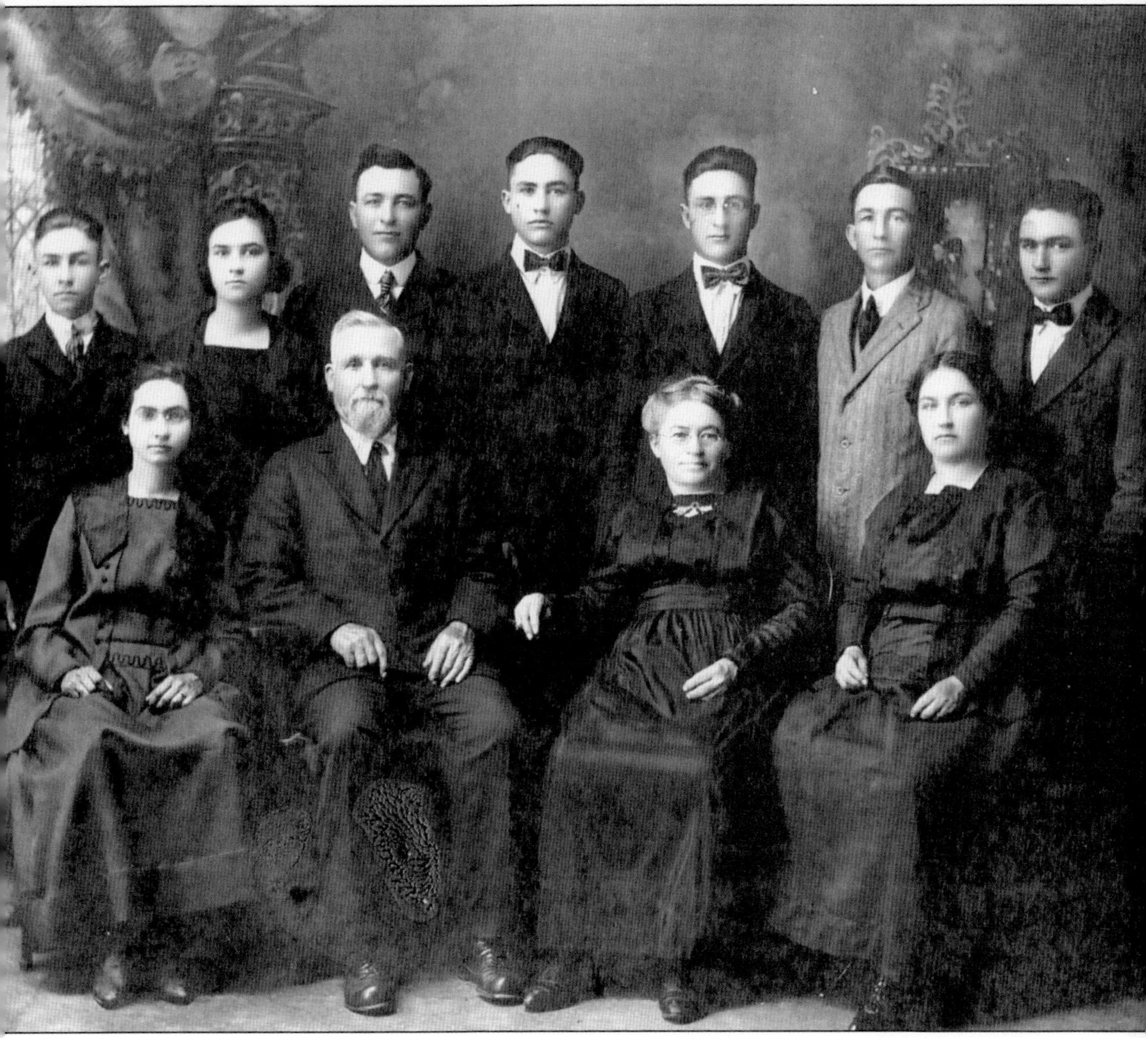

Valentine Dahlheimer was one of two brothers who homesteaded in the area from Ohio; John Dahlheimer is one of his sons. This is the John Dahlheimer family pictured, from left to right, as follow: (first row) Catherine, John, Mary, and Elizabeth; (second row) Ira, Petranilla, Philipp, Edmund, Matthew, William, and Rufus. The Dahlheimer women married men from the Scharber, Rouillard, Berg, and other families in the community. (Courtesy of Jack and Peggy Dahlheimer.)

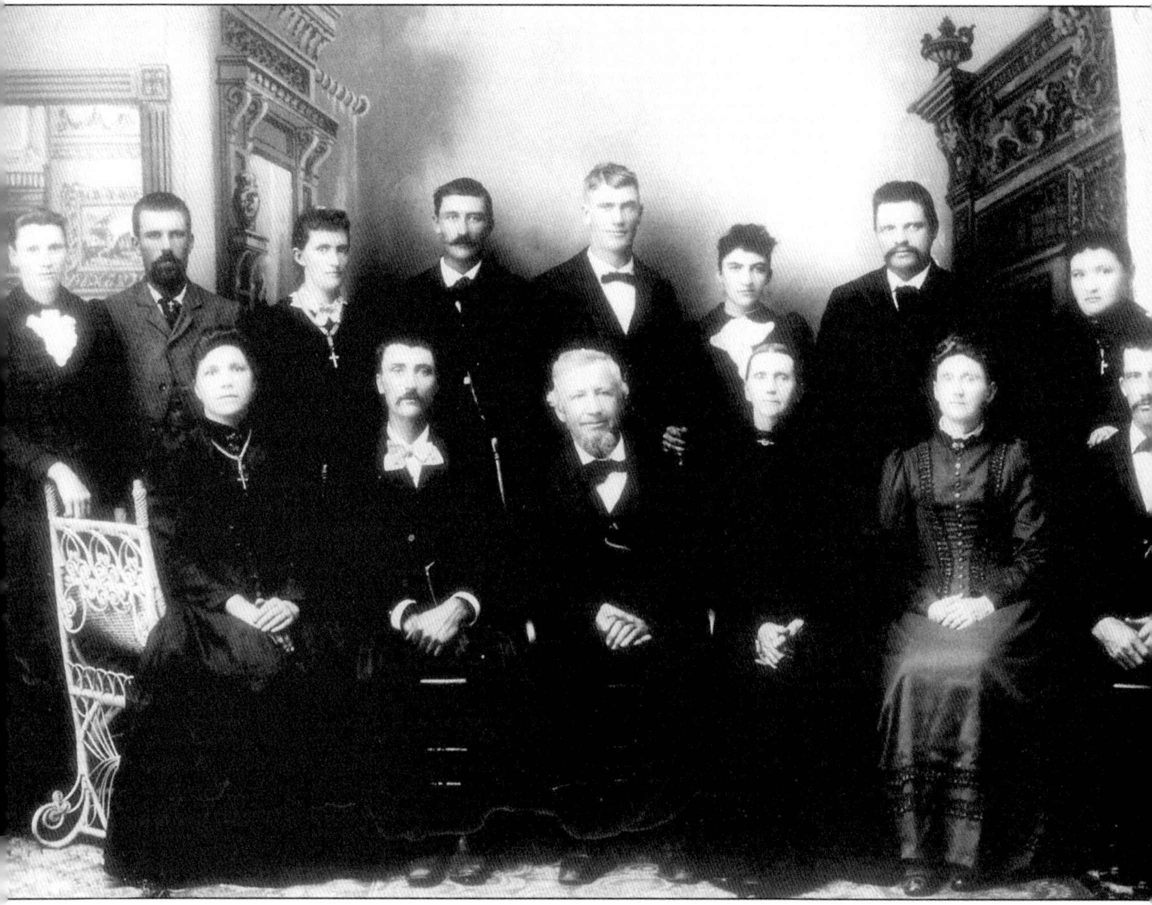

This Henry Dahlheimer family portrait was taken in 1907. Pictured from left to right are (first row) Mary (Lehn) Dahlheimer with her husband, Joseph Dahlheimer; Henry Dahlheimer and his wife, Maria; Elizabeth (Dahlheimer) Stenglein; and George Dahlheimer; (second row) Rose (Dahlheimer) Dehn and her husband, Andrew Dehn; Annie (Dahlheimer) Weber and her husband, John E. Weber; Frank Dahlheimer and his second wife, Sarah (Duffner) Dahlheimer; John Stenglein (husband of Elizabeth Dahlheimer); and Geraldine (Wahl) Dahlheimer, wife of George Dahlheimer. (Courtesy of Jane [Dahlheimer] Heinrich.)

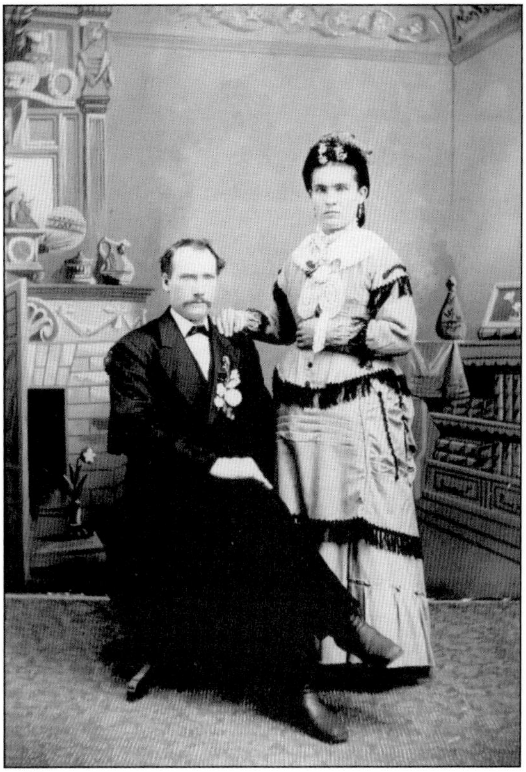

Pictured here in the top image are John Dahlheimer and Walburga (Temple) Dahlheimer. Pictured below are Andrew Dehn with his wife, Rose (Dahlheimer) Dehn, and children, from left to right, Rose, John, Henry, and Tillie (standing in back). (Courtesy of Norb Zahler.)

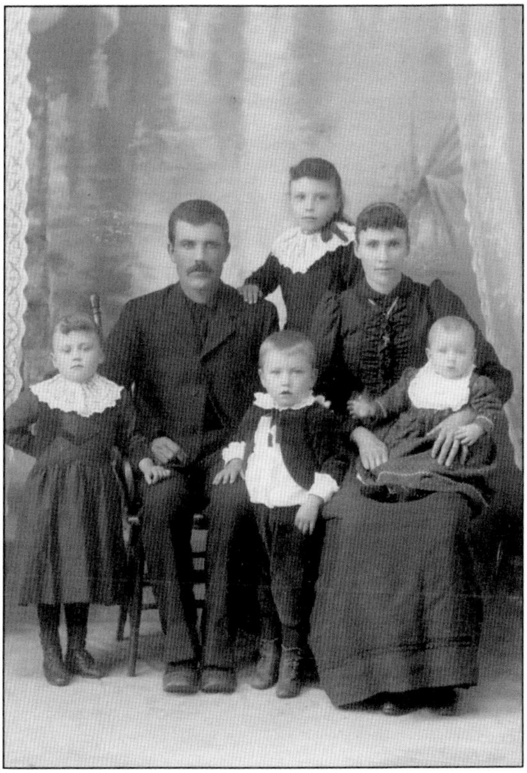

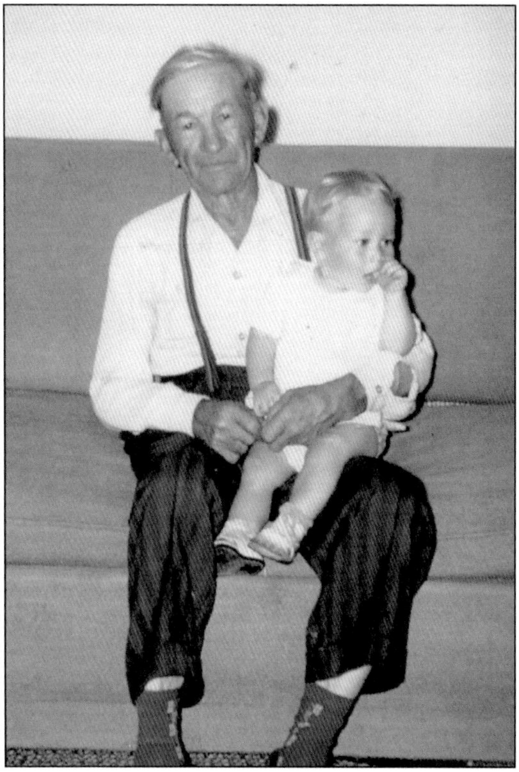

Willie Dahlheimer, pictured here with his great grandson Chuck, and Alice Dahlheimer, pictured below, were very active in the community. According to their son, Jack Dahlheimer, Willie was instrumental in helping form the village of Rogers, along with Otto Scharber and Mike Borck. Leadership continued in the family as Jack's wife, Peggy, helped start the Rogers Chamber of Commerce in 1986 at their kitchen table. She was the executive chair/president for three years. Kathleen Poate took over the position and continues to hold the role of president today. The organization is now known as the I-94 West Chamber and services seven cities. (Courtesy of Jack and Peggy Dahlheimer.)

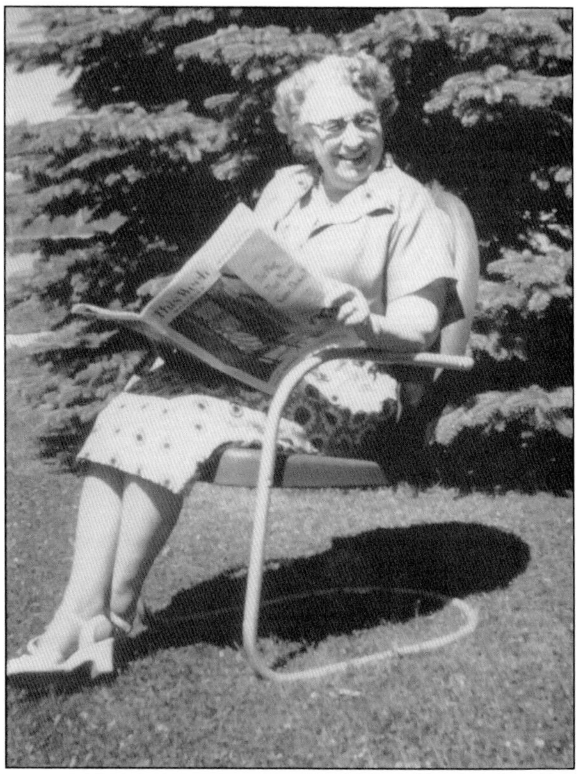

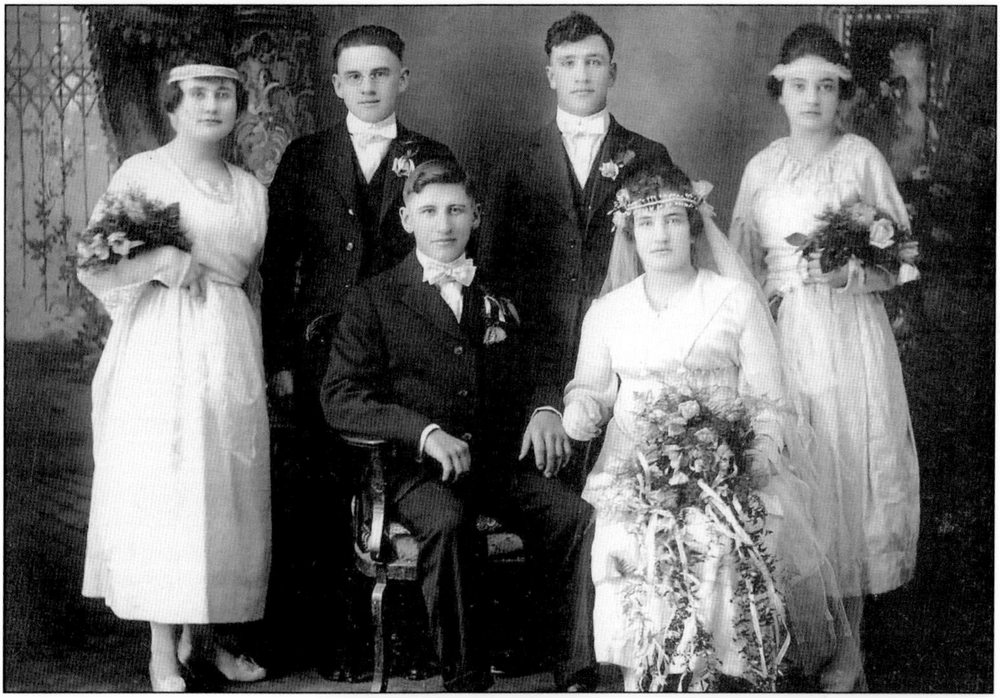

Werner and Emily Dahlheimer pose on their wedding day, and a few years later, the sons of Werner and Emily pose for the camera. From left to right, they are George, Howard, and Harvey. (Courtesy of Jane [Dahlheimer] Heinrich.)

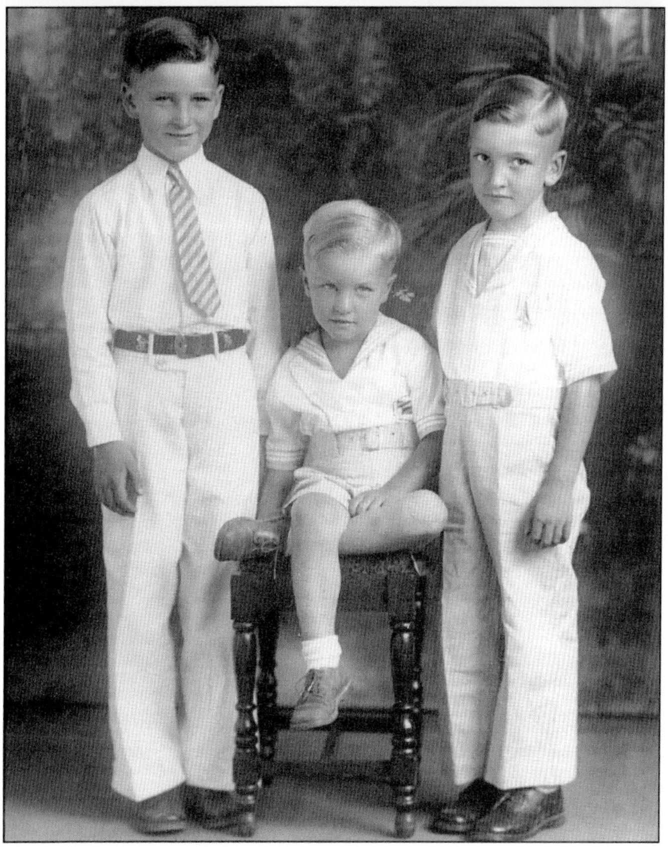

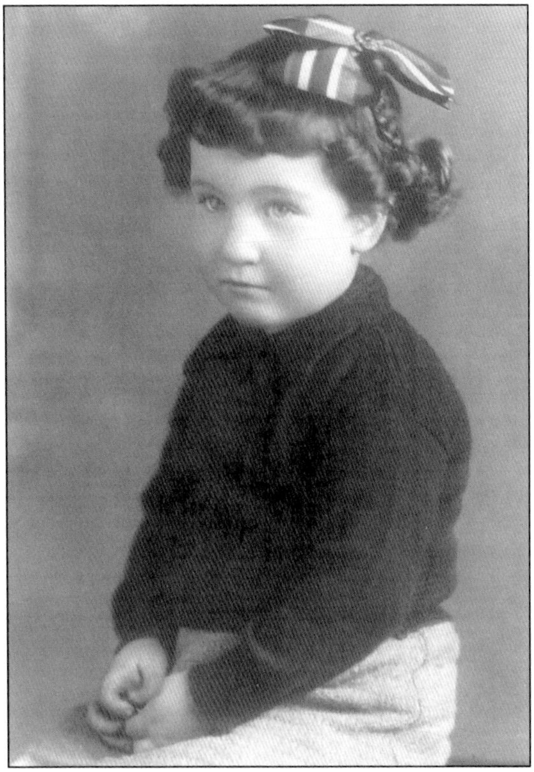

Marlene (Dahlheimer) Reinking, daughter of Werner and Emily Dahlheimer, is sitting pretty for a portrait. Pictured below is Lillian (Dahlheimer) Hughes (left) and Lucille (Dahlheimer) Gmach, two more of Werner and Emily's daughters, ready to capture the moment. (Courtesy of Jane [Dahlheimer] Heinrich.)

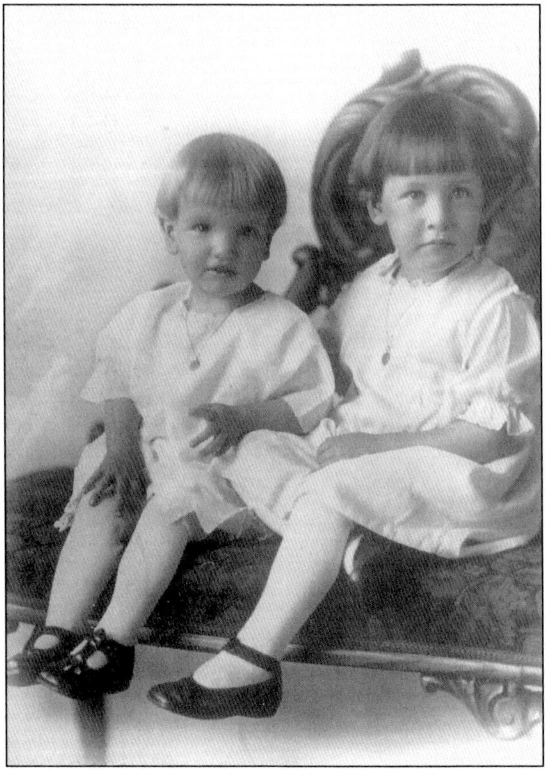

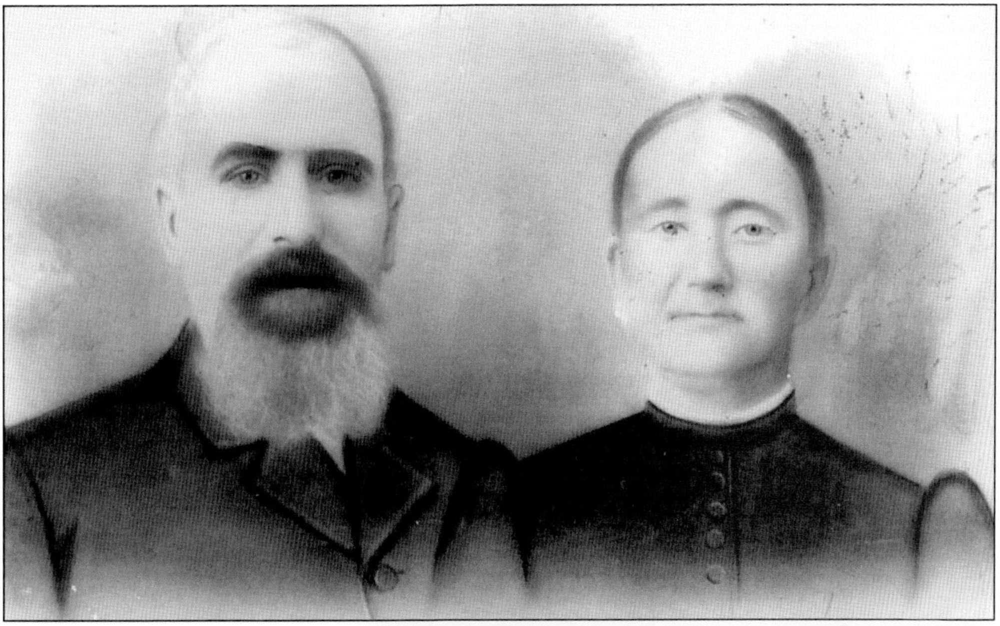

Elizabetha (Dahlheimer) Dehn, daughter of Caspar Dahlheimer, is pictured with her husband, Valentine Dehn. Also pictured is Tillie Dehn posing pretty on her first communion day. The Dehn family has farmed in the community since the beginning. (Above, courtesy of Jane [Dahlheimer] Heinrich; below, courtesy of Andrew Stueve.)

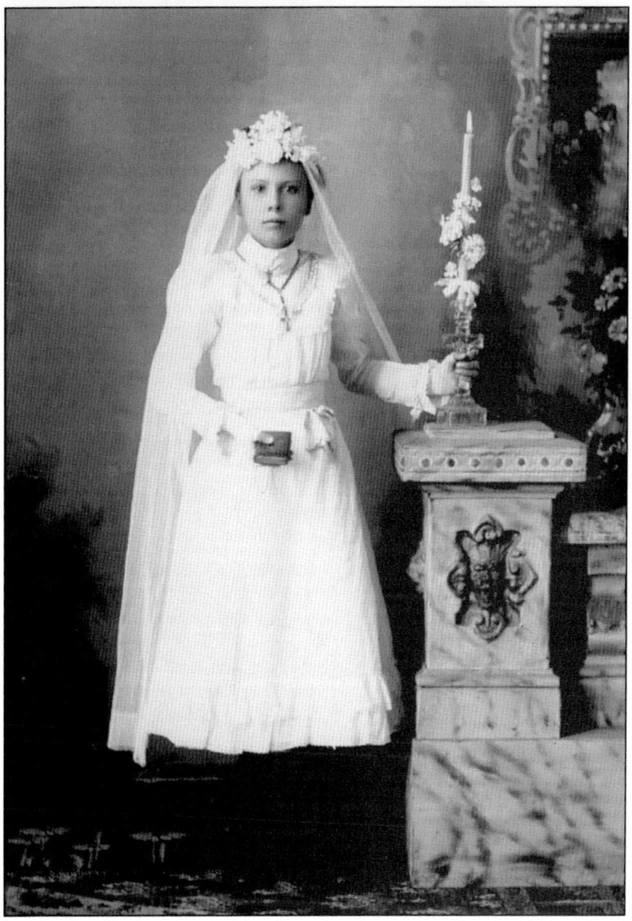

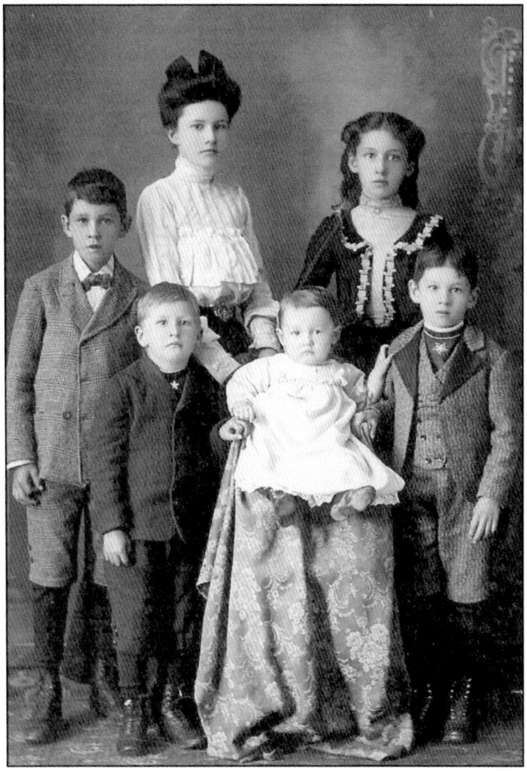

The children of George and Tina Dahlheimer included, from left to right, (first row) Werner, Walter, and Bernard; (second row) Leo, Emma, and Francis. The other picture includes the children of Joseph and Mary Dahlheimer: from left to right, (first row) Leonard and Monica; (second row) Elizabeth and Gertrude. (Courtesy of Jane [Dahlheimer] Heinrich.)

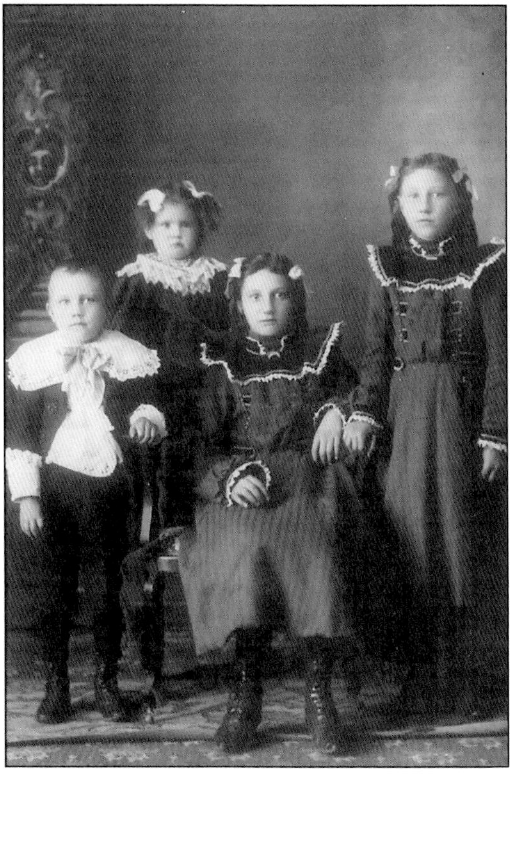

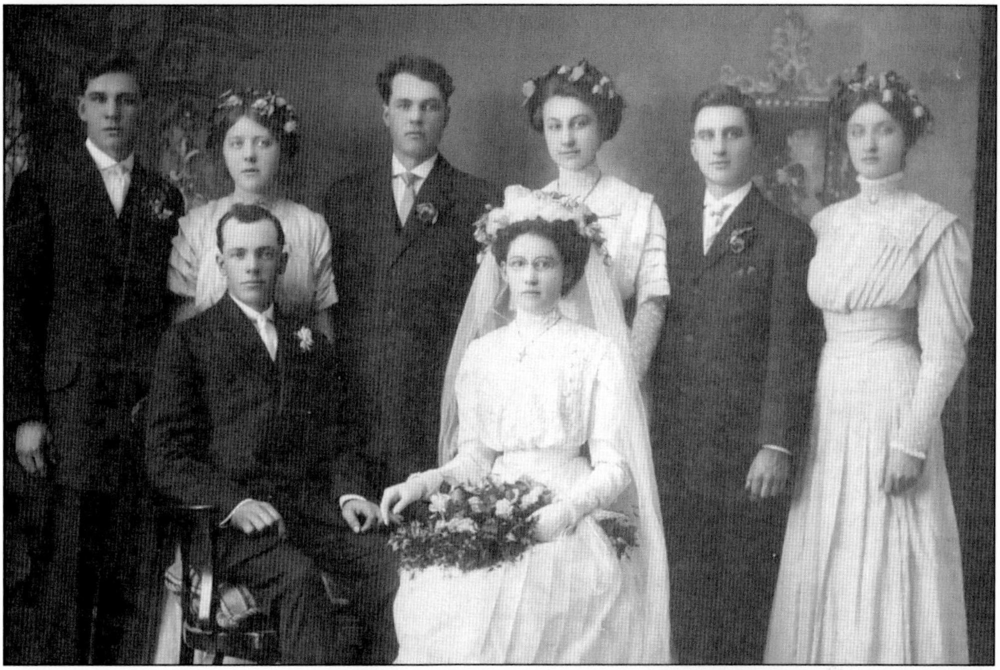

Pictured above is the marriage of Elmer Berg to Frances Dahlheimer, which took place on October 14, 1910. They were the paternal grandparents of Carol (Berg) Hines. Pictured below are Henry Scharber and Minnie Fournier on the day they exchanged wedding vows, November 22, 1904. (Courtesy of Jack and Carol Hines.)

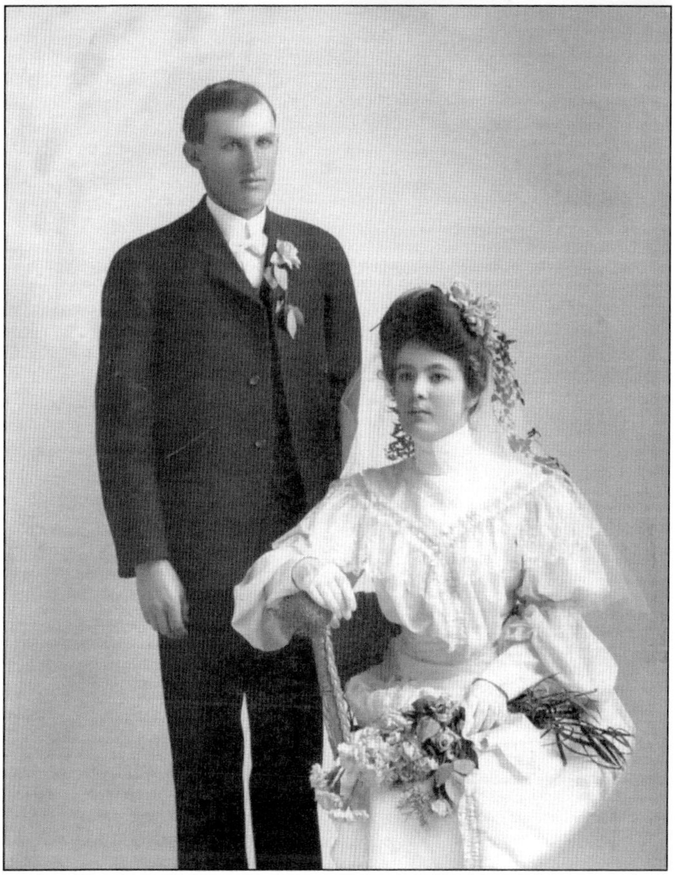

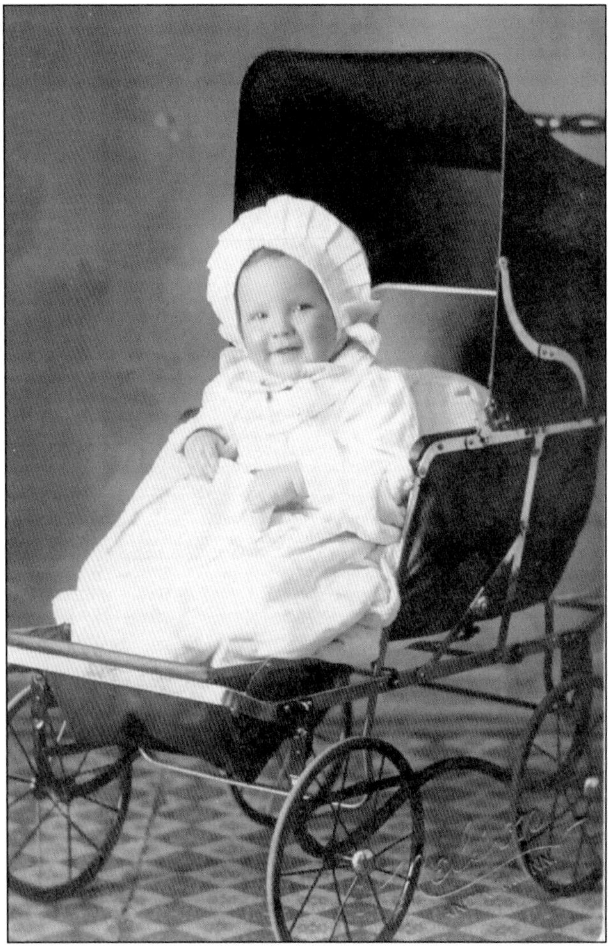

Carol (Berg) Hines's father was six months old in this picture taken on August 26, 1911. Also pictured is Cliff Berg with a sheep in 1928. Carol joked that she believed this was his best friend. (Courtesy of Jack and Carol Hines.)

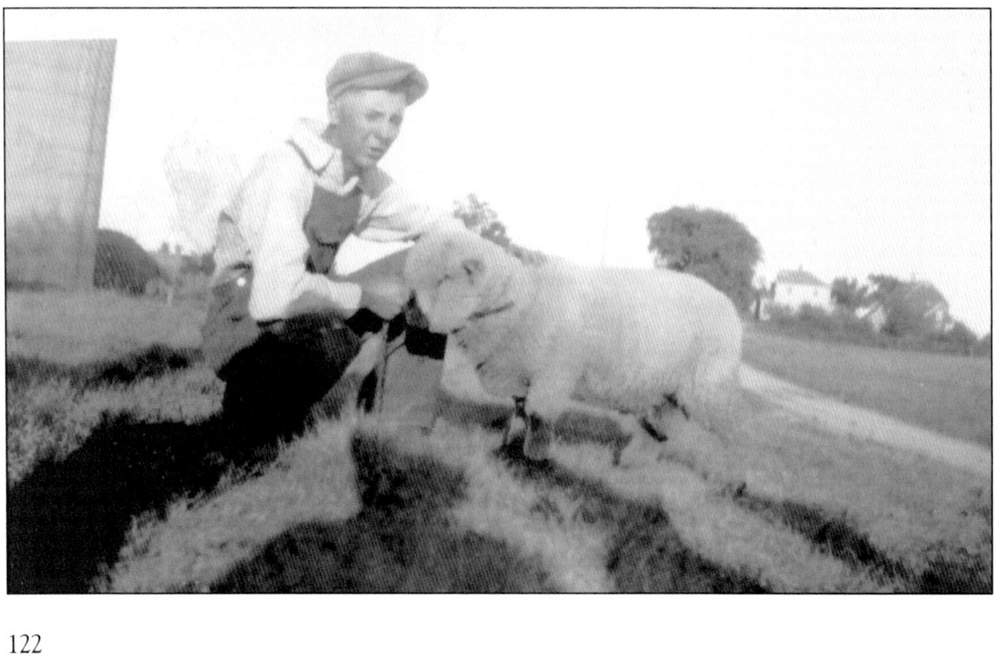

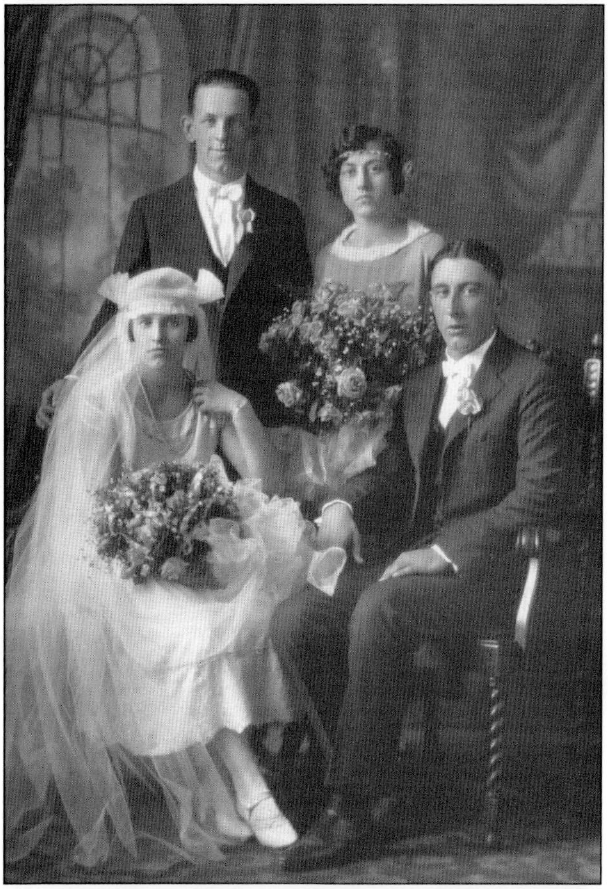

The wedding of Lillie Patnode to John Hines, Jack Hines's father, was held on October 22, 1923. Their attendants were Bob Lindsey and Zina (Patnode) Kreatz. The wedding between Jack Hines and Carol Berg, which was held in September 1962, is also captured here. Their parents are standing by their sides. (Courtesy of Jack and Carol Hines.)

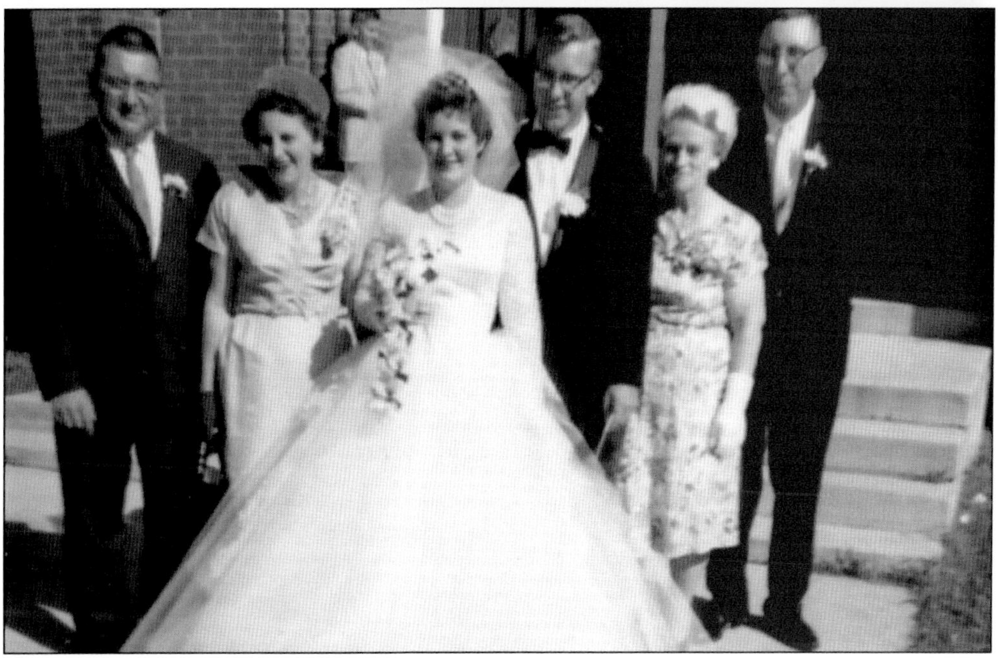

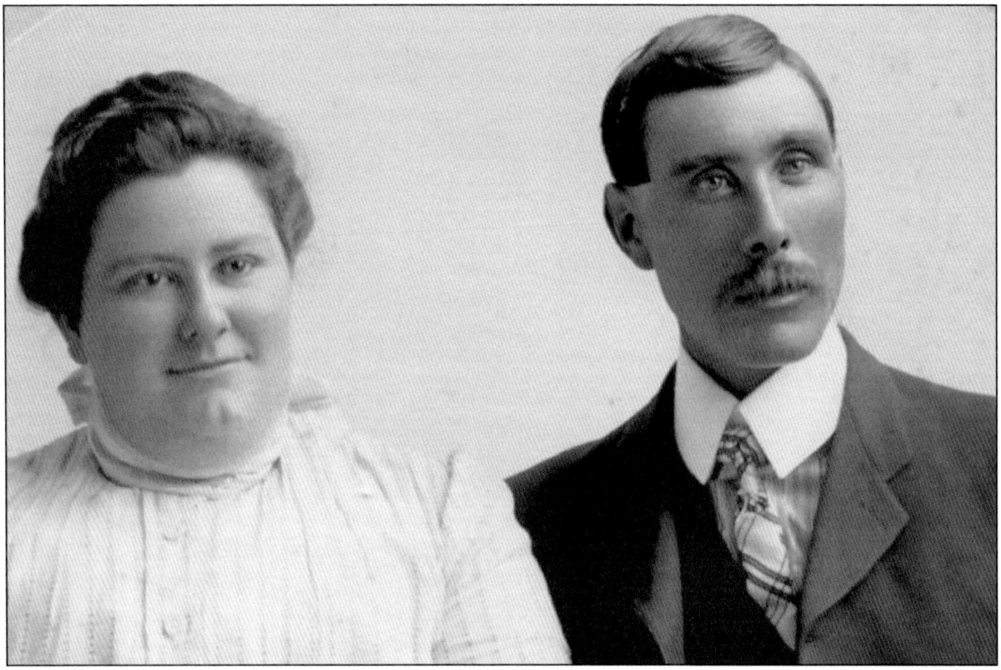

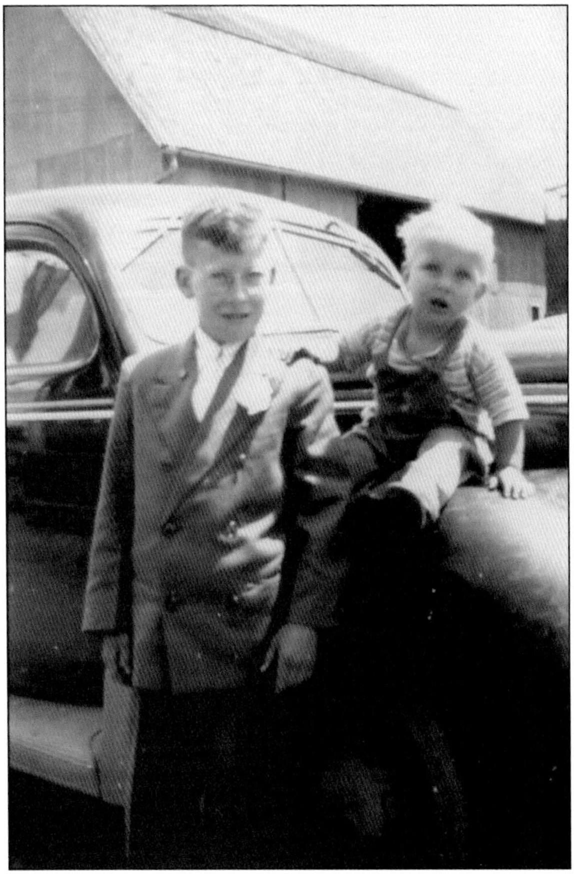

John and Ellen Hines were married in 1910. Jack Hines is not sure what brought his grandfather John to the area except that the family may be related to the original Hynes family. The picture below was taken in 1945 of Jack Hines, seated on his father's car, and his brother, Dennis, holding him steady. (Courtesy of Jack and Carol Hines.)

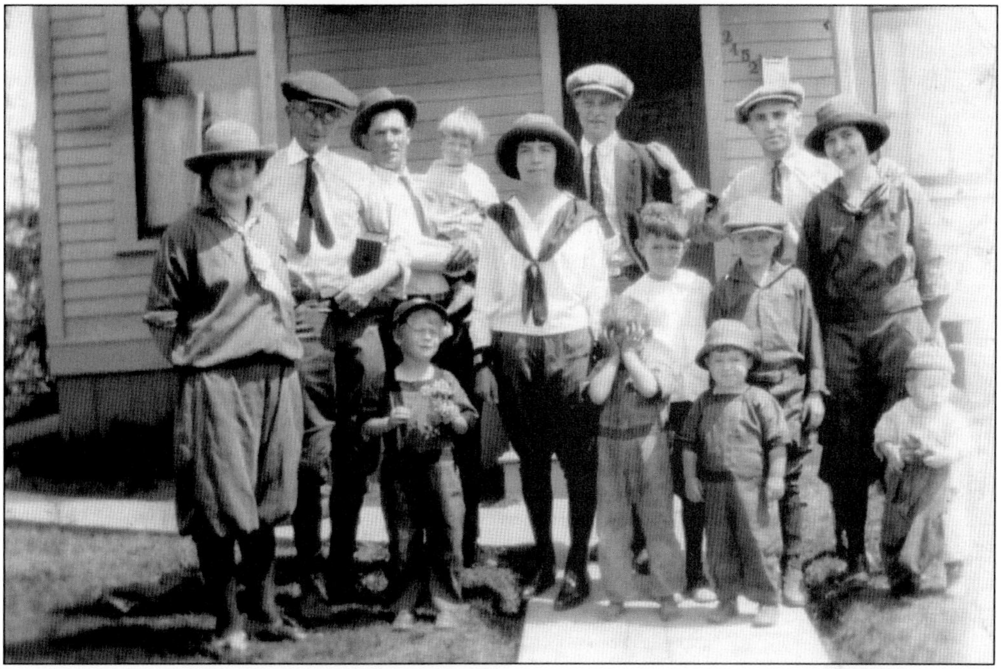

Pictured here are Joseph and Emma Stenglein, Henry Rouillard, Marvel Scharber, Eddie Rouillard, and Otto and Hazel Scharber and each of their children. Also pictured are Joseph Stenglein, Otto Scharber, Eddie Rouillard, and Henry Rouillard after a day of riding. They are all descendents of the original families who developed the area. (Courtesy of Melvin Rouillard.)

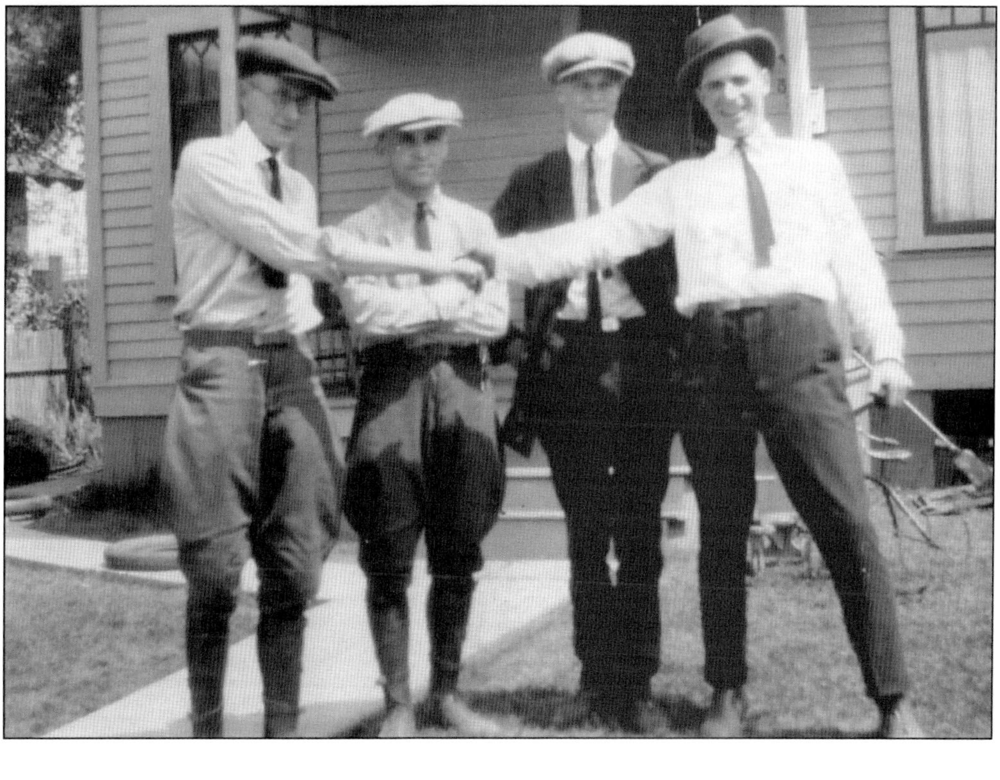

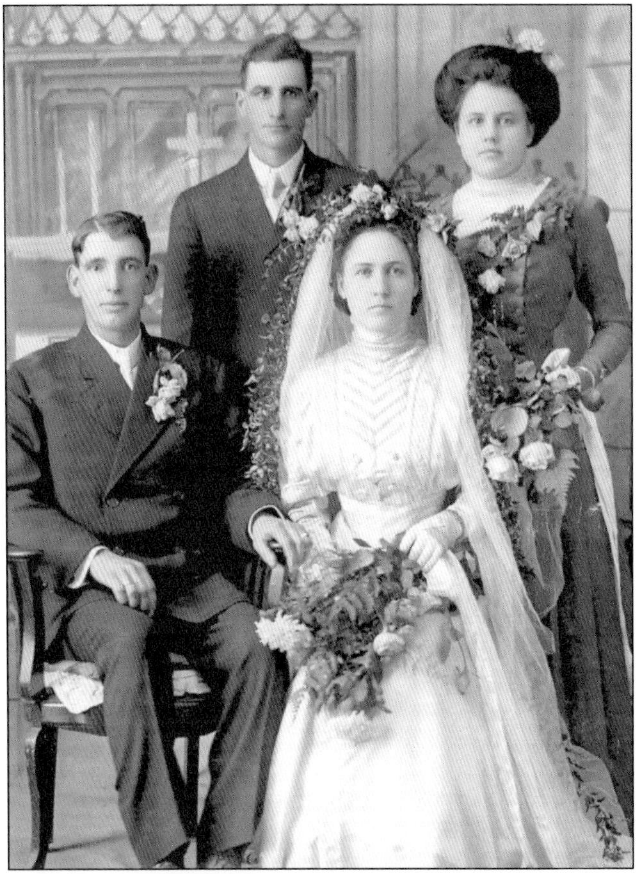

The John M. Milless family is a long-standing family in the community. There were 13 children in the family; most stayed in the community after graduating from school. The bottom image of the Goth family, which was taken in 1944, shows Rosa (Goth) Schlegel standing on the right. She was Lenny Schlegel's mother. (Above, courtesy of Bob Milless; below, courtesy of Lenny and Lila Schlegel.)

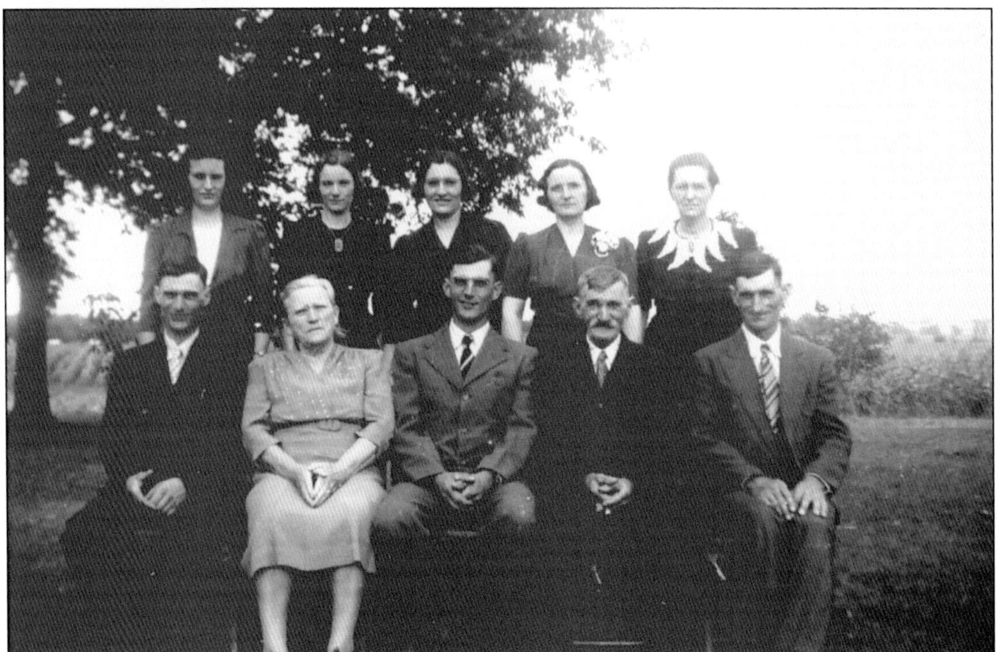

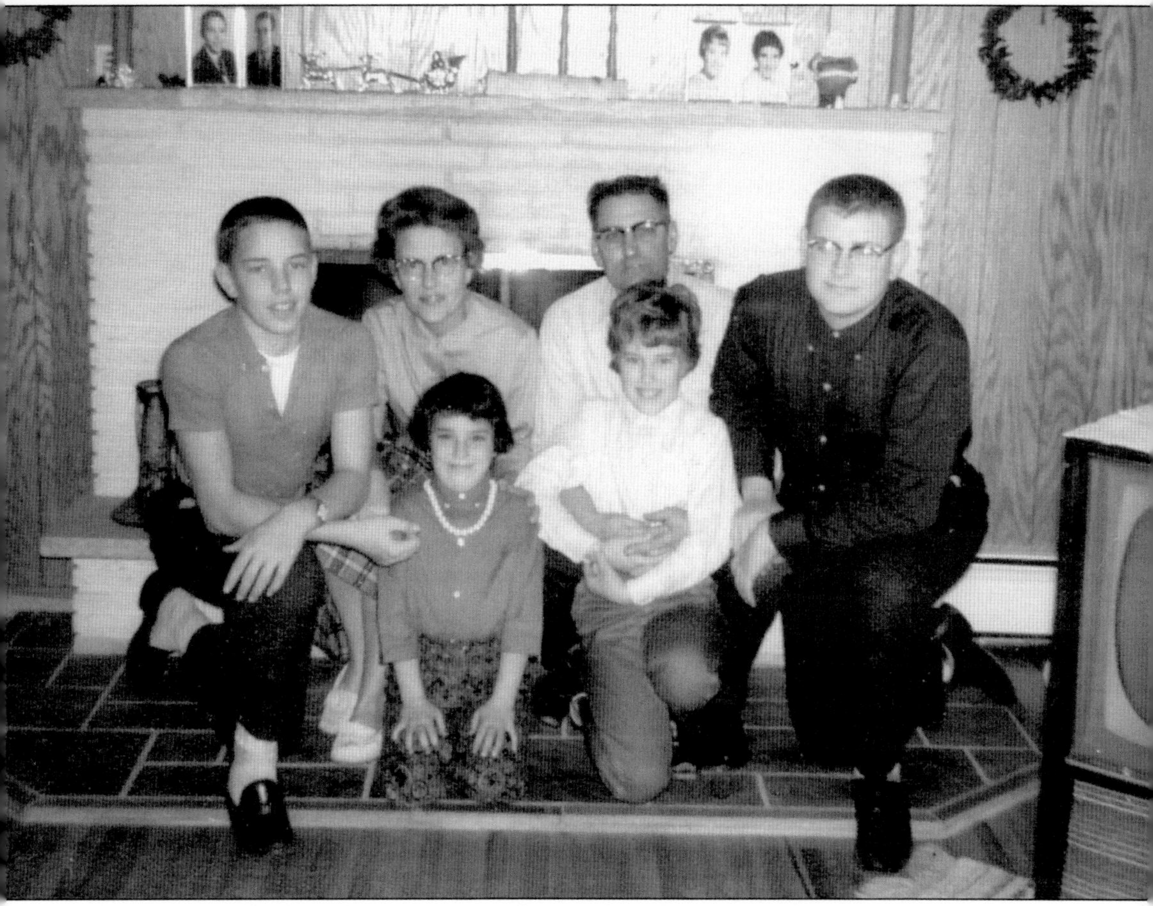

This Melvin Rouillard family picture was taken in the 1960s. Posing for the camera from left to right are Jim, Mary Katherine (Kay), Melvin, and Mike. Sherry and Mary Beth are kneeling in front.